NORTHERN PORTUGAL

PASSPORT'S REGIONAL GUIDES OF PORTUGAL

Algarve and Southern Portugal
Lisbon and Central Portugal (forthcoming)

Also available:
Passport's Regional Guides of France
Passport's Regional Guides of Italy

NORTHERN PORTUGAL

Brian and Eileen Anderson

PASSPORT BOOKS
a division of *NTC Publishing Group*
Lincolnwood, Illinois USA

Published in 1996 by Passport Books,
a division of NTC Publishing Group,
4255 West Touhy Avenue, Lincolnwood
(Chicago), Illinois 60646–1975 U.S.A.

Originally published by
A & C Black (Publishers) Limited,
35 Bedford Row, London WC1R 4JH

ISBN 0–8442–4544–5

Library of Congress Catalog, Card Number:
95–71161

Printed in Singapore by Imago

To Eddie and Vi Simpson for their friendship and shared love of wildlife.

Acknowledgements

A journey such as this is richly spiced with conversations along the way which add local colour or direct us here or there to ensure that nothing is missed. To all the people who have helped us we offer our thanks, not least to the staff of the local Turismos around the towns and villages. Deserving special mention are Mária Carneiro and António Carona of the ICEP office in Porto for their considerable help, Manuel Barros for entertaining us on the Barros estate during the busy harvest time, and similarly D. Eduardo Serpa Pimental of Quinta da Pacheca. Also in the Douro region, we must thank Manuel Pimental of Casal de Loivois for his kind hospitality and for sharing his knowledge of the region so freely. For special help in Ponte de Lima, and for passing on her collection of recipes to us, we thank Joannna Hewitt; in Coimbra thanks must go to the Tourist Office and to Hotel Astoria for providing complimentary accommodation. Last but not least we offer our thanks to Pilar Pereira of the Portuguese National Tourist Office in London who over the years has become a good friend.

CONTENTS

Maps and Plans

1. INTRODUCTION

Northern Portugal is tailor-made for the independent traveller. Historical sites and monuments apart, there is plenty of unspoilt countryside to explore. Rolling hills, verdant valleys and lazy rivers provide home to countless communities engrossed within their own self-perpetuating lifestyle which barely changes over decades. There are few other areas of Portugal which offer the thrill and challenge of exploration so transparently veiled with the promise of stepping beyond the edge of the guide book to new discoveries, perhaps to an unknown granite village where an old way of life prevails or simply to some mossy water mill grinding away by the edge of a stream. All this with good accommodation and good food never too far away!

The north, in terms of this guide, is virtually the old Portucale, the area between two rivers, between the Minho, the country's most northerly boundary with Spain, and the Douro which arises in Spain and forms an eastern boundary before battling its way west to emerge at Porto and the Atlantic Ocean. There is nothing too rigid in this demarcation, and boundaries are forgotten when Lamego, south of the Douro, draws too close to ignore and totally flouted by the lure of Coimbra sixty miles south of the Douro! There are few visitors, especially if arriving or departing through Porto, who would not entertain the idea of a brief excursion to the university city of Coimbra and the nearby Roman site of Conimbriga.

Portugal, around 350 miles long from north to south and 137 miles at its widest, embroiders the western edge of the Iberian peninsula. Although it has few natural boundaries with Spain, there is no doubting that it is a distinct country with its own language and customs. The people are different too, blessed with an old fashioned charm and politeness that is not just reserved for tourists. Men invariably greet each other with a formal brief handshake and women receive a polite kiss on each cheek and leave is taken in the same way. Men in suits is fairly normal for everyday business and since moustaches are common and smiles not always freely worn it leaves an impression that the Portuguese are a nation of serious and reserved people, which is not far from the truth. And they are conservative too, especially the people in this northern region. Do not be deceived by women still washing clothes in the river. Many families are improving their standard of living now and an automatic washing machine has a place in many homes but still women rotate their washing so that they receive at least one wash in the river every month because of the deeply held belief that it washes them better.

Friendliness is open but on a polite level and rarely is a visitor pressed to take hospitality at home as might happen in Greece or Turkey. If a visitor needs help then help is freely offered and their reserve is no impediment.

Geography and Geology

Mountain ranges, rivers and valleys punctuate much of Portugal and this is especially true in the northern region. Significant mountain ranges include Serra da Peneda and Serra do Gerês in the very north east which have largely been incorporated into the Peneda-Gerês National Park. A near-barrier of mountain ranges in the central region isolates the eastern Trás-os-Montes, which most aptly translates to 'behind-the-mountains'. Although these ranges have a dramatic presence, none reach particularly great heights, with the highest peak in the Peneda range reaching an elevation of 1416m (4646ft) which is equalled only by a peak in the Serra do Marão near Vila Real.

Granite dominates much of the north and western region presenting a grey landscape of rounded hills and steep sided valleys. The bare tops of the hills are often scattered with huge granite tors sculptured by the weather to unusual or weird shapes but sometimes resembling familiar objects like the giant tortoise near Castro Laboreiro. Abundant and fairly easily worked, granite is the natural choice for a building material. Churches are built from it, houses are built from it, the terrace walls are built from it, posts for the vines are cut from it and no building job fails to incorporate it. Where granite runs out the schist takes over. The Douro valley where the vines for port wine are grown and much of the Trás-os-Montes farm on schistose soils. In these regions, everything in sight is built of schist and slate but only the older houses still have slate roofs.

Virtually every drop of rain falling on these hard crystalline mountains is shed towards the Atlantic. Streams, rills, flosses, gills, brooks, rivulets and rivers flow down hillsides and valleys sustaining life for the farmers and providing energy to turn the mill wheels. Eventually the flow of water becomes organised into major rivers and there are a fair number including the Minho which separates Portugal from Spain, the Lima which flows through one of the loveliest valleys in Portugal and the Douro famous for its vineyards. The Douro has some major tributaries too like the rivers Tâmega and Tua.

View of Porto from Vila Nova de Gaia across the river Douro

Climate

Portugal is caught between the Atlantic and the Mediterranean and the climate reflects both these influences even in the north. Umbrella-carrying farmers and a verdant countryside tell their own story but, happily for the visitor, the rain falls mainly outside the summer months. Winter brings days of rain, often heavy, interspersed with short spells of fine weather with mild temperatures in coastal and lowland regions. The olive tree, a reliable guide to a Mediterranean climate of hot dry summers and mild wet winters, grows throughout much of the northern region. It grows throughout the Lima Valley as far inland as Ponte da Barca, along the Douro Valley, often amongst the vines, but is missing from the regions of high ground which suffer frost and snow in winter.

April brings showers and warmer days as spring moves quickly to summer. Summers in the north are perhaps a little less reliable than in other parts of the country. In a good year, and there are many, summers are long, hot and dry with temperatures well into the 30°C, but at other times Mediterranean highs yield a little to Atlantic westerlies allowing showers to penetrate. Even in the less settled summers temperatures often remain high. Towards the middle of October, sometimes a little later, there is a marked transition in the weather when the incursion of heavy showers heralds the start of the rainy season.

Trás-os-Montes and the higher reaches of the Douro valley tend to have hotter and perhaps more reliable summers than the rest of the region, with temperatures often in the 40°C. Spring and autumn are perhaps the best times to visit the northern region. The countryside is verdant all year but spring, particularly late April and May, has a vibrancy reinforced by a wealth of wild flowers and September, mostly a reliable month, has *vindima* when the grape harvesters are out in force. This is the time to visit the Quinta's of the famous name port houses in the Douro or tour the extensive Vinho Verde regions.

Flora and Fauna

Portugal is a meeting point of different geographical and climatic regions and this is fully reflected in the diversity of the flora. Species more typical of the Western Atlantic, like *Erica, Ulex* and *Daboecia* sit alongside western Mediterranean and circum-Mediterranean elements like the cork oak, *Quercus suber,* and oleander, *Nerium oleander.* The higher mountains show still more variation.

Amongst the forest trees, the stone pine, *Pinus pinea,* with its umbrella-shaped crown is easily recognised as is the ubiquitous chestnut tree, *Castanea sativa,* especially in autumn when dripping with spiny clad nuts. The cork oak, often with a bicoloured bole after being stripped of cork, is just one of a number of oaks found in the region which includes the deciduous Pyrenean oak, *Quercus pyrenaica* and the evergreen *Q. robur.* Birch grace the scene, and sycamore like *Acer pseudoplatanus,* the strawberry tree, *Arbutus unedo* and even holly, *Ilex aquifolium* are present to enrich the varied forest cover. Regretfully, eucalyptus forests are extensive in some areas. Introduced for its rapid growth and timber, mature plantations effectively suppress other species.

At shrub level there is an even wider spread of species with the heathers, brooms and rock roses dominant. The heaths include *Erica arborea, E.E. australis, cinerea, umbellata* and *Calluna vulgaris;* the *Cistacea, Cistus salvii-folius, C.C. psilosepalus, populifolius, laurifolius, Halimiun viscosum, H. alyssoides* and *H. umbellatum;* whilst the brooms include *Genista micrantha, G. falcata* and *G. florida.* Gorse, mainly *Ulex europaeus,* is particularly common in some areas forming an extensive cover over the hillsides.

At the lower levels the catalogue of species increases very significantly. Springtime is a riot with some real treasures to be found. Head for the uncult-ivated regions, which usually means the mountains, to find a host of narcissus, like *N. bulbocodium, N. triandrus* and *N. asturiensis. Scilla bifolia* is around too as is the dog's tooth violet, *Erythronium dens-canis,* which here is at the edge of its westerly range in Europe. The spring list seems endless but three more species which excite flower lovers are *Fritillaria lusitanica, Tulipa australis* and the delicate anemone, *A. trifolia.* Throughout summer there are still flowers from the small blue-flowered shrub *Lithodora diffusa* through blue forget-me-nots to blue-flowered *Iris boissieri* in the Peneda-Gerês National Park. The blues are well moderated by the pink heaths and the pink *Silene foetida* as well as whites of the paradise lily, *Paradisea lusitanica,* and the tall spikes of the ubiquitous asphodel. The small white daisy which seems to have colonised all the granite walls throughout the north, and the rest of Portugal, is out to prove that it can live with its name, *Erigeron karvinskianus.*

Do not look for brown bears, they disappeared around 1650, but the wild pony, *Equus caballus*, is still relatively common and there is a good possibility of seeing them in the Peneda Gerês National Park and other isolated regions. In these same regions are the wild boar, *Sus scrofa castillianus*, and the wolf, *Canis lupus*, but a chance encounter with either of these is most unlikely. There is more chance perhaps with the fox, *Vulpes vulpes*, the beech marten, *Martes foina*, the badger, *Meles meles*, or the otter, *Lutra lutra*, but it will require patience and a little luck.

There is plenty of bird life around but again it is a trek to the remote regions to see the golden eagle, *Aquila chrysaetus*, the buzzard, *Buteo buteo*, or the goshawk, *Accipiter gentillis*. Other notable species of the region include the red kite, *Milvus milvus*, the eagle owl, *Bubo bubo*, the tawny owl, *Stix aluco*, and Scops owl, *Otus scops*.

Visitors out striding in the countryside should be aware that the black viper, *Vipera latastei*, inhabits the area but its population is small. They tend to slide away without hurrying and are not confrontational unless provoked. The other two snakes, the grass snake, *Natrix natrix*, and the smooth snake, *Coronella austriaca*, present no threat. Amongst the lizard population, the water lizard, *Lacerta schreiberi*, often seen on the stonework of bridges over streams, is perhaps the most handsome.

Green Issues

There is an awareness of conservation on a broad front but Portugal remains with just one National Park, Peneda-Gerês, situated in the northern region and visited in Chapter 8. Whilst access within the park for motorists is improving with signposting and hard track services, walkers are not particularly catered for nor is there any significant attempt at conservation of the flora and fauna. Traditional activities, goat grazing and forest clearing, seem to continue as before. Information offices for the park are located in Arcos de Valdevez, Gerês and Montelegre where maps are available but do not expect any in depth information.

Apart from the National Parks there are some areas of natural beauty designated as Natural Parks. Natural Parks protect areas of natural beauty but are not subject to the same stringent rules and regulations as National Parks. The north has two such areas, Alvão Natural Park and Montesinho Natural Park. Although remote and isolated, both these protected areas are inhabited and have been through many centuries. Part of the protection is to preserve the old way of life and traditions which still survive and to encourage rural tourism to help sustain these regions. This means providing camp sites, encouraging handicrafts and suitable sports such as pony trekking. Other declared aims uphold lofty ideals such as protecting species and preserving genetic diversity. There is a more immediate problem which could negate all the good intentions within a short period of time, not just in the Natural Parks but in many other old, traditional villages through the region. The problem is that of émigrés returning with their new wealth to build modern houses in the villages where they were born. Built in modern materials, often in the heart of the village where the roads are sometimes too narrow to approach by car, these houses are totally incongruous, change the character of the place and destroy the heritage. The authorities are greatly concerned but the practice still continues.

There is no awareness of green issues in every day life although unleaded petrol is now freely available throughout the region except for small rural stations. Expect to see burning rubbish tips whilst touring around and plenty of unauthorised rubbish dumping. With increasing wealth over the last decade, the number of old cars for disposal is growing and the number littering the countryside is on the increase, a rare sight just a few years ago.

2. HISTORY

Before the Romans

Much of the early history is speculative. There are plenty of archaeological sites scattered throughout Portugal indicating early occupation but there seems to be no evidence of organised communities until the *castro* culture emerged in the second millennium BC. The idea of defended settlements built on strategic hilltops suited the Celts who arrived around 700–600 BC. They adapted and refined the system to allow these warring tribes to conduct primitive farming and goatherding close to a safe refuge. Later the Romans took over some of these castros which may explain why there are so many well-preserved examples to be seen. Two of these *citânias* in particular are worth a visit, the one at Briteiros, with its laid out streets and drainage system and a more recently excavated one on the hill behind Viana do Castelo, with its streets and well-preserved houses.

Whilst the Celts were taking refuge in the wild northern mountains, other tribes like the Phoenicians traded from coastal regions in the south exploiting metals mined inland. They were joined by the Greeks around the 6th century BC and by the Carthaginians who played a dominant role until the arrival of the Romans.

The Romans

As a consequence of the Second Punic War (218–202 BC) the peninsula as a whole passed to the control of the Romans and Portugal as it is known today simply became part of Hispania Ulterior. It was not an easy war for the Romans. Attacking from the south they had little trouble in colonising coastal areas but met serious resistance when attempting to capture the interior. Major resistance came from the Lusitani who lived north of the Tagus. Portugal's first legendary hero, **Viriathus**, emerged from the bitter fighting which continued for almost two centuries. He led resistance cleverly and held up the Roman advance until he was finally assassinated in 139 BC by three of his followers who had been bribed by the Romans. Within two years the legions of Decimus Junius Brutus had swept through and taken control.

Using Olisbo (Lisbon) as his capital, it was **Julius Caesar** in 60 BC who set about integrating the peninsula into the Roman Empire. Colonies were established at Ebora (Évora), Scallabis (Santarém), Pax Julia (Beja), Myrtilis (Mértola) and Bracara Augusta (Braga), although, with a few exceptions, little remains to excite the present day visitor. This page of history is not entirely closed since their 400 year rule has left lasting legacies in the Romance language, the legal system, roads and bridges, large scale farming in the crops of wheat, barley and the now ubiquitous vine.

Towards the end of the Romans' rule Christianity was established with important bishoprics at Évora and Braga. In the early 5th century, with the Romans in decline, waves of barbarians swept through Spain and Portugal from beyond the Pyrenees. First the Vandals settled in Galicia, then the Alani in Lusitani with the Suevi taking up the region between the Minho and the Douro. It was the Suevi who assimilated most readily with the Hispano-Roman population and the Suevi who soon became the dominant force. Before the end of the 5th century the Visigoths had established a tenuous rule over most of the peninsula which they managed to maintain for almost a century.

The Moors

The arrival in the south in 711 of the Moors from Africa seriously challenged the Visigoth rule. They overran Spain quickly and moved steadily northwards into Portugal pushing Christianity north of the Douro, an area which was never really conquered by the Muslims. Southern Portugal became part of Spain and was known by the Moors as **Al-Garb** (the West) which evolved eventually into the modern name of Algarve. They established a capital at Shelb, now Silves, and set about ruling with a great deal of tolerance, respecting the rights of the Christians and the Jews to practise their own religions. Social order brought considerable advances with the Moors allowing smallholders to rent land owned by the state and encouraging work to improve irrigation techniques introduced by the Romans and moves to introduce new crops including oranges, lemons and cotton. Centuries of harmony gradually decayed with the decentralisation of rule and with the arrival at the end of the 11th century of more militant Muslim groups like the Almoravids.

The Birth of a Nation

The victory of the Christians at the **battle of Covadonga** in the Asturias in 718 is regarded as the start of the long struggle for liberation from the Moors. From that small start the Muslims were pushed back slowly but steadily from León and Galicia southwards. Porto was taken in 868, Coimbra in 878 and raids were mounted against Lisbon by 955. South of the Douro there was no real consolidation of territory throughout this period and the land remained a fluctuating battle ground. Towards the end of the 9th century, the country that was to become Portugal started to emerge with the consolidation of the lands between the Lima and the Minho. This territory was called Portucale after its capital city. Although under the command of the kingdom of León, the region was stabilised by a dynasty of *duces* beginning with Gonçalo Mendes, but the incipient nation suffered control by division before its status as a country was finally accepted in the 11th century.

Towards a Kingdom

Alfonso VI succeeded his father, Ferdinand I of León, in 1065 and by 1073 he had declared himself emperor of the kingdoms of León, Castile, Galicia and Portucale. His call for crusaders to help fight the Almovarids brought, amongst others, Raymond of Burgundy and his cousin Henry who both married daughters of Alfonso, Henry marrying the illegitimate Teresa. Henry took charge of the County of Portucale and worked steadily towards confirming the autonomy of the state of Portugal, work carried on by Teresa after Henry's death around 1112 when she became regent for her son, Afonso Henriques.

After the death of Alfonso VI a war of succession broke out and the mantle of Emperor was assumed by **Alfonso VII**, son of Raymond and Urraca. Teresa's attempts to maintain Portugal's independence eventually failed when her armies fell and she accepted dominance by Alfonso VII in 1127. This inspired Teresa's 18 year old son, **Afonso Henriques** (1128/39–85), to rebellion and over the next decade and a half he constantly vied with his cousin for control of Portugal. The Treaty of Zamora, signed between them in 1143, made Afonso Henriques the first King of Portugal. Not feeling entirely secure, Afonso sought recognition from Pope Lucius II but it was not forthcoming since the Pope favoured a policy of supporting Iberian union as representing the best hope of holding back the Muslim tide. Later, in 1179, Pope Alexander III finally granted recognition to the 70 year old Afonso Henriques in exchange for a yearly tribute and other privileges.

The First Dynasty, House of Burgundy

Afonso Henriques I, o Conquistador (the Conqueror)	1128/39–1185
Sancho I, o Pavoador (the Resettler)	1185–1211
Afonso II, o Gordo (the Fat)	1211–1223
Sancho II	1223–1248
Afonso III	1248–1279
Dinis, o Lavrador (the Husbandman)	1279–1325
Afonso IV, a Bravo (the Brave)	1325–1357
Pedro I, o Justiceiro (the Justicer)	1357–1367
Fernando, o Formoso (the Beautiful)	1367–1383

Evicting the Moors

In his determination to establish Portugal and his kingdom, Afonso Henriques also enlisted the help of crusaders to fight against the Moors. Santarém and Lisbon were both taken in 1147 and joined with his emerging nation. Lisbon was taken by siege with the help of the English, French, Flemish and German crusaders who were passing through on their way to the Holy Land. Fighting for Christianity alone proved not persuasive enough but the offer of loot and land grants secured their services. The Reconquista was eventually backed by the Church, convinced by the argument that chasing out the Muslims here was just as important as fighting the infidel in the Holy Land. The Knights Templar and the Hospitallers lent their support and became extremely wealthy and powerful as a consequence of land grants.

Afonso Henriques fought his last battle in 1170 at Badajoz. Fernando II of León, concerned that land retaken from the Moors was in effect expanding Portugal instead of his own kingdom, joined forces with the powerful Almohads. Afonso Henriques broke a leg in the midst of the battle and was captured. He secured his release only by yielding land and castles to his enemy.

The final victory was still over a century away. Again with the help of passing crusaders, Sancho I invaded western Algarve and captured the capital Silves in 1189 but lost it together with much of the area south of the Tagus the following year in what proved to be the last great campaign of the Moors led by al-Mansur. Steady expansion under Sancho II and his successor Afonso III led to the recapture of territory in Alentejo and eastern Algarve until, in 1249, western Algarve too had been recovered and the Portuguese kingdom, endorsed by the Treaty of Alcanices in 1297, took its ultimate shape.

Organising a New Kingdom

New territories were divided between the Church, the Templars and other Holy Orders, and the most powerful nobles. Most of the population of 400,000 lived in the north so some internal recolonisation programmes were introduced to protect the new areas. There were problems of a social order too; the northerners with their Celtic genes had the arrogance of conquering invaders whilst the southerners had learnt gentler ways from a more settled existence under the rule of the Moors. An increase in social mobility amongst the lower classes did much to weld the divergent cultures but never completely so, not even to this day.

Some moves towards democracy started when the kings of the Burgundian line recognised the need for popular and financial support and began to consult with the nobles and clergy and later the wealthy merchants and townsmen. This was formalised into the *Cortes* (parliament), the first of which was held in Coimbra in 1211. In the 1254 *Cortes* at Leira, the king conceded the right of municipal representation in fiscal matters, an important concession since the king only called a *Cortes* when he needed to raise taxes. The Church was doing well with its extensive lands, freedom from taxation and its right to collect its own taxes from the population; rather too well and its increasing power was soon felt as a threat by the monarchy. Afonso II generally failed in his attempts to curb their power as did Sancho II who was ultimately excommunicated and dethroned in 1245.

The reign of **Dom Dinis** (1279–1325) proved significant in consolidating Portugal's independence and putting the monarchy firmly in control. Dinis was far-sighted in his reforms which were extensive and affected all walks of life. For security he financed the building of 50 castles along the frontier and started negotiations with Spain which eventually led to the 1294 Treaty of Alcanices by which Spain acknowledged Portugal's borders. He introduced agricultural reforms to produce export quantities of wine, olive oil, grain and dried fruit and afforestation schemes. He encouraged music and poetry and gave Lisbon a university in 1290 which was transferred to Coimbra in 1308. The Templars, in decline in Europe, were reorganised as the Order of Christ (of which Henry the Navigator was later to become a Grand Master) responsible to the King and not the Pope so the church was forced to accept a larger degree of state control.

Afonso IV (1325–57), who succeeded Dinis, had a much less happy reign. The Black Plague struck in 1348–49 and decimated the population, especially in the urban centres. It became a burden throughout his reign, indeed over the next century, as the pestilence returned again and again. Labour problems arose through migration to urban cities leaving insufficient agricultural workers to fill the nation's breadbasket, creating inflationary pressures and stagnation. Fears of Castilian domination persisted, not helped by continual intermarriage between the two royal families. But Portugal was bent on independence. Fear of a Castilian heir through his son's love affair with Inês de Castro, first a mistress and later his wife, was enough for Afonso to arrange her brutal murder (see feature p 176).

Just two years later, in 1357, **Pedro I** came to the throne after the death of his father and one of his first acts was to seek out the murderers of Inês to extract his revenge. Peaceful coexistence with Castile continued throughout his reign as the country started to recover from the ravages of the plague, but the growing power of the nobles and the emerging bourgeoisie was to create social unrest in the reign of his son **Fernando I** (1367–83). Alienating his subjects with an unpopular marriage to Leonor Teles and engaging the country in a series of unpopular wars against the Castilians, Fernando failed to produce a male heir and in 1383 the House of Burgundy came to an untidy end. Power passed to his wife Leonor but not for long as their daughter Beatriz, at the age of 12, married the widowed Juan I, King of Castile. By the terms of the marriage contract Beatriz, with her husband, would succeed to rule Portugal. Following the death of her father, Juan insisted that Beatriz be proclaimed queen and entered Portugal to take authority from Leonor. Although this move received support from the nobles, it incited the middle classes to riot and throw their weight behind the claims of João, the Grand Master of the Order of Avis and illegitimate son of King Pedro, who became regent. It started two years of war with Castile which was finally settled with the Battle of Aljubarrota (1385) which resulted in a decisive victory for João, backed by a force of English archers, against overwhelming odds. Later that year João was crowned at Coimbra to become **João I**, the first king of the House of Avis, and the great abbey of Batalha was ordered to commemorate the victory. Relations with England were sealed through the Treaty of Windsor of 1386 and by João's marriage to Phillipa of Lancaster, daughter of John of Gaunt, the following year.

Second Dynasty: House of Avis

João I, de Boa Memoria (of Good Memory)	1385–1433
Duarte, o Eloquente (the Eloquent)	1433–1438
Afonso V, o Africano (the African)	1438–1481
João II, o Principe Perfeito (the Perfect Prince)	1481–1495
Manuel I, o Venturoso (the Fortunate)	1495–1521
João III, o Piedoso (the Merciful)	1521–1557
Sebastião, o Desejado (the Awaited)	1557–1578
Henrique, o Casto (the Pure)	1578–1580

The new dynasty was much like the old, except the mercantile classes gained political representation, and skirmishes with Castile continued until peace was finally made in 1411. It was during this reign that Portugal started to look overseas to solve problems at home and the proximity of North Africa made it a natural target for overseas expansion.

Building an Empire

João's main contribution to building a new empire was in fathering some brilliant children including Pedro, who travelled widely sending home maps and works of geography, and **Henry the Navigator** (1394–1460) who played a very significant early role. Henry founded a school of navigation at Sagres in Algarve and used his power and wealth to staff it with the cream of Europe's cartographers, astronomers and navigators. During his lifetime Madeira (1419), the Azores (1427) and the Cape Verde Islands (1457) were all discovered and colonised and the west coast of Africa explored. Following the death of Henry the Navigator, who is also featured on p 52, there was a lull in the process of exploration.

The Age of Discovery

Portugal's explorations started haphazardly and were curiously motivated. Outflanking the Muslims and spreading the Christian faith lent a crusading element and respectability to their excursions but there were other issues like the need for gold, which was short throughout Europe, and the need to stabilise currency and support commerce. Maritime trade was of growing importance too and there was the unending search to discover the earthly paradise of Prester John. Prester John was known as a king and leader of a vast Christian empire somewhere in the middle of Africa. This deeply held belief stretched all the way back to Rome. The Pope granted Portugal the sole right to explore and colonise Africa except for those parts ruled by Prester John.

However faltering or motivated in the beginning, Portuguese sailors developed skills of seamanship superior to any in Europe and rapidly became intrepid explorers. A number of epic voyages took place around the dawning of the 16th century. Vasco da Gama (1497–99) sailed to India and back again, Pedro Alvares Cabral (1500) discovered Brazil and, from 1519–22, Ferdinand Magellan, ignoring pleas from his Portuguese masters, led the first navigation of the globe under the sponsorship of the Spanish. The Spanish, too, were taking to the seas creating fresh dispute between these two nations but, with Papal intervention, the Treaty of Tordesillas (1494) divided the world between them at an imaginary line 370 leagues west of the Cape Verdes. This gave Portugal the, as yet, undiscovered Orient and the key to great wealth.

Opening new trade routes brought with it enormous wealth and not just in gold. Spices from the east, cinnamon, cloves and peppers, grain, sugar and dyestuffs from Morocco, and slaves from Africa activated the merchants and stimulated the development of key overseas trading posts not always achieved without battles. On a more humble scale, one product from their discovery of Newfoundland, *balcalhau* (dried, salted cod), became virtually part of the staple diet and remains so even today.

This period of Portugal's history produced some epic heroes and a stable economy but no lasting wealth. Only the monarchy, taking a royal fifth from all trade revenues, benefited but even its wealth had no permanency.

Duarte (1433–38) succeeded João I but died in 1438 after only five years on the throne, some say from grief over the fate of his younger brother delivered as a hostage to the Muslims following an ill-fated expedition against Tangier in 1437. His son, **Afonso V** (1438–81), was too young to rule without a regent so Pedro stepped forward with the support of the populace to press his claim over that of Queen Leonor, Duarte's widow. Events took a dramatic turn when Afonso came of age and turned to the parties who opposed Pedro. Pedro fought the king in the battle of Alfarobeira in 1449 and lost his life. Two uncles who had proved trusted advisers, Fernão, the Duke of Bragança, and Henry the Navigator, were both rewarded with a large share of independent power. Afonso is remembered most for his crusading in North Africa which gave him the epithet of *o Africano*.

Overseas exploration became important again under **João II** (1481–95) especially when, in 1487, Bartolomeu Dias finally made it around the southern tip of Africa which he christened 'the Cape of Good Hope'. He started to assert more royal power over the nobles, particularly over the problem of land. A conspiracy gathered against the king but the perpetrators were quickly discovered and rapidly dispatched. In 1483 the Duke of Bragança, head of a family whose estate covered a third of the kingdom, was executed and his lands recovered by the crown, and the following year the Queen's brother, the Duke of Viseu, was treated in a similar way.

Dom Manuel I (1495–1521) succeeded João and continued centralising power in the crown. However, he appeased the nobles by restoring their estates although not their political power. It was an enlightened reign in which a postal service was instituted, the taxation of the districts was regulated and exercise of justice brought under royal control. He presided over Portugal's greatest period of exploration and enjoyed the wealth flowing from it. The exuberance of this age lead to the development of a new architectural style involving twisted forms in the columns, ribs and corbels which later became known as Manueline (featured on p 152).

However, Portugal's hitherto lenient attitude with its Jewish minority was gathering resentment amongst the people of the country.

An Age of Decline

João III (1481–95) continued Manuel's policies of establishing royal authority and expanding trade. Literature was flowing from the printing presses and the humanistic influences of Europe were making a noticeable impression. Colleges were established and the university at Lisbon was moved permanently to Coimbra in 1537. Permitting the establishment of the Inquisition was a turning point that led Portugal into decline. Slowly and steadily a whole entrepreneurial class was snubbed out robbing the country of the engine to drive the huge commercial empire it had striven so hard to build. Humanism and the Inquisition proved incompatible bedfellows and it was the Inquisition which gathered force.

Stability still held with the ascension of the young **Dom Sebastião** in 1557 and it was during his reign (1572) that Luís de Camões published his epic *The Lusiads* which was to achieve lasting fame. Strains in the economy were showing which became overpowering around the 1570s when increasing

The Jews and the Inquisition

As physicians, astronomers, bankers, money lenders and tax collectors, the Jews had lived in Portugal for a thousand years or more without gathering any great resentment. Their influence was growing and it was the Jews who opened Portugal's first presses with their first eleven books all in Hebrew. Complaints against the Jews raised in the *Cortes* in 1490 indicated changing attitudes and events in Spain were to compound their difficulties further.

Some 60,000 Jews expelled from Spain in 1462 were allowed to settle peacefully in Portugal. Unfortunately for the Jews, Dom Manuel was forced to take a hardened attitude against them as a condition of his marriage to Princess Isabela of Spain just four years later. There was a considerable reluctance on the part of the King in ordering the expulsion of such a valuable sector of the community so he offered the option of baptism to expulsion. Some did leave for the Netherlands but many were baptised as 'New Christians', accepting assurances that there would be a 20 year period of grace before their new faith was tested. New Christians and Old Christians intermarried freely but it was to offer no protection for the Jewish heritage.

Dom João III in 1536 eventually persuaded the Pope of the need to introduce the Inquisition in spite of the fact that there was no disunity threatening the faith in Portugal. Intended as a tool of the monarchy, it quickly took on a life and force of its own with the inquisitor-generals responding directly to the Pope. The main target was the New Christians and thousands were tortured, left to rot in prison cells or burnt at the stake as the Inquisition became nothing more than a reign of terror until it was finally suppressed in 1820.

Small Jewish communities still exist in Portugal and there are traces of Jewish quarters in the towns where they first settled, including Viana do Castelo, Bragança, Lamego, Guarda and Castelo de Vide. The latter houses the oldest synagogue in Portugal, founded in the 13th century, hidden away down a small side street. In Tomar, too, there is a 14th century synagogue which now contains a museum named after Abraham Zacuto. A brilliant astronomer and mathematician, it was Zacuto who first published *Almanac Perpetuum*, in Hebrew, which enabled mariners to calculate latitude at sea by declination of the sun. He was amongst those who declined to convert at the bidding of Dom Manuel and left the country.

competition, falling prices, foreign debts and a drop in productivity signalled a serious decline.

Sebastião, an unstable and idealistic king, yearned for a crusade against the Moors in North Africa and when he sensed the time was right he emptied his coffers to equip an 18,000 strong force. It sailed to Morocco from Algarve in 1578 but met a superior force at Alcacer-Quiber and was effectively annihilated. Around 8000 were left dead on the battlefield including the king and many young nobles, and most of the rest were taken prisoner, with only a 100 or so escaping capture.

Cardinal Henrique, an elderly uncle, assumed control and further weakened the country by paying ruinous ransoms for the release of prisoners. He died after only two years in power leaving no male heirs. King Philip II of Spain invaded and was installed as King Filipe I of Portugal in 1581.

The Castilian Usurpers

Although this rule was initially unpopular, the union with Spain brought short term advantages to the economy. Spanish wheat helped to feed the people and the Spanish helped to guard the Portuguese empire. Filipe started well by observing Portuguese autonomy and leaving control of the *Cortes* and the judicial system entirely with the Portuguese while promising that the Portuguese language would remain and that their empire overseas would still be ruled by Portugal. Apart from the first two years, the whole of the Castilian reign was conducted from Spain.

The balance of power was tilting from Spain to Europe around this period. 1588 witnessed the failure of the Spanish Armada which was supported by boats built in Lisbon and crewed by Portuguese. Portuguese ports were closed to English ships and the seizure of 50 Dutch ships in Lisbon by Filipe in 1594 brought a Dutch retaliation aimed at the Portuguese in India. By 1602, with both the English and the Dutch established in India, the Portuguese monopoly was broken. Much of their maritime empire was under threat with the country no longer powerful enough to mount a robust defence.

Filipe II (1581–98), not as diplomatic as his father, started to advance the power of Spain by appointing Spaniards to the Council of Portugal in Madrid. Although he still retained favour with the *Cortes*, seeds of resistance were sown amongst the populace. In 1621 Filipe III succeeded to the throne but his reign continued to erode and undermine the union. Portugal was drawn into Spain's 30 year war with France and its troops were pressed into battle to quell an uprising in Catalonia. 1 December 1640 dawned as any other but on this day Spanish rule was effectively overthrown creating a landmark in Portuguese history remembered to this day as a national holiday. A group of conspirators stormed the palace in Lisbon to depose the Duchess of Mantua, governor of Portugal, and install the Duke of Bragança, head of one of the oldest families in Portugal and reluctant leader of the uprising, as king.

Third Dynasty: the Hapsburgs

Filipe I, o Prudente (the Prudent)	1581–1598
Filipe II, o Pio (the Pious)	1598–1621
Filipe III, o Grande (the Grand)	1621–1640

The House of Bragança

The Duke of Bragança was crowned **João IV** (1640–56) in 1640, and with Spain seriously distracted on other fronts there was no immediate opposition. Dom João focused his efforts on rebuilding the country, placing its independence beyond doubt and gaining recognition abroad. England agreed to renew the old alliance of 1386 and treaties were signed with Charles I (1642) and Oliver Cromwell (1654). Later, in 1661, the alliance was strengthened by the marriage of Charles II to Catherine of Bragança. Although skirmishes with Spain had waxed and waned, and taxes had been raised to fairly high levels, it was a quietly successful reign which had also seen the emphasis in trade swing from India to Brazil.

Consolidation continued under Luisa, the Spanish wife of João IV, acting as regent for her son, Afonso IV, and a peace treaty was signed with Holland. Young Afonso, just 13 years old, was a problematic child associating with street gangs and criminal elements. His mother was deposed as regent by the Count of Costelho Melhor who promptly married off Afonso to a French Princess, Marie-Françoise. The count himself became subject of a conspiracy and fled, whereupon Marie-Françoise immediately entered a convent and asked for an annulment of the marriage on the grounds that it had never been consummated. This was agreed by *Cortes* and the princess promptly married Afonso's younger brother who assumed the role of regent.

Luisa's third child, Catherine, was married to Charles II in 1662 to give Portugal another treaty of alliance with England and England provided forces to help fight off the Spanish at Évora. The treaty gave England a handsome dowry and trading rights in all Portuguese territories, Tangiers and Bombay. Spain, on the other hand, now seriously weakened, finally agreed peace in the Treaty of Lisbon of 1668.

Remarkably, all Luisa's three children ascended to a throne, Afonso and Pedro as kings of Portugal and Catherine as queen of England.

Pedro acted as regent for his brother from 1668 until he was crowned King **Pedro II** in 1683. Economic problems beset the country throughout this period reflecting a decline in maritime commerce, the loss of the spice trade and greater competition in the sugar trade. Agriculture at home was not so productive and wheat shortages continued so efforts were directed towards increasing manufacturing output to solve the difficulties. Tariff-protected glass and textile industries were developed, exports boosted and the import of luxury goods was controlled, and this together with concessions from the English for Portuguese wines (Methuen Treaty) did much to stabilise the economy. The discovery of gold in Brazil poured in a new wealth and the growing new industries instantly faltered.

When **João V** succeeded Pedro II in 1706 he had Brazilian gold to spend. The Crown's revenues soared as it took one fifth of all the revenues and the money was spent on building palaces, churches and monasteries including the monastery-church at Mafra which virtually bankrupted the monarchy. Scholarship also flourished under his patronage, and, with his concern also for the poor, João became known as the *Magnanimo*. Palaces were also built to house João's bastard sons, three from nuns.

Fourth Dynasty: House of Bragança

João IV, o Restaurador (the Restorer)	1640–1656
Afonso VI, o Vitrioso (the Victorious)	1656–1683
Pedro II, o Pacifico (regent from 1668) (the Peace Lover)	1683–1706
João V, o Magnanimo (the Magnanimous)	1706–1750
José, o Reformador (the Reformer)	1750–1777
Maria I, a Piedosa (the Merciful)	1777–1816
João VI, o Clemente (the Merciful)	1816–1826
Pedro IV, o Libertador (the Liberator)	1826 (abdicated)
Miguel, o Usurpador (the Usurper)	1828–1834
Maria II, a Educadora (the Educator)	1834–1853
Pedro V, o Esperancoso (the Hopeful)	1853–1861
Luís, o Popular (the Popular)	1861–1889
Carlos, o Martirizado (the Martyr)	1889–1908
Manuel II, o Desventuroso (the Unfortunate)	1908–1910

José (1750–77), Dom João's successor, was genial and easy going. He shared his father's love of the arts, particularly opera, and was happy to leave the affairs of state in the capable hands of his minister, the **Marquês de Pombal**. He was to go down in history as one of Portugal's greatest statesman, admired by some but reviled and hated by others. His was an oppressive dictatorial rule exercised by using the royal prerogative rather than his own personal power.

It was church as usual for the people of Lisbon on All Saints' Day, 1 November 1755, when a terrifying and furious **earthquake** suddenly hit the town. Buildings collapsed everywhere and fires from the many church candles added further devastation. After nine days of raging fires the heart of the city was reduced to ashes. Much of the surrounding country was also seriously affected as shock waves spread as far as France in the north and Algarve to the south yet the north of the country escaped serious damage. The

Jesuits laid the blame for this divine retribution entirely on Pombal. After surviving an assassination attempt, Pombal declared the Jesuits and certain nobles as responsible and took his revenge with executions and by disbanding the Jesuit movement in 1759. Granted emergency powers by the king, Pombal set about building Lisbon in a simple grid fashion with houses in a neo-classical style.

Oppressive though his regime was, his policies helped to reform Portugal's economy and lay the foundation of the modern Portuguese state. Towards the end of King José's life, Pombal plotted to force Maria to renounce her rights to the throne in favour of her son, José, who was a disciple of Pombal. It failed and, on her accession, **Maria** (1777–1816) tried Pombal for crimes against the state and confined him to his estates.

A pious woman, Maria revived many of the religious elements of government but left Pombal's economic reforms undisturbed. Roads and canals were built, agricultural methods improved and industry again supported including the textile industry. Slowly and steadily Portugal started to make economic progress until the French Revolution of 1789 reverberated around Europe. Maria, deeply disturbed by the loss of loved ones, including her eldest son to smallpox after she had forbidden vaccination, and other events, suffered hallucinations and slipped towards insanity. In 1791 she was declared insane and her son, João, took over as regent until his mother died in 1816, when he was ultimately crowned King **João VI** (1816–20).

The Era of Napoleon

In 1807 Napoleon delivered an ultimatum that Portugal declare war on Britain and close its ports to British shipping. Since Portugal was dependent for half her trade on Britain and on British sea power to protect her trade routes there was little option but to reject Napoleon and face the inevitable war. The monarchy immediately slipped off to Brazil to set up court there as the French, under General Junot, entered Lisbon. The Portuguese invoked the alliance with Britain and an expeditionary force commanded by the brilliant tactician Sir Arthur Wellesley (later the Duke of Wellington) quickly defeated the French. In all there were three waves of French attacks in the Peninsular War, all repelled, but it left the country fatally weakened. The French failed to pay the agreed compensation and another Anglo-Portuguese treaty, this one in 1810, gave Britain the right to trade freely with Brazil eliminating Portugal's lucrative middle-man's role. Brazil itself was proclaimed a kingdom in 1815.

From 1808 to 1821, Portugal effectively became a British protectorate governed by **Marshal William Beresford**. He ruled with a heavy hand which brought about bitter resentment. Liberal ideas introduced from France were spread by secret societies including the Masonic order of which Lisbon had 13 groups. A plot was hatched to dispose of Beresford but it was discovered and 12 conspirators were executed in October 1817. In 1820, Beresford, alarmed at the growing strength of the liberals in Spain and the support spilling over the border, went to Brazil to request more powers from the king. In his absence the liberals rose to seize power and João VI was forced to return from Brazil, but he was too late to resist the new liberal ideologies.

Constitutional Wrangles

A new constitution was adopted in 1822 which assured the establishment of broad voting rights, no special prerogatives for nobles or clergy, a liberal *Cortes* more truly representing the people and the end of the Inquisition. On a divergent course from the King, the Queen remained firmly against its adoption and used ill health as an excuse to avoid becoming a signatory.

In the same year, Crown Prince Pedro, who had remained in Brazil, was stirred by attempts at home to restrict Brazilian autonomy and promptly declared Brazil independent. Portugal had troubles enough at home with an uprising to restore absolute monarchy by the anti-liberals headed by Miguel, the Queen's youngest son, and backed by the Queen. They won a victory and the constitution was suspended in 1824. This almost destabilised the monarchy which left the King no option but to send his son Miguel into exile.

By 1825 Portugal had conceded and recognised Brazil as an independent empire with Pedro as Emperor of Brazil. On João's death the following year, the Regency council declared **Pedro IV** king. He hardly knew Portugal or his younger brother Miguel but he had conceived a plan to settle all the problems. He proposed a new compromise constitution in which a chamber of deputies was partly elected and partly nominated with an upper house of hereditary peers. Pedro IV then abdicated on condition that **Miguel** marry Maria, his seven year old daughter, and rule as her regent under the new constitution. Miguel happily agreed, returned to Portugal, swore his oath of loyalty and promptly abolished the constitution. He recalled the old *Cortes* and, in 1828, proclaimed himself king. Maria, still in transit when the news reached her, diverted to England. The Azores, out in the Atlantic, were not in favour of accepting Miguel so declared Pedro regent in the name of his daughter. Pedro abdicated his Brazilian empire to establish his daughter's claim to the throne and promptly set sail for the Azores where he made his base. The 'War of Two Brothers' led to capitulation by Miguel and in 1834 he was back in exile. Pedro died in the same year and his 15 year old daughter took the throne as **Maria II**.

The Decline of a Monarchy

At 16, Maria married the Duke of Leuchtenburg but he died soon after his arrival in Lisbon. A year later she married the German Duke Ferdinand of Saxe-Coburg-Gotha, had 11 children and died, still only 36, giving birth to her twelfth. Her reign was to witness the birth of political parties.

Disputes still continued over the constitution. Some favoured the charter introduced by Pedro II, strongly supported by Maria herself, whilst the liberals wanted a return to the constitution of 1822. The liberals themselves failed to present a unified view and soon divided into conservatives and progressives, the latter calling themselves the **Septembrists** after their revolutionary victory of September 1836 brought them to power. Their first demand was the restoration of the 1822 constitution but in 1838 they adopted a more moderate version. The **Chartists** made a return in 1842 and, under Costa Cabral, restored the Charter of 1826. It proved a firm government which re-established free trade and set Portugal on a track back towards prosperity. Cabral foundered on a relatively minor issue but one which struck at the very heart of age old custom. He declared that burials inside church were unhygienic and must stop. Devout women from the north were outraged and one in particular, Maria da Fonte, became the symbol of unrest which grew into a national rebellion in 1846. Feeling personally threatened, Cabral fled in disguise to Spain. On the edge of a civil war, English and French intervention steadied the unrest and restored Costa Cabral. In 1851 Cabral was ousted for good by another Chartist, Saldanha.

Maria II died in childbirth in 1853 and her husband, Duke Ferdinand of Saxe-Coburg-Gotha, ruled as regent for the next two years until their son, **Pedro V**, came of age. It was a brief reign and he died in 1861. He was succeeded by his brother Luís who became king at 23. **Dom Luís** (1861–89) was generally judged a popular king but then he left politics to the politicians and concentrated on things he did best, like translating Shakespeare and playing the cello. Two sons were born from his marriage to Maria Pia, daughter of Victor Emmanuel of Savoy who later became king of Italy.

Although it was a popular and peaceful reign, Portugal continued to lag behind the rest of Europe. An improved infrastructure encouraged foreign investment but the growth of industry was slow. It was tenacious on holding on to its colonial claims and territories in Africa but these too were a burden on the country's finances.

Carlos succeeded Luís in 1889 and inherited a crisis. In 1887 the Portuguese announced their intention to bring all the lands between the Angolan and Mozambican coasts under their control. This brought them into conflict with British interests and in 1890 Lord Salisbury issued an ultimatum: Portugal was to withdraw from that territory. There was no compromise on offer and the old alliance was at stake so Portugal had little option but to concede. The Progressist government fell, the Regenerators formed a government and fell, and a coalition government failed. Crisis followed crisis but Portugal was broke and forced to declare itself bankrupt.

The real threat to the establishment of the monarchy came from Republicanism, a radical and nationalist movement arising from the middle and lower classes. This movement attacked the government for its corruption and inefficiency but the pendulum of power started to swing in their favour with the collapse of the governing parties in the crisis of the 1890s.

Carlos, still dreaming of restoring the empire, could do little about growing republicanism, socialism and trade unionism. Struggling to maintain some sort of control, he appointed João Franco as Prime Minister in 1906 and endowed him with dictatorial powers. He promptly dismissed the *Cortes* and ruled by decree, but it had the effect of driving more liberals over to the Republican movement. Demonstrations against his dictatorship frequently ended in violence. An attempted Republican revolt in 1908 was followed by the assassination of the King and the Crown Prince. The Republicans denied involvement yet it benefited their cause.

Portugal's last king, **Manuel II** ascended the throne in 1908. His attempts to appease the Republicans also proved futile and the monarchy was violently overthrown on 5 October 1910. Dom Manuel, the Unfortunate, went into exile in England where he died in 1932.

The Republic

It can hardly be said that the Republicans grasped their opportunity with both hands. It is true that they won an overwhelming victory in 1911 with strong support from the urban and rural poor but they promptly disenfranchised much of their support by introducing electoral laws based on literacy. Unrealistically high hopes of the Republican supporters never materialised and there were further measures which alienated support, like the Law of Separation passed by parliament in an attempt to divide the Church from the State and gain control of the Catholic Church. Weak economic factors, cyclical revival of the monarchists and general political turmoil brought about 45 changes of government in the years up to 1926.

The Salazar Dictatorship

A bloodless coup on 28 May 1926 overthrew the Democratic party and put the military in control. Portugal's first Republic was at an end. There was an instant jostling for power but General Carmona emerged finally and became president.

One of Carmona's first acts was to invite the well-known professor of economics from Coimbra University, **António de Oliveira Salazar**, to take the post of finance minister, but he quickly resigned when he realised his control was too limited. In 1928, with the country's finances in an even worse mess, Salazar was re-appointed, this time with full powers, to put the economy in order. Now he had complete and utter control over government and departmental expenses and by using strict monetarist policies he brought the budget into balance for the first time in many years. In 1932 he was appointed Prime Minister and held that position until an accident with a deck chair in 1968 brought on a stroke.

In 1933 a new political constitution converted the military dictatorship into an authoritarian, nationalistic and pro-Catholic regime. A special police force kept vigilant guard against subversive activities and censorship was rigid, especially over journalism. Salazar had no appetite for party politics so he permitted just one, the National Union, but it was without power. Numerous coup attempts were put down but Salazar's leadership was never seriously threatened and he continued to govern virtually as a dictator. Improvements in the infrastructure included bridges over the Tejo, Douro and other important waterways, new roads and hospitals, while the economy in general grew steadily.

Portugal remained formally neutral throughout the Spanish Civil War but sent an unofficial army of some magnitude to aid Franco's Nationalistic forces. Although Salazar and his ministers were admirers of Germany, Portugal remained neutral again in World War II. Under pressure to sell the metal wolfram to the Germans, a balancing act was achieved by allowing Britain the use of a base on the Azores and in giving generous credit. Refugees flooded into neutral Portugal including the rich and the famous, and also spies of all nationalities. There was no doubt where the sympathies of the ordinary people lay and the allied victory was widely celebrated throughout the country.

Following the end of the war, Salazar called free elections allowing a role for a newly formed liberal party, the Movement of Democratic Unity. It was the first legal opposition party permitted under Salazar's rule. Some electioneering was permitted in the month preceding elections but the disenchantment of the new party was immediate when they were listed by the police as dissidents. Portugal's strategic location proved more important than their record on democracy when membership of the North Atlantic Treaty Organisation was mooted, and they joined in 1949.

By 1960, events in the colonies were causing concern to Portugal, especially the violent uprising in Angola in 1961. It proved the spark to ignite war across all of Portugal's African colonies. Portugal reacted by crushing the revolts and, without offering concessions, tried to appease them by speeding up economic reforms. India, too, seized Goa in 1961. Greater military involvement in the colonies, now renamed 'Overseas Provinces´, was draining the country's finances. Salazar's tight control of the nation's purse strings had ensured the country was free from national debt but, equally, had no foreign investment. With the tasteful conversion of some of the country's historic buildings into *pousadas*, tourism was playing a more important role and bringing in a new source of wealth but not enough and, by 1965, Salazar, on his 76th birthday, agreed to allow foreign investment.

Revolution

A deck chair accident in 1968 brought Salazar's active term in office to a close. Acting Prime Minister Marcelo Caetano had the vision but not the strength to reform the New State at home and solve the colonial problems overseas. His limited liberal changes only stimulated demand for further democratisation. The clandestine Communist party, which had been in existence for around 20 years, gained ground and military unrest led to the formation of the Armed Forces Movement (MFA) in 1973. In February 1974, the ageing **General António de Spínola**, a member of government but dismissed, published *Portugal and the Future* which was a comprehensive critique of the country and its problems. The solution proffered was a military coup. After a couple of abortive attempts, it happened bloodlessly on 25 April 1974. The populace was euphoric sensing the end of a long nightmare.

The following day Spínola announced a Junta of National Salvation comprising seven military officers, co-ordinating committees and a council of state. Censorship was immediately abolished and elections promised. On 15 May, Spínola was inaugurated as president and a provisional government formed from a coalition of Communists, Socialists and Centrists led by Adelino da Palma Carlos with socialist Mário Soares as foreign secretary. Discontent festered with waves of strikes, shortages and general unrest which brought Carlos' resignation. Colonel Vasco Gonçalves, military governor of Lisbon, took over. Spínola himself, opposed to early decolonisation, consented to the independence of Guinea in 1974 but was reluctant to hand over Angola. He was pushed aside as president in 1974 and succeeded by General Costa Gomes who lasted for two years. Decolonisation did continue with Mozambique and the Cape Verde islands going peacefully but Angola and East Timor only after civil wars.

Towards Democracy

Elections for a constituent assembly on 25 April attracted almost 92 per cent of the registered voters and was won by the Socialists and Centrists, but it did not bring stability. In the two years after the revolution Portugal had six governments and in the following two years, between July 1976 and July 1978, they elected ten. By 1976 the economy was in poor shape, banks and insurance companies had been nationalised and giant monopolies taken over by the workers. A new constitution attempted to uphold democracy and socialism while giving greater powers to the president. Elections of 1976 favoured General Eanes as president who appointed **Mário Soares** as Prime Minister.

The next decade brought no greater stability since elections invariably failed to give any party overall majority, at least until 1987. Mário Soares held office as prime minister three times in that politically volatile period. In 1986 the presidential elections were narrowly won on the second round by Mário Soares who became the first civilian head of state in 60 years.

In 1986 Portugal entered the European Community which initiated changes greater than at any time since the revolution. Funds poured in to help modernise the infrastructure and, with increased foreign investment, the country enjoyed a sustained period of economic growth. Today there is a new wealth about with many now enjoying a good standard of living but it masks a deep poverty still experienced in parts of the countryside.

3. TOURING THE REGION

National Tourist Offices

Useful information leaflets are usually available on just about all areas of Portugal, as are brochures on the *pousadas*. Enquiries should be made to:

UK
Portuguese National Tourist Office, 22/25A Sackville Street, London W1X 1DE. Tel: 0171 494 1441

USA
Portuguese National Tourist Office, 590 Fifth Avenue, New York, NY 10036–4704. Tel: 212 354 4403/4/5/6/7/8

Canada
Portuguese National Tourist Office, 60 Bloor Street West, Suite 1005, Toronto, Ontario M4W 3B8. Tel: 416 921 7376

Other enquiries not directly connected with the promotion of tourism, such as visa applications, should be directed to the Embassy or consulate.

Passport Requirements

A valid passport allows entry for EU nationals for a period of 90 days and for North American citizens for a period of 60 days. To extend this period it is necessary to apply before the time expires to the Foreigners' Registration Service, Rua Conselheiro José Silvestre Ribeiro, 22, 1600 Lisbon.

Embassies and Consulates

Consular help is available in emergency situations and is largely advisory. The following indicates some areas in which they can help but it does not fully define the powers of the office:

- in the event of a lost or stolen passport they can issue an emergency one if necessary
- help with problems over lost or stolen money or tickets but only by contacting relatives or friends at your request to ask for financial assistance
- advise on details of transfering funds
- encash a cheque supported by a banker's card but only in an emergency
- make a loan to cover repatriation expenses but only as a last resort
- arrange for the next of kin to be informed following an accident or death and advise on procedures
- act for nationals arrested or imprisoned to inform relatives
- provide a list of local interpreters, English speaking doctors and solicitors
- give guidance on organisations experienced in tracing missing people.

Useful addresses in this context are:

British Embassy,
35–37 Rua São Domingos à Lapa,
Lisbon.
Tel: 01 661 191

British Consulate,
3072 Avenida da Boa Vista,
Porto.
Tel: 02 684 789

British Consulate,
21 Rua de Santa Isabel,
Portimão,
Algarve.
Tel: 082 23 071

British Consulate,
4 Rua General Humberto Delgardo,
Vila Real de Santo António,
Algarve.
Tel: 081 43 729

British Consulate,
Quinta de Santa Maria,
Estrada de Tavereve 3080,
Figueira da Foz.
Tel: 033 22 235

United States Embassy,
Avenida das Forças Armadas,
Lisbon.
Tel: 01 726 6600

United States Consulate,
826–3° Rua do Júlio Dinis,
Porto.
Tel: 02 63 094

Canadian Embassy,
2 Rua de Rosa Araújo,
Lisbon.
Tel: 01 562 547 or 563 821

Getting There

The easiest way to explore the northern region is to take a **fly-drive** package to Porto. The airport lies to the north of Porto which, although the airport is surrounded by a confusion of new roads, offers an easy escape for those who want to head directly into the country without visiting Porto itself.

Using the **ferry** from Plymouth to Santander in Spain is another popular route. Crossing the border into Portugal offers no difficulty whatsoever since virtually all the crossing points are now unmanned. The route via Lindoso is convenient for the north-west corner of the country whilst crossing into Bragança gives access to Trás-os-Montes and the central area. In either event, it is easy to join in at the appropriate chapter to follow the tours outlined.

By Air

TAP, the Portuguese National airline runs scheduled flights between London Heathrow and Porto, Lisbon and Faro; similar services are also offered by *British Airways*. In North America *TAP* operates services to Lisbon from New York, Boston, Los Angeles and Toronto. Some American carriers also offer direct flights to Portugal and other Spanish cities which may be equally convenient on a fly-drive holiday.

Charter flights from the UK, especially to Faro and Lisbon, vastly outnumber scheduled services and offer the most economical way to travel. If a seat only is required then these can be booked through a travel agent. *TAP* and some tour operators sometimes offer fly-drive holidays but it is just as convenient, and often more economical, to book a car in the UK before departure. All the major car hire companies are present in Portugal and can arrange car hire before departure but the most competitive of these is *Transhire* (Tel: 0171 978 1922, Fax: 0171 978 1797) which operate through *Auto Jardim*, a leading car hire company in Portugal with offices at all airports. Portugal is one of the cheaper countries in Europe for car hire.

Charter flights including a package holiday offer such good value that visitors from North America sometimes find it more economical to fly to Britain to take advantage of them. There are many tour operators listing holidays in Portugal. Travel agents mostly deal with a limited number of tour operators and may not be able to offer the destination required. All of them have directories and, on request, will check which operators do offer the preferred destination although it may be necessary to book elsewhere.

By Ferry

Car ferries link the south coast of England with ports in northern Spain which are convenient for Portugal. There are no services directly to Portugal itself. *Brittany Ferries* offer services between Plymouth and Santander in northern Spain while *P&O* operate ferries from Southampton to Bilbão. The choice of which route to follow from Spain into Portugal will be dictated by the intended destination. Since the borders are now open, crossing between Spain and Portugal offers no problems. Facilities for money exchange and refreshments exist only at major crossing points. *Brittany Ferries* also offer inclusive holidays which can be booked through travel agents.

Travel in Portugal

By Car

The vast network of minor roads in the north and the countless small villages and hamlets is far too challenging for most road map publishers, who tend to settle for a compromise by showing a selection of the more important roads. Many of the smaller roads are well surfaced, good to drive on and lead through rustic areas which are often more interesting than the main road routes. A compass is handy for these roads, even with a good map, for they wind and twist so much that it is easy to lose orientation.

Motorways and major roads are growing apace and few maps show them accurately or have marked in roads which have not yet been constructed. Some motorways, but not too many, are subjected to a toll which, considered against the rate of pay in Portugal, are expensive. A consequence is that they generally enjoy much lighter traffic and for longer journeys — for example, from Porto down to Lisbon — they are worth considering for their comfort and speed compared to the busy national roads.

The Portuguese drive on the right. Main roads are generally well surfaced and there is an increasing network of motorways, some of which are toll roads. Minor roads are mostly reasonable but potholes can be a danger. Road markings have improved considerably in recent years making driving much safer but there is a need to keep a watchful eye on the local drivers who lack awareness of others and have a compulsion to overtake any vehicle in front without necessarily waiting for an opportune moment. Warning signs, especially temporary ones, are not necessarily in English so words to look out for are *perigo* = danger; *desvio* = diversion, *obras* = road works and *lombas* which is a ridge in the road to calm traffic flow. As far as road maps are concerned, *Hildebrand's Travel Map*, 1:400,000 series, is reasonably accurate (few maps are particularly accurate for the web of minor roads) and, available in Portugal, the *Turinta* maps are fairly good.

Drivers must be over the age of 18, seat belts are compulsory and speed limits for cars without trailers are 60kph (37mph) in built up areas, 90kph (55mph) in rural areas and 120kph (75mph) on motorways. Certain items of equipment are obligatory and these include a fire extinguisher, a warning triangle in case of breakdown or accident, a spare set of light bulbs and a small first aid kit. If the car is a right-hand drive then headlight deflectors must also be fitted.

Police checks are frequent and drivers must be able to produce their passport, driver's licence and papers relevant to the vehicle or face a heavy fine.

In the event of an accident it is essential to call the police before the vehicle is moved. Emergency SOS telephones (orange coloured) are available along main roads for reporting accidents and emergencies. Otherwise the emergency telephone number nationwide is 151.

Petrol stations are plentiful along main routes, although it pays to fill before leaving if a route is chosen following minor roads. Unleaded petrol (*sem chumbro*) is freely available and major credit cards are accepted at main petrol stations although a small surcharge is sometimes levied.

By Train

There is an extensive rail network in Portugal connecting most of the major towns. Long-distance services by *rapido* trains are excellent. They are fast and comfortable usually offering restaurant and refreshment facilities. The *directo* trains stop rather more frequently whilst the *tranvia* service is primarily local and stops at every lamppost. Main services are listed in the Thomas Cook Continental timetable, available both in the UK and USA, and other timetables can be picked up locally. Tickets must be purchased before boarding.

By Bus

Comfortable express buses, some with toilet and refreshment facilities, connect most major towns to Lisbon and Porto. Until recently they carried the RN logo but privatising has replaced Rodoviária Nacional by at least nine new companies so the operating company varies with the region. In spite of this division, it remains an integrated nationwide service and the various regions work in harmony. Timetables are available locally and tickets must be obtained before boarding. Otherwise there is a good network of local buses which operate reliably to timetable.

Accommodation

Portugal offers accommodation in different types of establishments which need some introduction.

Pousadas
Pousadas are mostly located in outstanding beauty spots and often in buildings of great historical interest, like a converted castle or monastery. They are the equivalent of the Spanish paradores and represent the flagship of luxury accommodation. Unfortunately, these state run establishments do not always meet the high standards intended and the warm welcome and personalised service are not always evident but, as always, some succeed more than others. They are priced according to three categories from B, lowest, through C to CH which are the most expensive. Bookings are made through ENATUR, a central agency, on Av. Santa Joana a Princesa, 10–1700 Lisbon, telephone 01 848 1221. There are nine *pousadas* in the northern region and one hotel which belongs to the same organisation. Advance bookings for the more popular *pousadas* is essential for high season.

Ponies and trap

Solares de Portugal

This is one of the most confusing organisations likely to be encountered in Portugal, quite defying any lucid explanation. The confusion starts with its name since it is also known as Turihab and Turismo de Habitação and used to be known as manor houses. It is an organisation which controls the letting of the houses which have joined the association and many have, especially in the north. The houses in the scheme are mainly of great distinction. Some are very old family homes dating back to the 16th and 17th centuries, others may have once been water mills or *quintas*, great estate farmhouses of character. All of them are private and were in some state of decay just a decade or so ago but a contract with the government advanced them money to renovate in return for opening them up to tourism for a minimum period.

These houses are classified into three distinct groups: *casa antigas, quintas* and *herdades* and *casa rusticas*.

Casa Antigas are elegant manor houses and country estates mostly originating from the 17th and 18th centuries. They are furnished with period furniture and may contain valued works of art.

Quintas and Herdades are agricultural farms and estates with a rural setting and atmosphere. These often have their own distinctive architectural style which is rather grand and their estates are enclosed by tall walls.

Casa Rusticas are generally of a simpler architectural style and located in the heart of the country or within a farm.

Very few are in town locations, most are well off the beaten track and personal transport is essential. Booking conditions specify a minimum of three nights and there is no high and low season, prices for January and

August are exactly the same. The houses, which may also be self-contained apartments or cottages, fall into three categories, A, B and C, depending on certain criteria which include: the building's architectural style; interior decoration and antique furnishings; historical value of the house; facilities, swimming pool, tennis courts etc.; atmosphere: tranquillity and hospitality; enthusiastic proprietors with local knowledge and language skills; service: well-trained staff, well-presented food, daily change of bed linen etc.

One selling point is that families still live in the houses so guests can observe the local customs and way of life at first hand.

Although all the properties look good, they do not always meet the high ideals set. Living with dark antique furniture in a gloomy room with a remote owner and staff who do not speak English can be a trial rather than a relaxing experience. Breakfast is always included and often served in the room since the view prevails that guests prefer privacy. Although many advertise the availability of evening meals, these are not always on offer which, in remote locations, can be a source of irritation. On the positive side, staying in a good house with a thoughtful owner can be an exhilarating experience.

Some of the self-catering establishments (breakfast is still provided) have excellent character, like the converted water mill Minho de Estorãos, near Ponte de Lima, and provide a more relaxing atmosphere.

There are many houses in the scheme throughout Portugal with the northern region having perhaps the majority. Most of them, but by no means all of them, can be booked through TURIHAB, Praça da Republica, 4900 Ponte de Lima, telephone 058 741672. There are two other organisations offering a similar service, PRIVETUR, Rua de João Penha, 10–Sala 15, 1200 Lisbon, telephone 01 690549 and ANTER, which specialise in rural tourism, at Quinta do Campo, Valado do Frades, 2450 Nazaré, telephone 062 577135.

Other Accommodation

Several other categories of accommodation are available which are as baffling to unravel as the manor house system. There are hotels in various categories from one to five stars, but in addition there are **albergarias** and **estalagems**, both of which are described as inns. *Albergarias* offer a four-star comfort whereas the *estalagems* may be four or five-star. Both seem indistinguishable from hotels. A **residencial** slots in somewhere between a hotel and a **pensão** and offers one to four-star accommodation. Some hotels prefer to operate as *residencials* as do some pensions. Pensions form the lowest stratum and can be a mixed bag best sorted out by actual inspection.

Crime and Theft

Portugal is normally a safe destination and a relatively crime free country but recently there has been a rise in non violent crime, particularly involving theft from car boots. Motorists are strongly advised to leave nothing on display in the car nor to leave valuables locked in the boot and not to let their car out of sight if it is loaded with luggage. Some areas are worse in this respect than others and the Lisbon region is one of the worst.

Otherwise, it is wise to protect valuables, including camera, with as much care as at home and not make it easy for any casual thief. All losses must be reported to the police, especially if an insurance claim is anticipated. In towns seek out the PSP (Policia de Segurança Pública) who deal with tourist incidents but in rural areas this function is taken over by the GNR (Guarda National Rebulicana) who normally carry out traffic responsibilities and police the motorways. The chances of finding an English speaking policeman are only fair. Old fashioned courtesy and respect goes a long way in Portugal in all walks of life and is particularly recommended in dealing with the police.

Disabled Travellers

Portugal is only slowly coming to terms with the needs of the disabled and only the more recently built hotels offer anything like good facilities. Airports and main stations have generally adapted toilet facilities and there are specially reserved spaces in most towns for disabled motorists. Local tourist offices (addresses at the end of each chapter) can sometimes supply a list of wheelchair accessible hotels and campsites but the Institute for the Promotion of Tourism, Rua Alexandre Herculano 51, 1200 Lisbon publishes a list of hotels which are more suitable to wheelchair users. Ramps for crossing roads are still in short supply as are pavements outside main towns.

Money Matters

Most towns of any size have a bank where money can be changed, either from bank notes, travellers cheques or eurocheques. Bank hours are from 8.30am to 3.00pm during weekdays. Exchange bureaux can also be found in popular tourist areas. In addition there is a growing network of automatic teller machines called Multibanco which dispense cash 24 hours a day and can be used with a wide selection of cards including Visa, Eurocheque, Eurocard and American Express. There is a daily limit of 40,000 *escudos*.

Museums and Galleries

Portugal's major museums are undergoing extensive renovations which seem to be taking years rather than months. These are closed to the public so it has not been possible to give any detailed description nor is it known how the displays will be arranged when they finally reopen. In general, museums are closed on a Monday and, like the rest of Portugal, closed for a couple of hours midday. Although not closing officially until 12.30pm, last entry is usually 12noon and is strictly enforced.

Public Holidays

Since virtually every town has one or more religious festivals it sometimes seems that the country is on permanent holiday but the list of National Holidays celebrated nationwide is appreciably shorter. Easter is consistent with the rest of Europe and the holidays associated with it include Shrove Tuesday and Good Friday. Corpus Christi, late May or early June, is another variable holiday but the remainder are fixed as follows:

1 January	New Year's Day	5 October	Republic Day
25 April	Liberation Day	1 November	All Saints
1 May	May Day	1 December	Independence Day
10 June	Camões Day	8 December	Immaculate Conception
15 August	Assumption	25 December	Christmas Day

Restaurant Closing Days

Most eating places close on at least one day each week. Rather surprisingly, popular closing days are clustered around weekend, especially Friday, Saturday and Sunday and in some places there is a very limited selection on these days. The closing day is usually posted on the door and it pays to take note of this at favoured restaurants.

Sport

Portugal is a haven for golfers, especially Algarve which is well endowed with courses and where the climate allows the sport to be enjoyed the whole year around, although new courses seem to be opening steadily in other parts. The latest of these is near Ponte de Lima. Tennis facilities are mostly associated with hotels, some of which allow public access, but also there are clubs which open their courts to non members. Similarly horse riding stables are usually to be found in centres of tourism. There is plenty of opportunity for walking but no officially marked trails. Some holiday companies lead organised walks, but the best guides are three books published by Sunflower books, *Landscapes of Algarve*, *Landscapes of Costa Verde* and *Landscapes of Sintra, Estoril & Cascais*, all by the authors of this book, which detail long and short walks.

Hunting mainly for wild boar, partridge and pheasant, is a new growth area and reserves and lodges are on the steady increase. Further details can be obtained from the Federação Portuguesa de Tiro com Armas de Caça, Avenida Júlio Dinis, 10–4° Esq°, 1200 Lisboa.

There are plenty of opportunities for water sports in the main resort areas, conditions for surfing are often good, especially on the west coast, but there are also good spots for wind surfing. Sailing too is popular with marinas spread around the coast, the majority in the south.

Particular details of facilities are listed at the end of each chapter, as appropriate.

Tax Free Shopping

Visitors from outside the European Union can take advantage of the tax free system by shopping at any of the 1500 shops which display the tax free logo. A receipt must be obtained for which a reimbursement of tax will be made at the airport on departure, either in cash or by credit if a credit card was used in the first instance.

4. FOOD AND WINE

Some of the huge kitchens in the older manor houses tell how the Portuguese discovered the art of good eating and lavish entertainment many centuries ago. As a nation of explorers, their great seafarers brought back more than gold and metals, they brought back pepper and spices of which cinnamon was the real prize. It is often said one boatload of cinnamon raised enough money to pay for an entire expedition to India. Vasco da Gama brought curry powder for the kitchen which continues to find frequent use but rarely in overpowering quantities, more to add a background oriental flavour to a wide range of soups and stews. The hot chilli pepper so successfully cultivated in Angola is another favourite of Portuguese chefs but it turns up under its African name of piri-piri, and is frequently used as a sauce mixed in oil and vinegar. It is these hints of other cultures, the taste of Africa, the smell of the Orient, which brings a uniqueness to Portuguese cuisine.

Like the French, the Portuguese are devoted to their food and will happily drive long distances to their favourite restaurant or to try out a friend's recommendation. On the whole, they have farmer-size appetites which is reflected in massive portions and some restaurants list half portions (*meia dose*) on the menu which are more or less half price. Where there is an option, the half *dose* is normally adequate and, in any case, there is always the opportunity of ordering another portion, or even something different, if it is not enough. The size of the portions do vary and tend to be smaller — actually not so much smaller as normal — in restaurants which cater more for tourists. Many restaurants will still provide half *doses* even though they may not be listed and it pays to look around other tables before ordering. If unsure, two people can always order one and a half *doses* between them.

Restaurants are not the only places to eat in Portugal, there is also a café culture which primarily meets the needs of the locals for coffee and cakes, but many provide food as well. These cafés are often a good bet for a lunch time meal — the special of the day is often excellent value and some provide remarkably good food. Many continue to serve food in the evening from a limited menu but it is best to proceed on recommendations where possible.

Soup

A meal starts invariably with soup and, for the Portuguese, may also end with a soup. One of the specialities of the north but equally popular throughout

Coffee and Cakes

The Portuguese are renowned for genteel afternoon tea, a custom which Catherine of Bragança introduced to the English. Visitors are unlikely to see any evidence of this but will certainly witness the Portuguese calling in to a local café during the morning for a quick coffee and cake. This is a national pastime. The larger shops act as a gathering place for those happy to while away the hours, morning, noon or night. No matter where it is bought, the coffee is always excellent which is perhaps not too surprising for a country which once ranked some of the great coffee producing countries, like Brazil, Angola and Timor, amongst its colonies. **Coffee** is served in a bewildering variety of ways. The Portuguese mainly prefer a *bica*, a small strong coffee, which is good for a quick fix of caffeine but hardly slakes a thirst. Worse still, the small cup is only half full, so for a full cup ask for a *cheio* which simply means full. A *pingo* will bring a small strong coffee with a drop (*pingo*) of milk, but for a larger coffee ask for a *meia de leite* which is usually a normal cup size, half of strong coffee filled up with hot frothed up milk. In tourist areas, *café com leite* is well understood and it usually produces a white coffee, but if less milk is preferred then *só pouco leite* added to the order should result in a less milky coffee. To be sure to get a large cup the word *grande* can be added to the order. Terms for coffee tend to be very local and do not always apply in other parts of the country. On one occasion, a request for *meia de leite*, literally half of milk, which works well in the north, produced a cup of milk and a cup of coffee in a part of the country where *café com leite* is more normally used. Two more coffees which are invariably on the list are *galão*, weak, milky coffee served in a glass and *galão direita* which is half milk, half coffee served in a glass. Other descriptions of coffee may appear on the menu but these are mainly alternative names of the types described. Tea drinkers should beware that many of the shops make tea very badly often trying to brew it from hot rather than boiling water. If there is an opportunity, head for a tea shop for the best brew where herbal teas may also be available. *Chá* will bring tea, *chá com leite* will bring tea with milk and *chá com limão* a refreshing tea with lemon.

Few coffee shops sell coffee without selling **cakes** (*bolos*). Whilst the north has no particular specialities, there is still a good range available. Rice cakes (*arroz*) offer a light sponge which is not usually so sweet, *bolo da rocha* is a delicious bun with a coconut top and filled with custard, whilst coconut cakes, *cocos*, are also good. Donuts are mostly filled with custard; but for something plainer try the *palmier* which look like butterfly wings. *Pão de ló*, a light sponge cake, is another popular choice which, although baked as a large ring, is sold in slices.

the country is **caldo verde**, a jade-green soup rich with potatoes, garlic, shreds of green cabbage and olive oil with a slice of a spicy sausage lurking at the bottom. Although it originated in the Minho, just about every region of Portugal is prepared to call this soup its own and it does vary around the country. The cabbage used is a non-heading variety with tender leaves which are taken from the plant as desired leaving a progressively longer bare stalk, rather like a sprout plant with all the sprouts removed. Cutting the cabbage is the secret to *calde verde* soup. A stack of cabbage leaves are rolled into a cigar shape and then cut from the end into extremely fine shreds, the finer the shreds the better the colour of the soup, and these shreds are added at the last minute with minimum cooking before the soup is served. There is another soup frequently on the menu, not from the north this time but one that has achieved widespread popularity, **açorda á Alentejana** or Alentejo bread soup. It is more than a soup, it is a meal in itself. Coriander, salt and garlic are ground to a paste, let down with olive oil and poured into boiling water. Bread is added, sometimes in pieces or sometimes whole slices, and one or two eggs are dropped in. Even the Portuguese may struggle to start and finish a meal with this soup.

Bacalhau

Fish and meat dishes appear on the menu in almost equal ratio. Surrounded by sea and with several major rivers, fresh fish is constantly available. But it is not the fresh fish which has become the national dish but **bacalhau**, the dried salted cod. Looking more like pieces of board, it is distinctly un-appetising and smelly in the dry state and it advertises itself strongly on passing one of the shops. As early as the 16th century sailors learnt to salt cod at sea and sun dry it for the long journey home. It dries down to thin, stiff slabs which can be safely kept for months and quickly reconstituted by soaking in water. Almost since Columbus discovered America, Newfoundland's Grand Banks have been the traditional fishing ground for cod and it has provided catches enough to be a source of cheap food which has served the tables of the poor particularly well. The over-fished Grand Banks no longer yield enough to meet the nation's demands and it has become necessary to import *bacalhau* from Norway at a price which the poor can now hardly afford.

The Portuguese claim at least 365 ways to prepare *bacalhau*, one for every day of the year. All the recipes start by soaking the cod in water for 24 to 48 hours with frequent changes of water to remove the salt. Afterwards the cod is usually boiled gently until soft then mixed with potatoes in some form, covered with a cheese sauce and baked in the oven. Only the more popular recipes appear on restaurant menus which include *bacalhau à bràs*, with egg, onion and thinly sliced fried potatoes, and *bacalhau à gomes de sá* which is a casserole dish with onions and sliced potatoes then garnished with black olives and hard boiled eggs.

Bacalhau com Broa

One of the northern specialities is *bacalhau com broa*, *broa* being the dark brown maize bread so popular in the maize growing areas of the north. The recipe is as follows: take 600g of *bacalhau*, preferably thick pieces which have been prepared by soaking, and season with pepper, a bay leaf and chopped garlic (two cloves) then add five tablespoons of white wine. Cut open both sides of the fish to the bone and stuff with six pieces of *presunto* (smoked, cooked ham) or pork sausage. Coat the fish with crumbled *broa*, place in an oven dish, add half a chopped onion and olive oil then roast until ready. Serve with boiled potatoes and brussel sprouts.

Some fish items on the menu are easily recognised like *truta* and *sardinhas* but others are less obvious:

robalo	bass	*salmão*	salmon
pargo	bream	*salmonete*	red mullet
cirós	eels	*linguado*	sole
pescada	hake	*espadarte*	sword fish
carapau	mackerel	*atum*	tuna
solha	plaice	*lampreia*	lamprey

Both salmon and trout are fished from the rivers in the northern region, salmon from the Minho. Local sardines are in season from June to October, which is the best time to buy them, but they are available all the year round although the Portuguese claim they are too bony to eat between November and April. They are barbecued at just about every outdoor fair or celebration throughout the country. In restaurants, sardines are traditionally served with boiled potatoes.

The Cataplana

A speciality introduced by the Arabs and particularly popular in Algarve is the *cataplana*. This seafood dish has a place on menus throughout the country, particularly in the larger restaurants. The *cataplana* is a hinged metal pan with a long handle which can be thrust into the fire. A close fitting heavy lid retains the steam so that the pan behaves a little like a pressure cooker which can be safely shaken and turned over whilst cooking. In the modern version, the *cataplana* is without a handle. There are various recipes in which clams feature prominently but one of the most popular uses clams, pork, onions, herbs and white wine. Often the *cataplana* is brought to the table so that diners can enjoy the rich aroma released when opened.

Copper stills at Ponte de Lima market

Pork

Pork figures strongly on the meat menu and with good reason, the meat is truly tender and succulent. Pigs in Portugal live the high life on a diet of acorns and chestnuts, with probably a few truffles thrown in, and are highly prized for the production of *presunto*, smoked ham. Pork is also used in endless garlicky sausages which are popular throughout the north and a speciality of Trás-os-Montes. *Chouriço* is a dark sausage, around six or seven inches long and an inch thick, which is made from cured pork and spiced with garlic and paprika. *Murcela* is a blood sausage and one commonly used to add to *calde verde* soup. *Linguica* is like *chouriço* but slimmer, while *alheira* is a fresh sausage made from pork. Thin slices of ham are used in a number of recipes in which they may be used to wrap around fish or chicken. One speciality of the north is *rójoes*, deep fried nuggets of pork, which turns up in various combinations sometimes with slices of sausage.

Other Meat Dishes

Steak turns up mostly as *bife à Portuguesa* which is either grilled or cooked with a port wine sauce. *Cabrito*, kid, is also highly favoured by the Portuguese and finds its way on to most menus in some dish or other and is usually excellent. Recipes for roast kid often read like Mrs Beeton ... kill the kid, cleanse and hang it in the cellar, while still warm wash well with water and salt ... this is followed by frequent painting with a garlicky seasoning while still hanging before it reaches the oven two days later. Both chicken (*frango*) and turkey (*peru*) appear on the menu but are mostly served simply, although the locals prefer chicken with *piri-piri* sauce. Turkey is mostly served as steaks.

Vegetables

Vegetables abound on local markets and they are good quality vegetables too. There is just about everything imaginable from carrots, through cauliflower to turnips, leeks or whatever is in season. None of this shows up on the dinner plate in the restaurant, unless *cozido* is ordered The recipe featured here shows how the vegetables are used and the quantities that the Portuguese eat.

Salads are sometimes served with the meal in place of vegetables but invariably there is rice involved somewhere, served mostly in separate dishes in kilo quantities!

Desserts

The Portuguese have a sweet tooth so there is certain to be a sweet trolley hovering at the end of the main course or a *sobremesa* list on the menu. Eggs and sugar are used in abundance to produce the fantasies so loved by the Portuguese. Fantasies they are too judging by some of the descriptive and

Portuguese Cozido

These quantities are for six people! Boil 500g of beef in water using a large pan and, a little while later, add half a chicken and season with salt. Cook in a separate pan, 300g ham, 500g salted pigs ears, 500g fresh bacon, 500g salted pork ribs, one meat sausage and one blood sausage. Add no salt since the meat is already salted. To the beef pan add now the vegetables comprising two good green cabbages, one white cabbage and three large carrots but tie the vegetables with white thread so that they can easily be removed. After 30 minutes, boil six halved potatoes separately until partly cooked and transfer to the beef pan followed by all the meat, now cooked, from the other pan. The *cozido* is ready as soon as the potatoes have finished cooking. Carefully remove the vegetables, place all the meat suitably cut onto a serving dish and decorate with the vegetables after removing all the threads.

The stock from the large pan can later be used to make soup by adding cooked, small white beans and small noodles.

colourful names, like *barriga de freiras* (nun's belly) and *papos de anjo* (angel's breasts). Two sweets ever present on the menu are *arroz doce*, a cold rice pudding liberally sprinkled with cinnamon and usually very sweet, and the ubiquitous *pudim de flan* which is none other than crème caramel of which the Portuguese are extraordinarily fond. The calorie count is so high for most sweets that the energy released is best measured on the Richter scale; check out some of the recipes featured here.

Cheese

If the puddings are all too sweet there is always the cheese which is some-times put on the table with olives to provide nibbles at the start of a meal. *Broa*, the dark brown moist bread which is especially appetising when fresh, turns up in the bread basket alongside white bread in regions where maize is grown as a major crop. The pick of Portugal's limited cheeses, which are mostly expensive to buy in the shops, is the brie-like *queijo da serra* made strictly from the milk of sheep grazing on the mountains of Serra da Estrela. *Serpa*, cured in caves and brushed regularly with an olive oil/paprika mixture, is from Alentejo and is equally delicious but much stronger after ageing. Tangy and creamy *azeitão*, from the Arrábida peninsula across the Tagus south of Lisbon is another of the more famous cheeses as is *beja*, a semi hard cheese again from Alentejo. For the calorie counters there is always *queijos frescos* which is an uncured soft cheese rather like cottage cheese.

Nun's Thighs and All That

There is an endless selection of recipes for sweets but they have two things in common, a huge quantity of sugar and countless eggs in some form.

Leite Pudim (Custard Cream)
Beat eight egg yolks with 250g sugar and the rind of one lemon for over 20 minutes. Blend two tablespoons of cornflour into one litre of milk, beat well and add to the egg yolk mixture. Heat to bring to the boil while stirring constantly, remove the lemon rind and pour into a dish. Before serving, sprinkle the surface with sugar and place under a grill to caramelise the surface.

Viana Pie
A fairly large tray is needed for this Swiss roll type sweet. Beat ten egg yolks with 200g sugar and add grated lemon (or orange rind). Beat the whites stiffly and add to the dough and sift in 170g flour. Beat lightly and bake on a tray lined with paper. Do not over bake otherwise it becomes difficult to roll. To make the filling, boil 100g sugar to a soft syrup, add the whisked yolks of four eggs and heat until the mixture comes to the boil.

Take the cake from the tray and place on a sugared surface, spread the egg filling and roll carefully.

Rabanadas Minhotas
These are essentially cooked bread slices which can be eaten for breakfast or at any time of the day.

Boil a little red Vinho Verde wine with sugar and cinnamon and dip slices of bread into the mixture until well soaked. Dip the bread next into beaten egg and fry in olive oil. Sprinkle with sugar and cinnamon before eating.

Egg cigars (speciality from Arcos de Valdevez)
Make the filling by boiling 250g sugar with a little water until the syrup reaches the thread stage and adding 250g ground almonds, eight egg yolks, a tablespoon of butter and the rind of a lemon.

Dampen some round filo pastry sheets with egg white, add the filling and roll into cigar shapes. Deep fry and coat with sugar before eating.

Wines

Port

Port wine is Portugal's most eminent ambassador. It has had a place on the dinner tables of Europe and beyond for more than three centuries, and is a household name. But there is no better place to drink port than in Portugal. A tour around the great port houses in Gaia, as described in Chapter 5, gives some insight into some of the stages in the manufacture and provides the opportunity to try out a few labels. The full range of styles is quite bewildering but the chief variables are the ageing process and the age. All ports start in casks for two years but after that they are either matured in wood or in bottles and may be a single vintage or a blend of different years. Some of the major styles are:

Ruby port: this is made for drinking as soon as it is bottled which is usually after about three years in wood. This full-bodied fruity wine of good ruby colour is still the biggest selling port wine. More sophisticated 'Reserve' and 'Vintage Character' rubies are also made. Both of these are aged longer in the casks, usually to around four or more years, and the Vintage Character may be from selected harvests from different years but it will not continue to improve in the bottle.

White port: made and fortified in exactly the same way as ruby but made from white grapes. It may be sweet or dry but the modern tendency is for dry or extra dry. Taylors produced the first white port, Chip Dry, in 1935 and it is still one of the best and great as an apéritif.

Crusted: it starts life earmarked as vintage but it does not meet the standards so it is blended and aged for at least three years in a cask and two years in a bottle. During bottle storage it throws a deposit, or crust, and needs to be decanted before drinking.

Tawny: usually made from grapes from the lower Douro which are less heavily pigmented. It is matured in wood for much longer than the ruby so that the wine loses its red colour and acquires a brownish tawny colour. Smooth and mellow, the tawnies are very popular, especially the older ones. There are strict regulations controlling the labelling of port wines and a date on the label is not permitted except for exceptional wines of a single harvest under certain conditions. Even though they start life as blends, good quality tawnies can, with special approval from the Port Wine Institute, show their age as 10, 20, 30 or over 40 years old.

All the above wines are blends of several years but the following are only from single years and sometimes from particular *quintas*. The wines are allowed to carry the date on the label.

Single Quinta: this is an unblended wine usually from a single harvest. It is vintage in character but without the full depth and character. It usually requires long ageing in the bottle to reach perfection.

Vintage: this is the flagship of the port wine industry. Hopes are raised for a vintage in years when the climate has been favourable and the harvest good but they remain no more than hopes at that stage. Only after two years in the cask is a decision made and, if declared a vintage, it is bottled straight away. When mature it has a different quality to the cask aged ports. Vintage declarations are not taken lightly and reflect the individuality of each of the port houses. The Douro has such a multitude of vineyard sites with different grape varieties and different micro-climates that declared vintages are not universal but mostly quite specific to a particular manufacturer. The larger port houses which have a wider variety of farms have more chance of producing a vintage than the smaller firms. Vintage ports take some years to reach their optimum and they do not all mature at the same rate. Cockburn's declare their 1963 vintage as drinking well and one of their finest vintages of recent times, the 1970 vintage, as ready soon and the 1975 vintage as light but of good quality and just ready.

Late Bottled Vintage: is port of a single year, aged in wood for 4–6 years and filtered before bottling to prevent crusting.

The Port Wine Institute is the controlling body which guarantees that standards are maintained. The Institute has a bar in Porto (see Chapter 5) where port wines can be tried by the glass. Every port wine made from all the manufacturers is on the menu listed by style and by manufacturer so it is a great place to sample the various ports (except the expensive vintages) without having to buy full bottles.

Something like 83 million litres of port are consumed annually and most of it in Europe with France drinking the lion's share. The UK has fallen down the league table of port consumption to be overtaken by Portugal itself. The USA is a low market taking only around 1.5 per cent of the annual production but it is strongly biased to premium styles.

Many of the familiar names of port are now being taken over but they still trade under the same labels. Sandeman remains the major port shipper followed by the Symington group which includes Dow and Graham and third is Royal Oporto. The history of port is featured on p 68 (chapter 5) and the making of port wine on p 80 (chapter 6).

Vinho Verde and Douro Wines

Apart from port, Portugal has many very fine wines to offer apart from the well known Mateus rosé, and some very ordinary ones too. The Portuguese themselves drink gallons of wine but rarely get drunk. They tend to buy their wine in five litre flasks. Throughout just about all of the northern region, apart from the colder parts of Trás-os-Montes, vines are farmed by anyone with a square yard of land, which means that there is a lot of wine made for home consumption. This in turn is reflected in the stocks carried by the local shops who are without a good market and therefore tend to offer a small selection of predominantly local wines. Bigger supermarkets often give the best choice. There are some excellent labels which have only a very local and limited distribution. *Quinta da Pacheca*, in the Alto Douro, is an excellent red Douro wine but only rarely can it be found in shops or in restaurants away from the region where it is made. At least there is a sense of adventure in trying different wines with a chance of some rewarding discoveries.

The country has a number of regions of demarcation, two in the northern area, Vinho Verde and the Douro. Although Vinho Verde translates to green wine it really means young or fresh wine and is usually listed separately on the wine list in restaurants, the other wines are listed under *Vinhos maduros*, or mature wines, which means everything other than the Vinho Verdes. *Garrafeira* on the wine label means that the wine has been aged for a minimum of two years in the barrel and one in the bottle, but often much longer, whilst *Reservas* spend even longer in the wood.

Douro wines arise from grapes grown in the Alto Douro in areas generally away from the river. The land close to the River Douro is prized for the port wine grapes. Even away from the river the earth is the same impossibly dry and impoverished stony soil which looks as though it will not sustain any sort of plant growth. This region produces some very fine and exciting wines including one of the country's best red wines, *Barca Velha*, made in limited quantity. Some of the best years which are still around are 81, 82, 83 and 84. *Quinta do Cotto* produces dense fruity wines which are well worth searching out and laying down.

The area of demarcation for **Vinho Verde** is quite extensive and covers much of the region outside the Douro. In fact the only region north of the Douro which is not dedicated to vineyards is the higher part of Trás-os-Montes. Details on the growth of the vines and the production of the wine is included in chapter 8, p 127. Vinho Verde is a light, refreshing, acidic wine with a slight sparkle induced by a shot of carbon dioxide. In alcohol strength it is on the low side, eight to nine percent, and comes in two colours red and white. Only the white has achieved any fame outside Portugal whilst the red in virtually unknown. This is in total contrast to the area where it is grown, here the red is drunk almost exclusively by the locals but be warned, it is an acquired taste. The red is a wine on its own. Its harshness lies outside the boundaries of the flowing eloquence of descriptive terms used by wine buffs, it is acidic, scours the taste buds with the subtlety of raw acetic acid and adds a piquancy even to a highly spiced lunch. Perhaps it is only necessary to quote the description of the red wine from the leaflet produced by the *Ponte de Lima* wine co-operative 'light and aromatic, should be drunk at 16–18 degrees and is good to accompany pig's blood rice, stewed giblets and catfish rice and cod´. Intrepid explorers determined to journey into this particular unknown might start with the Ponte da Lima red and, palate withstanding, move on from this gentle introduction. The very best reds are those freshly made in the villages which are not gassed up and never reach the shops.

White Vinho Verde, although stimulatingly acidic, is a very different wine. With so many small producers in the north, the list of labels is endless but the *Ponte de Lima* whites have a good reputation. The white made from a single grape variety, the *loureiro* grape, and called by that name is especially worth trying. *Casa de Sezim*, which is one of the more comfortable manor houses in the Solares scheme, is another small producer with a good reputation.

Bairrada and Dão Wines

Two demarcated areas south of the River Douro produce good wine and are close enough to the northern region for their wines to appear on restaurant lists. These are the Bairrada wines which come from an area south of Porto and the Dão wines from the region south of the Alto Douro. The mountainous Dão region is served by a river of the same name which filters down to the sea through Coimbra. The **Dão wines** built up a good reputation in the past but they have not advanced in quality in recent years as other regions have, notably Alentejo. With considerable capital investment in new stainless steel plant and new technology, wine making in Portugal is in a mobile phase which is advancing some of the newer wines over old favourites. A new high-tech Sogrape plant in Viseu is producing some worthwhile **Grão Vasco** wines both white and red.

Bairrada wines are made in the area south of Porto stretching all the way down to Coimbra. Although wine manufacture has been in hand here as long as most other areas in Portugal, it was recognised as a demarcated region only as recently as 1979. Vineyards are dominated by the *baga* grape and make good red wines which take some years to reach maturity. It pays to buy the *garrafeiras* and the older the better. The last years of the 1970s, from '75 onwards, are all worth buying. Guests at the Palace Hotel in Buçaco Forest have the opportunity to try their legendary red wine, *Buçaco*, which is unavailable outside their chain of hotels. Much of the white wine of this region is converted to a sparkling wine by the champagne method.

Colares, Carcavelos, Bucelos and Setúbal

Nearer to Lisbon there are four small demarcated areas: Colares (see feature) and Carcavelos, both very small, with the slightly larger Bucelos all on the north side of the Tagus and the Setúbal vineyards on the south. With the expansion of the holiday resorts of Estoril and Cascais south of Lisbon, the **Carcavelos** area is under threat; it is small and getting smaller. It produces a Madeira style sweet aperitif or dessert wine of around 19 per cent strength but it is difficult to find. Look for the *Quinta do Barão* label. Some 24km (15 miles) north of Lisbon lies the **Bucelos** wine area centred around the Trancão river. Predominantly two white grape varieties, *arinto* and *esgana cão*, are grown on the clay slopes and floor of the river valley. These produce reliable

Colares Wines

Colares, near Sintra, produces one of the best and most distinctive wines in Portugal from vineyards which are not just unique, they defy belief. The practice is by no means new, it can be traced back as far as 1154. Vines are planted into clay but to reach the clay it is first necessary to dig through a depth of sand which may be as much as 10m (33ft). Digging a trench so deep through sand is not without danger and it was commonplace for workers to cover their heads with a wicker basket while excavating at depth to give them protection and air to breath should the trench collapse. Once planted, the vines are encouraged to produce lateral shoots which are pegged down at intervals and allowed to root thus producing a whole row of seemingly individual vines. As the vines start to grow the sand is slowly replaced until, eventually, the vines reach normal surface level. Once above ground, the vines are grown along wire strainers without achieving any great height and the vineyards are protected by high fences of fine netting to prevent the Atlantic winds from disturbing the sand. One unexpected and invaluable advantage of this method was that the depth and density of the sand gave protection to the vine roots from the ravages of the phylloxera beetle which decimated the vineyards of Europe last century. This beetle operates by burrowing through the soil and feeding from the rootstock which eventually sickens the vine. It was introduced from the United States during viticultural exchanges and, oddly enough, the solution to the problem also came from the States in the form of more rugged root stocks which had proved immune to the scourge. European vines were then universally grafted onto these rootstocks. Colares still uses the original pre-phylloxera vines. The red wines are generally better than the whites but must be matured in oak casks for several years, at least 10, before reaching their best. The one to try is the award winning *Colares Chita* which is a very quaffable, aromatic and fruity red wine.

wines of moderate strength, 11–12 per cent, which are clean and dry with a slight acidity. As in the other small areas here, production is in the hands of one main producer, Camillio Alves, and the label to look for is *Caves Velhas*.

South of the Tagus is **Setúbal** which produces another of Portugal's distinctive and famous wines. This is the sweet and perfumed *Moscatel de Setúbal*. The vines are grown around the villages of Palmela and Azeitão and Setúbal muscles in on the name only because it is the nearest port. The crushed grapes are fermented in cement vats and arrested by the addition of grape brandy at the required sugar level, the same technique as used in the production of port wine. The secret of this wine lies in the next stage when it is transferred to fresh cement vats and lightly crushed grapes and skins are added to impart to the wine the signature of the moscatel grape with its delightful aroma. After pressing again, the wine is held in casks until ready for bottling. This highly aromatic dessert wine is usually available in two ages, six and 20 year old. First one to try is Fonseca's *Muscatel de Setúbal*.

Algarve and Alentejo Wines

The final area of demarcation is in Algarve which has been growing vines since the time of the Romans but its wines have no great reputation. Some 31 new areas are seeking recognition in Portugal and were accepted in 1990 as IPRs (*Indicacões de Proveniência Regulamentada*) on six years probation for official wine region status (DOC). Both Lagos and Lagoa in Algarve are amongst the new applicants.

Alentejo has only IPRs but is already producing some of the country's most exciting wines and the areas worth trying include Redondo, Reguengos and Vidigueira.

Brandy

To accompany coffee at the end of a meal there is always the local brandy-like *aguardente* made from distilled wine or the *bagaceira* distilled from the alcoholic left-overs from the wine making. Two brandies which are popularly found on the shelves are *Macieira* and *Croft*'s, neither of which is particularly expensive which makes them rather good value for money.

Water

Water usually has a place on the dining table and bottled water may be offered as carbonated (*com gas*) or natural (*sem gas*). One of the really outstanding bottled waters is from Carvalhelhos, visited in Chapter 7.

5. PORTO

A sprawl of industry, nondescript suburbs and a population close on half a million may fail to excite the imagination but if first impressions were to be relied upon then Porto, or Oporto as it is known in English, would long since have become a backwater on the tourist trail. The reason it has not is due in no small measure to its reputation as the port capital of the world. Visitors, initially lured more by their taste buds than by a desire to sightsee, soon find themselves embarking on their own voyage of discovery. Across the river from the port wine houses, which are sited on the south bank of the River Douro, lies the pulsating heart of old Porto. Soulless modernity and creeping industrialisation are forgotten at the sight of the hotchpotch of red-tiled roofs tumbling like a precarious stack of playing cards down to the water's edge. Shabby it may be but the narrow alleyways beg exploration. The tall narrow façades of decadent houses, with their iron balconies, *azulejos* and billowing washing, jostle for space. Little chance of the sun's bright light penetrating here but splashes of yellow-painted plaster glow dully in the deep shadow. In sharp contrast, strong granite medieval buildings stand stoically amongst this precarious assortment of dwellings, their outer starkness concealing a wealth of treasures within. It is in the Barredo and Ribeiro quarters that the vibrancy, character and energy of the real Porto seep into the senses and capture the imagination. Fortunately, most of the sights can be found in or around this relatively small area, but be prepared for plenty of uphill work, there is nothing much on the level in this part of the city.

Portucale was renamed o Porto (meaning 'the port') sometime during the early medieval period when Portucale became the name of the region between the Rivers Douro and Minho. Since that time the Portuguese have dropped the definite article 'o' leaving Porto, which slips more easily off the tongue.

Porto's chequered history stretches back over 3000 years but subsequent development and natural catastrophes have erased much of the evidence. **Penaventosa Hill**, on which the cathedral now stands, has been identified as the site of pre-Celtic and Celtic settlements. The Celtic inhabitants were of the areas dominant Celtiberian tribe and are known to have traded with Phoenician merchants who came in search of metal.

Development gathered pace after the Roman conquest in the 2nd century BC when it became a strategic river crossing point on the main Lisbon to Braga route. The subdued Celtic town was fortified and given the name Portus

View from the Clérigos tower towards the cathedral, Porto

and a new town, Cale, constructed on the opposite south bank of the Douro which collectively became known as Portucale. Once the Romans departed, the Suevi and Visigoths laid claim to the town but found themselves, in 711, expelled by the conquering Moors. The Moors' tenuous hold on Portucale (Porto) lasted one and a half centuries until they too were finally ousted by the Christians in 868.

Despite most of the administrative action being transferred from Portucale to centres such as Braga, Guimarães and Coimbra over the following centuries, Porto still retained its importance in the new country of Portugal.

In the 12th century, Teresa, widow of Henry of Burgundy and mother of Afonso Henriques, endowed Porto with its cathedral. A century later, a bitter dispute erupted over the collection of tolls and unloading of merchandise between the crown on the one hand and the nobles and a now rich and powerful church on the other. During this period the royal borough of Gaia, renamed Vila Nova de Gaia soon afterwards, was founded by the crown in a bid to consolidate royal commercial interests in the area. The resourceful merchants of the city supported the crown in its long struggle to reduce the power and influence of the nobles and church and their loyalty was eventually rewarded by a royal decree, in 1478, which forbade the nobility from residing within the city walls.

Whilst in the midst of this power struggle, Dom Joao I married Phillipa of Lancaster in Porto cathedral, appropriately on St Valentine's Day 1387. Seven years later their third and most famous son, Henry the Navigator, was born in the same city. Henry's influence and money helped the merchants of Porto to develop shipyards and finance overseas exploration. On one of the few expeditions on which Henry actually sailed, to Ceuta on the Moroccan coast, an enthusiastic local populace deprived itself of meat to help provision the ships leaving only tripe for the inhabitants themselves to eat. Centuries later, tripe still figures strongly in local dishes and the nickname '*tripeiros*' (tripe eaters), given then to Porto's inhabitants, has withstood the test of time.

The colonial expansion of the 15th and 16th centuries produced many a fortune but the merchants suffered a setback with the loss of their spice monopoly at the end of that time. Fortunes were revived with the Methuen Treaty of 1703 which lowered the import duty of Portuguese wines shipped to Britain. Over the next century the wine trade flourished and grew, despite Pombal's decree that it should be controlled by a state monopoly.

After the Napoleonic invasions of Porto in 1808 and 1809 were finally repelled by Sir Arthur Wellesley the future Duke of Wellington, the seeds of republican fervour were sown. Turmoil and confusion reigned, compounded by the royal family's reluctance to return from Brazil where it had fled from Napoleon's advance. The resulting uprising began in Porto in 1820 and paved the way for constitutional changes which limited the power of the crown, nobles and church. Porto itself was besieged for a year and its population reputedly reduced to eating cats and dogs. Yet despite such deprivation the merchant classes bounced back with renewed commercial vigour.

Infante Dom Henrique—Henry the Navigator 1394–1460

Foundations of the British connection with Portugal were cemented in 1385 when, with the aid of English archers, João I defeated the Castilians at the battle of Aljubarotta. In gratitude for English assistance in securing Portugal's independence, the Treaty of Windsor was signed in 1386 as a declaration of lasting peace between the two countries. More than anything, it served as formal confirmation of an earlier Anglo-Portuguese Alliance of 1373. As a further seal of good intent, John of Gaunt, Duke of Lancaster, a signatory to the Treaty, gave his daughter Philippa of Lancaster in marriage to João I. They were married in Porto cathedral on 14 February 1387 and their third son Henry, later known as Henry the Navigator, was born in 1394.

A serious son of an equally studious and serious mother, Henry's curiosity regarding seafaring matters was most likely developed whilst as a child growing up close to the Douro riverside in Porto. What motivated Henry is a matter of conjecture but expeditions were still very much bound up with the Crusades. Interest in voyages of discovery were fuelled by talk of the legendary Christian Kingdom of Prester John, and its untold riches, said to lie somewhere in Africa. Conquering Moorish lands in North Africa was a prerequisite to gaining access into the hinterland of that continent; the seeds had been sown to think of wider possibilites.

With a fleet of 200 ships, the building of which Henry himself supervised, he set sail from Porto with his father and brother on a Crusade against Ceuta in North Africa where they won a resounding victory. A lasting impression on Henry was not so much the victory itself but the oriental riches they looted. What of these lands from where such a wealth of gold, silver, silks and spices originated? Henry returned to Portugal a thoughtful man but his energies were still chan-nelled into taming the north coast of Africa. Only later, on hearing tales from other sailors, was Henry drawn into the search further afield although he himself remained a landlubber after his foray to North Africa.

Taking himself off down to the untamed wilderness of Sagres in Algarve, Henry established an observatory and school of navigation, where he devoted time, effort and money to improve navigational aids and boat design. Using revenue from his position as Duke of Viseu, Governor of the Algarve and also Governor of the Order of Christ, he gathered together experts in astronomy and astrology, cartography and geography as well as knowledgeable mariners. His shipyard at Lagos built the boats, from where they set sail; the red Cross of Christ, emblem of the Order of Christ, prominently displayed on their white sails. Trading gradually took over precedence from crusading as Henry developed a tidy business from financing and equipping excursions down the west coast of Africa.

A huge leap forward came in the form of a new boat, the caravel, which Henry and his team designed and perfected. The caravel's light weight gave it manoeuvrability and speed, and a shallow draught the ability to sail close inshore. Another advantage was the need for a smaller crew and thus more storage space for goods.

Under Henry's patronage Gil Eanes finally passed Cape Bojador on Africa's west coast in 1434, a barrier beyond which 15 earlier expeditions had been too afraid to penetrate. Explorers were encouraged to set up trading posts at each new landing place, where they erected stone pillars (padrões) topped by crosses and engraved with the Portuguese coat of arms. They also brought back samples of plant life, fruit and nuts. It was to be a further decade before Gil Eanes returned with the first human cargo of African slaves, which prompted an escalation of trade along the west coast of Africa.

An austere man who shunned wordly pleasures in favour of a monkish existence, Henry remains something of an enigma. His striving after wealth is inconsistent with his frugal personal image: wealth to fuel his life's interest at Sagres seems a more probably explanation than personal gain. By the time he died at Sagres in 1460, his expeditions had reached as far as Sierra Leone.

A period of relative stability in the latter half of the 19th century saw the completion of two major bridge building programmes. Both provided an important economic link with the south of the country, the first, designed by Eiffel, being the Ponte de Dona Maria Pia railway bridge (1876) and ten years later, the spectacular two-tier Ponte Dom Luís I road bridge.

Although the port wine trade has declined since the Second World War, Porto has continued to build on the enterprise of its earlier merchants to become the centre of Portugal's manufacturing industry. Lisbon might be the capital city but the roots of the Portuguese nation are firmly embedded in Porto which gave the country its name and language. The people of this northern city are proud of their heritage which is succinctly expressed in the following popular saying: 'Coimbra sings, Braga prays, Lisbon shows off and Porto works.'

A minimum stay of two days allows for time to savour port wine and absorb some of the atmosphere and sights of the old town. Add an extra day or two for forays to the coast and trips along the Douro. On the other hand, those with stamina may well find one day sufficient to satisfy a fleeting curiosity before moving on. Without question, the best way to capture the flavour of Porto is on foot. Most of what there is to see is encompassed within

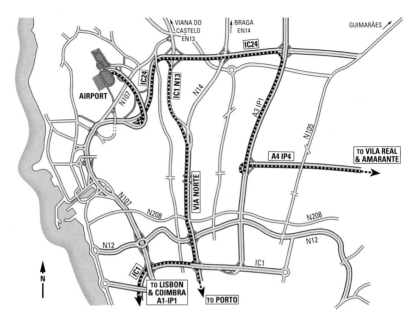

a relatively compact area, the main drawback being the energy required for the steep haul up to the centre from the river. Driving in Porto is a nightmare of traffic congestion, one-way systems and parking restrictions. It is better to leave the car behind. Although taxis seem in adequate supply at designated taxi ranks, they are invariably thin on the ground to flag down en route. Fortunately, the problem is easily solved as it is accepted practice to nip into the nearest bar and ask them to call a taxi.

Vila Nova de Gaia

There is little doubt as to where to start a tour of Porto. **Vila Nova de Gaia** is a logical choice since it encompasses all that is Porto in the minds of the majority of visitors. Time for further exploration after fortification with a few glasses of the local nectar, maybe!

Gaia's position on the north facing bank of the Douro is ideal for wine storage purposes. Its cellars are kept cool and damp by the higher humidity and cooler air which slow down the evaporation rate of the wine, and flood level markers stand testament to the days when flash floods were a constant problem. Erratic water levels have now been tamed by a series of *barragems* (dams) along the upper reaches of the Douro. In reality, the word cellar is a misnomer as the wine is mainly stored above ground on account of the danger of flooding and difficult geology. To all intents and purposes, the south bank of the Douro is one glorious wine vault.

Vintage port in a cellar at Porto

An approach along the lower level of the Ponte Dom Luís I bridge leads straight to the riverside **port wine lodges**. Buildings shelve a little less steeply up the river bank on the Gaia side of the river and the lodges announce their position with an array of huge signs. Company names are also emblazoned on the unfurled sails of the *barcos rabelos* moored in a line along the quay. It is hard to imagine these seemingly delicate vessels surviving the vagaries of the once untamed Douro as they battled downstream with their cargo of wine. Now they are just a picturesque reminder of times gone by. Views of old Porto across the river can be admired over a coffee at one of the many outdoor cafés lining the quay.

'Spoilt for choice' is an adage which springs readily to mind when confronted by the problem of where to start. If time is of the essence, it is a case of diving into the nearest lodge to hand. Calem and Sandeman are the first two encountered along the riverside with Sandeman having the edge as the most inviting. Sandeman's slick tours are conducted in a choice of languages and is very much on the tour operators' trail. A Scotsman, George Sandeman, started the company in 1790, in what was once a 16th century Jesuit monastery, but it is now owned by Seagrams of Canada although descendants of the founder still work in the business. The Sandeman logo of a black silhouetted student in cape and hat is familiar in many corners of the world. A similar operation to that of Sandeman and Calem is offered by Real Vinicola whilst other companies are smaller, less slick and exude a more traditional ambience.

Tours of the lodges concentrate on the blending and ageing aspects of the operation with generous free sampling. Some visitors may be lucky to chance upon coopers still producing oak casks with tools handed down through the generations. What is most striking is a refreshing lack of sales pressure at the end. Most of the lodges have conducted tours in English five days a week, except during lunchtime 12.30–13.30, until 17.30pm. One exception is Taylor's which boasts a restaurant. Calem and Sandeman are also open Saturday so these may be the only options for weekend visitors. Check with Turismo as they may also open on Sunday. Of the few score lodges housed in the area some of the other well known names are Barros, Cintra, Cockburn, Croft, Dow, Ferreira, Fonseca, Graham, Kopke and Taylor.

A more personal and less frenetic tour can be enjoyed by searching out the lodges up the narrow cobbled streets. Many are signposted from the water-front and can be amazingly ambient oases, tucked away as they are behind tall boundary stone walls. Many of these lodges are quite happy to conduct small groups or individuals around their premises. Amongst the choices are interesting and intimate Cockburn's; Graham's, with its magnificent view of the Ponte Dom Luís I; and Taylor's, where garden views from the wine tasting salon add an extra dimension. The salon at Taylor's houses a small collection of artefacts relating to the wine industry and, if lunch calls, the moderately priced restaurant offers good food and elevated views down to the Douro and Porto. A glass of Taylor's *Chip Dry* white port, chilled, makes an excellent aperitif. With the exception of Croft and Cintra, which are closed to the public, remaining vertical is the only restriction placed on the number of lodges which can be visited in one day.

Energetic art lovers may be inclined to hike further uphill, to Rua Candido dos Reis and the **Casa-Museu de Teixeira Lopes**. The museum contains the work of sculptor Lopes (António Teixeira Lopes, 1866–1942), a pupil of António Soares dos Reis, and his contemporaries. Lopes was the linchpin of an active artistic and intellectual circle centred in Gaia at the beginning of the 20th century. The museum contains mainly sculptures and paintings with a selection of books, coins and ceramics.

If vertigo is not a problem, the effort of climbing to join the upper road, which crosses the high level bridge, is rewarded with panoramic views. Even better is to make the small diversion up to the terrace of the former **Monastery of Serra do Pilar** built high above the Douro. This provides the best overview of the city and remains of the 14th century Fernandina city wall. From here, the eye can follow the river west, beyond the more recent Ponte da Arrabida (1963), to its mouth at Foz. Views inland are more restricted but, beyond the old and new (1991) railway bridges, the EN 108 makes its way tortuously along the river bank to Entre-os-Rios. The monastery building is now given over to military use but the 16th century church, with its barrel-vaulted roof and round Renaissance cloister, is open to the public. Sir Arthur Wellesley (later the Duke of Wellington) used the monastery as a base in 1809 when he drove the French out of Porto during the Peninsular War. A *festa* in honour of the patron saint of the monastery takes place there in August.

Gaia's major **festival** takes places early in the year. Phallus-shaped cakes figure predominantly in the Festas de São Gonçalo e Cristovão on the second Sunday in January. Christian overtones mask its probable origins as a pagan fertility rite and São Gonçalo allotted the role of husband-finder. An image of São Gonçalo found in the river centuries ago is paraded through the streets, along with images of São Cristovão and São Roque, to the deafening sound of accompanying drums. As can be expected, copious quantities of port and wine are consumed along with the cakes. *Festas* are usually associated with a particular saint, the religious connection part and parcel of the high jinks.

City Centre

A compact area encompassing east, west and south of Avenida dos Aliados contains Porto's commercial heart and heritage. No Pombal grid layout here, Porto is a confusing maze of streets and alleys which add a touch of spice to exploration. Ribeira is the venue for the major **festa** of the year. Dedicated to São Joao (St John the Baptist), the patron saint of Porto, it begins on the night of 23 June and continues non-stop over the following day. As with most of the *festas*, its origins lie in pagan rites, in this case associated with the summer-solstice, which have been Christianised and adopted by the Church. A whale of a time is had by all with dancing in the street, bonfires and a running banquet of roast kid, grilled sardines and rivers of vinho verde. Lemon balm and leeks also figure in the ritual, the latter used to hit people over the head, although plastic hammers are fast replacing leeks as a modern-day equivalent. Even the *barcos rabelos* are given an airing and take part in a race on the river.

East of the Centre

Head back across the bridge from Gaia towards Porto centre. If on the lower tier, cross Avenida Gustavo Eiffel and take the steps up right on the corner. These lead up a stepped street to Rua Saraiva de Carvalho between houses which encapsulate everyday life. Women gossip over endless washing whilst lazy dogs make little attempt to move out of the way. Walkers along the upper tier of the bridge, on the inland side, enjoy a bird's-eye view of the same street before a right turn into Rua Saraiva de Carvalho. Tucked away at the rear of a square off this street can be found the **Igreja de Santa Clara**, the former church of the Convento de Santa Clara.

The simple lines of Santa Clara's original Romanesque structure (1416) have been adulterated over the centuries. Obvious external influences can be found in the confusing mix of Gothic, Manueline and Renaissance styles of the church doors but give little clue to the Baroque opulence enshrined within. Gold gleams from every corner, the intricately carved and gilded woodwork covering most available space. A touch of relief from all the gold is a panel of the Immaculate Conception by Joaquim Raphael and a Mudejar (Moorish style) painted ceiling. Those intent on closer inspection of the seemingly inaccessible **Fernandina Wall** need to turn right immediately on leaving

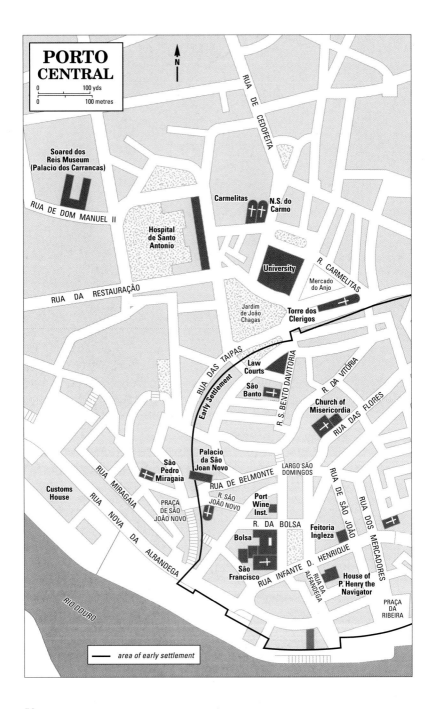

PORTO CENTRAL

0   100 yds
0   100 metres

N

Soared dos Reis Museum (Palacio dos Carrancas)

RUA DE DOM MANUEL II

RUA DE CEDOFEITA

Carmelitas

N.S. do Carmo

Hospital de Santo Antonio

University

R. CARMELITAS

Mercado do Anjo

RUA DA RESTAURAÇÃO

Jardim de João Chagas

Torre dos Clerigos

RUA DAS TAIPAS

Early Settlement

Law Courts

São Banto

R. S. BENTO DAVITORIA

R. DA VITÓRIA

Church of Misericordia

RUA DAS FLORES

RUA MIRAGAIA

São Pedro Miragaia

Palacio da São Joan Novo

RUA DE BELMONTE

LARGO SÃO DOMINGOS

RUA DE SÃO JOÃO

RUA DOS MERCADORES

Customs House

RUA NOVA DA ALRANDEGA

PRAÇA DE SÃO JOÃO NOVO

R. SÃO JOÃO NOVO

Port Wine Inst.

R. DA BOLSA

Feitoria Ingleza

Bolsa

São Francisco

RUA INFANTE D. HENRIQUE

RUA DA ALFANDEGA

House of P. Henry the Navigator

PRAÇA DA RIBEIRA

RIO DOURO

— area of early settlement

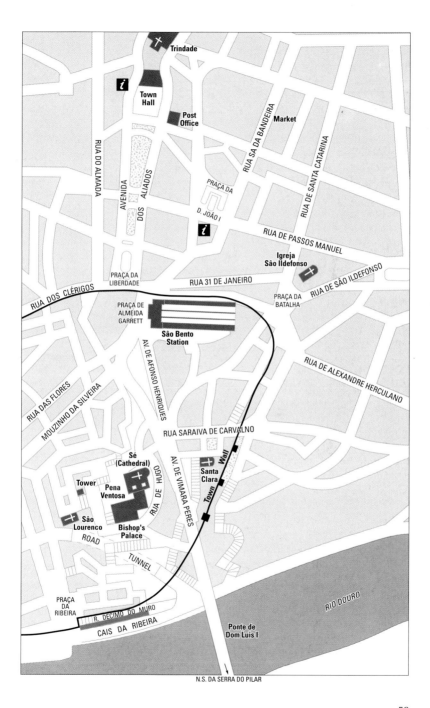

the church. A further right turn, at the end of the church, and across a small courtyard solves the puzzle. Steps lead up onto the unfenced ramparts, which are in a reasonable state of repair, to give a different perspective over the river. Built to replace the 'Sueve' wall, which circled Penaventosa Hill, it was named after King Ferdinand who was on the throne at the time of its completion in 1376. It stood on average 11m high, was 3km in length and took 40 years to build. Unfortunately, the wall has been systematically destroyed over the past 200 years to accommodate expansion of the city limits. Further sections can be found along the Cais da Ribeira where buildings are incorporated into remnants of the wall.

Rua Augusto Rosa leads to the **Praça da Batalha**. A recent face-lift for the Teatro São João (National Theatre) here commands attention, the dazzling golden glow of its façade far outshining the drabness of its surrounds. A daily craft market sets up stall in the square, beneath the indifferent gaze of the tiled façade of the neglected 18th century Igreja São Idlefonso and a statue of Dom Pedro V. Avenida Rodrigues de Freitas, east from the square, leads to the Museu Militar (Military Museum) and beyond to the Estação de Campanhã where the nearby restaurant *Aleixo* serves typical local food.

Pass through Praça da Batalha into **Rua de Santa Catarina**. This street soon becomes pedestrianised and, along with the surrounding maze of streets, is a magnet for shopaholics. Its numerous outlets, now joined by a major British chain store, sell fashionable clothing, gifts, leather goods and linen. During the week and Saturday morning Santa Catarina buzzes with activity, as street traders tout their wares side by side with the occasional entertainer. Garlanded cherubs over the doorway announce No. 112, the *Majestic Café*, one of the oldest coffeehouses in the city, where the restored gilt and mirrored interior is a fitting foil for those who wish to see and be seen. Close by, on the same street, is the refurbished *Grande Hotel do Porto*. Once the doyen of Porto hotels, its central position and comfortable rooms ensure its continuing popularity. For something different and a quieter ambience, the *Residencial Castelo de Santa Catarina* might prove a good choice. Situated way up Rua de Santa Catarina near Praça Marqués de Pombal, its off street parking and easy access to the airport make it especially convenient for those with a car. Set well back off the road, this once grand castellated edifice has a chapel and a private garden which offers a blissful haven after the heat of the city.

Sandwiched between Bandeira and Santa Catarina, the large oblong building of the **Bolhão Market** is not obvious at first. The blue tiled façade of the Chapel of Souls on the corner of Santa Catarina and Rua de Fernandes Tómas provides a good landmark. Turn left here along Tómas and the market is the building on the left after crossing Rua Alexandre Braga. Nothing prepares the visitor for such a hive of activity. The two tier building encloses a large open central area which is crammed with stalls selling just about everything. Seeming chaos is really quite organised with different areas for particular produce. Guinea pigs, quails and rabbits share space with hens which are popped into plastic bags to carry away. Shops line the perimeter on the ground floor whilst the gallery above is given over to the vegetable sellers so there is plenty to see. From Balhão, head west along Rua Formosa in the direction of Avenida dos Aliados to emerge by the Town Hall. A diversion here up Rua do Almada leads through the Praça da Republica beyond which lies **Igreja da Lapa**. The claim to fame of this 18th century church, with its rabbit-eared double towers, is the history attached to the mausoleum housed within it which contained a golden heart. This heart was presented to the city by a grateful Dom Pedro IV in recognition of Porto's support during the 19th century War of Succession.

The early 20th century Town Hall (Câmara Municipal) dominates the sloping Avenida dos Aliados and is open to the public on weekdays. Gardens fill the space between the twin avenues all the way down to the statue of Dom Pedro IV in **Praça Liberdade**. This busy square marks what was once the northern entrance to the old medieval city. Now it is the hub of the Baixa, Porto's shopping and commercial area. Cafés and pastry shops feature strongly here, their tables spilling out onto the pavement. One of the oldest is *Arcadia*, with its tempting display of delicious pastries served in Belle Epoque mirrored surrounds, and opposite is the similar styled *Café Imperial*. On Sunday mornings, activity centres around the flower market in Praça Liberdade as many of the city centre cafés are closed. Belle Epoque also figures strongly in the genteel establishments of the early 20th century, one such being *Hotel Infante de Sagres* in Praça Dona Filipa de Lencastre, to the west of Avenida dos Aliados. Shoppers may be tempted to search out gold, silver and antiques in this same area but **Rua das Flores** has the best reputation for gold and silver buys.

West of the Centre

Make for Turismo at the side of the Town Hall and take the next unassuming uphill street left, Rua Dr. Ricardo Jorge. Along here, in **Largo de Mompilher**, can still be found one of the original style wooden kiosks (*quiosque*). Much more user friendly than the modern green metal replacement with its domed tube-like appearance. Keeping along in the same direction, the narrow road soon becomes Travessa Cedofeita. If mention of *Pão de Ló* keeps cropping up in conversation then this is where to find the genuine article. Originally an import from Japan, it became part of the Easter tradition but is now eaten all year round. Locals buy and eat the large distinctive ring shaped cake in huge quantities. Pieces are sold separately if required, and its sponge-like texture is an ideal accompaniment to coffee or hot chocolate in pastry shops and cafés. Although found in many shops throughout the region, the inconspicuous bakery of *Casa Margaridense* is renowned for making the best *Pão de Ló* in Porto.

Continue ahead into Rua de Cedofeita and take a left turn back towards the river. Church enthusiasts with energy could turn right here and take a 15 minute walk to the oldest church in Porto, the 12th century Romanesque **Igreja de Cedofeita** on Rua Aníbal Cunha. King Theodomir of the Suevi is reputed to have been responsible for the 6th century foundation of the church which could make it one of the oldest in this corner of Europe. The church was seemingly constructed in a hurry to house relics of St Martin, sent from Tours, and its name derives from *cito facta* meaning 'built quickly'. Palms add an exotic air to **Praça Gomes Teixeira**, graced with the 19th century Fountain of the Lions. It comes into view on reaching a wall of 20th century *azulejos* on the right, which belong to the 18th century **Igreja do Carmo**. Designed by Silvestro Silvestri, the tiles depict the battle between Christians and pagans on Mount Carmel. Next door is its twin, the 17th century classical and Baroque styled **Igreja das Carmelitas**, one time monastery now a barracks. The church is open to the public during the summer months. Across the square, the enormous granite main university building, founded in 1807 with the grand title of Polytechnical Academy, still maintains its function as a seat of learning.

Overlooking the Jardim de João Chagas, which lies behind the university, are the Palaçio da Justiça, south of the hospital, and the smaller Cadeia da Relação (Old Prison) opposite. More gilt carvings and panels depicting the life of St Benedict can be seen in the 17th century Igreja São Bento da Vitória in the block below the Old Prison. Art lovers with a fully charged credit card might be tempted to seek out the commercial galleries, located in the quarter below the university. The colonnaded façade of the **Hospital de Santo António** fills the view to the west. Work commenced in 1770 on this mammoth edifice which was the first neo-Palladian building in Portugal. Quips about its unfinished state down the centuries still hold true today as feverish construction carries on apace. To the south west can be spotted the main reason for a trip to this part of the city: the tower of the **Igreja dos Clérigos**. It is not the Igreja dos Clérigos which attracts immediate attention but the 76m/250ft **Torre dos Clérigos**. Long a dominant landmark, the Torre dos Clérigos remains an unequalled vantage point from which to enjoy stunning panoramic views over the city. Designed by the Italian architect Nicolau Nasoni, the tower itself was completed in 1763, 14 years after the construction of the unusual oval-shaped Baroque-style church and the later House of the Clergy which links the two. It is well worth huffing and puffing up the 225 or so steps to reach the top.

Next port of call is the former royal **Palácio dos Carrancas**, reached by heading back through Praça Gomes Teixeira to the Hospital de Santo António then around the north side into Rua de Dom Manuel II. The palace was used by Marshall Soult as the French headquarters during the Peninsular War. It was from here that Soult fled in a hurry in 1809, as Sir Arthur Wellesley and his troops advanced across the Douro, leaving a banquet for them to enjoy. Built by a rich Jewish family in 1795 the neo-classical structure has suffered a chequered history. After Marshall Soult's sojourn, Dom Pedro IV installed himself here for a brief period during the Civil War and it was eventually bought by Dom Pedro V in 1861, when the owner's fortunes were reduced. In the 1930s Salazar overturned the wishes of the last king of Portugal, Dom Manuel II, that it become a hospital, and established the **Soares dos Reis Museu** instead. It is named after Portuguese sculptor António Soares dos Reis

(1847–89), many of whose works are exhibited here, including his best known work *O Desterrado* (The Exile). Also housed in the same building are a comprehensive collection of Portuguese paintings, which date back over the past 500 years, early gold and silver jewellery, Bohemian glassware, ceramics which include a fine dinner service made for the Bishop of Porto, and a sword that belonged to the first king of Portugal, Dom Afonso Henriques.

A stone's throw further along Rua Dom Manuel II lies the Jardim do Palácio de Cristal, recognised by the huge glass dome of the **Pavilhão Rosa Mota**. A prominent landmark in the city, it was the site of the 19th century `Crystal Palace' which was demolished and replaced in 1952 by a sports and exhibition pavilion. The formal gardens provide a restful oasis and a gathering point where the locals engage in chatter and a game of *petanca*, similar to the French game of *boules*.

Leave the noise and bustle of Rua Dom Manuel II and disappear down Rua de Entre Quintas at the western side of the garden. Almost immediately, there is a feeling of being transported back in time. The narrow, leafy cobbled road seems to be leading nowhere in particular and a notice by a gate, announcing the **Museu Romântico** (Romantic Museum) at No. 220, is the only indication that this is the correct location. Initial reaction, of disbelief that this could possibly be the location of a museum, is soon replaced by pleasure at being in such a tranquil spot. The doll's house quality of the 19th century Quinta da Maceirinha suits its role as the Romantic Museum admirably. Because of its size, only ten people are admitted at any one time to view this recreation of a wealthy residence of the 19th century. There is little to announce the presence of the Solar do Vinho do Porto though, tucked away down some outside steps in the basement below the museum. Here, a discreet 20th century gentleman's club atmosphere prevails, in sharp contrast to the 19th century opulence upstairs; but it is not a gentleman's club and ladies are equally as welcome. After a hectic day touring the sites it is bliss to sink into one of the comfortable seats, glass of port in hand, of course, doing nothing more energetic than admiring the small garden through arched glass doors or selecting from the comprehensive wine list. Except for vintage ports, it is possible to try any port by the glass from the different port wine houses at very low cost, the courteous and friendly staff only too willing to bring you as many different ports to sample as you wish. The views from the terrace are unexpected, with the land falling sharply away to the Douro below and extending past the Ponte da Arrâbida to its estuary.

Tram enthusiasts might consider staggering further downhill to the banks of the Douro. A fairly recent introduction to the museum scene is the Museu do Carro Eléctrico (Electric Tram Museum) on Alameda Basilio Teles. Converging tramlines mark the spot! Close by, near the start of Rua da Restauração, is **Igreja de Massarelos**. Not usually given a mention, it is nevertheless a significant part of Porto's history. Originally founded, in what was then the village of Massarelos as a Chapel of Corpus Christi in 1394, it was dedicated to St Pedro Gonçalves Telmo, the patron saint of navigators. Round about the same time, an association was formed by the maritime fraternity and given the long-winded title the Brotherhood of the Souls of Corpus Christi. This developed into a vibrant body of people connected with life on the water. Such was its importance, Infante Dom Henrique (Henry the Navigator), born in the year of the association's inception (1394), became its first Honorary Chairman. Figures of Prince Henry and the church's patron saint can be found on the outside wall of the present day church, facing the river. There is also a recent tiled picture depicting the Portuguese Discoveries. A direct way back to the centre is up Rua da Restauração, close below the gardens of the Palaçio de Cristal, which leads to the Torre dos Clérigos and Praça da Liberdade beyond.

South of the Centre

Leaving Praça da Liberdade to head south, pass the cheerful tiled exterior of Igreja dos Congregados on the left and maybe sample a coffee in the nearby *A Brasileira*, on Rua do Bonjardim, another of the city's famous cafés. Traffic surges through the Praça de Almeida Garrett, named to honour Portugal's great 19th century poet and novelist, in its headlong rush to cross the high level Ponte Dom Luís I. The **Estação de São Bento** (Porto's central railway station) stands aloof from the mêlée outside intent on less frantic activity. Its main draw, for those with time to stand and stare, is the famous *azulejos* of Jorge Colaço which decorate the walls of the main entrance hall. Many of the panels illustrate the development of the railways, but some are of Portuguese historical events. The station was constructed early in the 20th century on the site of the Convento do Avé Maria and trains still depart from here for the spectacular run along the Douro. Rua da Madeira, down the side of the station, is the regular Sunday morning venue for a bird market.

The **Sé** (cathedral) is only a few minutes' walk south from the station, its twin towers clearly in view. Calçada de Vandoma, tucked in the shadow of the Sé, is passed on the way. A flea market takes place here most days but Saturday morning finds it at its best. Climb up to the windswept plateau of aptly named **Penaventosa** (Ventosa means windy), on which the cathedral stands; it was also the site of a much earlier citadel. An ornate *pelourinho* (pillory) is the only decoration on the otherwise barren expanse of the Terreiro da Sé, the square in front of the Sé. The views from the edge of this lofty perch are magnificent. Beyond the jumbled rooftops of the ancient quarters of the Barredo and waterfront Ribeira, which tumble away below, the eye can travel over most of the old city and beyond, to the river estuary.

First impressions of the Sé are that it looks more imposing from a distance. Close to, the severe lines of its façade contrast unfavourably with the more impressive frontage of the Palácio Episcopal (Archbishop's Palace) next door. Little remains of the original 12th century Sé, founded by Dona Teresa, mother of the first King of Portugal. The Sé of today is an amalgam of 13th century Romanesque, built more to resemble a fortress than a church, and additions over the centuries which culminated in inept 18th century Baroque extensions. King João I and the English Philippa of Lancaster married here in 1387 but would be hard pressed to recognise the present day Sé. The austere external image extends to the disappointingly gloomy interior. Fluted columns support a lofty barrel-vaulted roof, which seem to add to rather than dispel the all-pervading gloom inside. The only chinks of brightness come from the elaborate gilded Baroque carving' above the main altar and the notable silver altarpiece in the north transept. Nicolau Nasoni, the 18th century architect, had a hand in some of the Baroque additions and was responsible for the completion of the silver altarpiece. Its saving grace is to escape into the Gothic cloister and up stairs, designed by Nasoni, to the chapterhouse with its rich furnishings. This diversion also gives the opportunity to see *azulejos* from the 18th century, depicting scenes from the life of the Virgin and Ovid's *Metamorphoses*. Nasoni also designed the porch on the city side of the Sé but is better remembered for the adjoining imposing **Palácio Episcopal**. The Palácio has been converted into offices and is not open to the public. Behind the Sé complex, on Rua de Dom Hugo, is the **Casa Museu de Guerra Junqueiro** in the 18th century Baroque mansion that was home to the poet Guerra Junqueiro (1850–1923). The house and gardens seem to excite more attention than does the poet's collection of furniture, paintings, sculpture, silver and ceramics. Its future as a museum seems uncertain, as it has been closed for a while and no date is projected for its reopening.

Leave the Sé by plunging into the narrow alleys of the Barredo in the direction of the waterfront Ribeira. Remnants of the 6th century Suevian wall, which circled Penaventosa Hill, are evident at the start of the descent. In the vicinity are the ruins of the 15th century Casa Torre (Tower House), once the seat of municipal power, and the Jesuit church (1570) of São Lourenço, better known as **Igreja dos Grilos** (1577), and one of the earliest examples of Portuguese Baroque. Also close by, at Largo de Pedro Vitorino, is the **Museu de Arte Sacra** containing religious treasures which were concealed by the citizens from Napoleon's troops. The narrow, sometimes stepped, alleyways which all seem to converge on the waterfront are reminiscent of the medieval past. Rickety houses close in until they form bridges in parts, the ever present washing flapping above as the way twists tortuously downhill. Although fascinating, these alleys reflect the poverty of the area and it is wise to keep a tight hold on bags and cameras.

Tourism has been absorbed into the fabric of the **Ribeira** without altering its structure to any great extent. Tall narrow houses, with their ubiquitous balconies, still peer down on the dark green waters of the Douro much as they have always done. The **Cais da Ribeira** (quay) extends along the riverside where even remnants of the Fernandino Wall have been commandeered to do service as *tascas* (taverns) and restaurants. A daily market held along the *cais* is as much for visitors as locals but boating activity is now reduced to pleasure trips along the river, one of which is a sail in a *barcos rabelos*. A longer trip (for a price) sails up-river as far as Regua and includes breakfast and lunch with a first class seat on the Douro train return. This lively part of

Praça da Ribeira, Porto

Porto, the **Praça da Ribeira**, is a favourite spot to sit and watch the world go by from one of the outdoor cafés. For a local meeting place, the insipid, nondescript cubed sculpture in the Praça da Ribeira makes an odd focal point for such an historic setting.

Ribeira is renowned for its fish restaurants and *tascas* which has made it a popular venue for eating out. The small rooms and discreet ambience of the restaurants create an atmospheric intimacy which, along with superb food, has no equal elsewhere in the city. One worth seeking out is *Restaurante do Terreirinho,* tucked away in Largo do Terreirinho amid the warren of alleys behind the Cais. This delightful restaurant has small dining areas on different levels and its choice menu includes a mouth-watering seafood *cataplana* (Sesimbra style). The food is fresh and there is a persuasive wine list. Among other options are restaurants *Mercearia* in Praça da Ribeira, *Chez Lapin* along Rua Canastreiro and *Dom Tonho* along the Cais da Ribeira. For a real local *tasca* experience, the *Tasca do Bebobos* on Cais da Ribeira is very popular.

From the Praça da Ribeira move into Largo do Terreir. To the left, along Rua Reboleira, is the **Centro Regional de Artes Tradicionais** (Centre of Traditional Arts), sometimes referred to simply as CRAT. The building has been renovated to house a permanent craft exhibition and sales room. This is the place to come to buy genuine regional souvenirs.

Moving on up into Rua da Alfândega, the austere granite façade on the right fronts the 14th century building in which, purportedly, the Infante Dom Henrique (Henry the Navigator) was born in 1394, now known as the **Casa do Infante**. Evidence that this was actually the place is not wholly persuasive, but documents of the time and the fact that the building was once part of a civil administrative complex, which included the mint and treasury and trade exchange along with residences for treasury officials and noble families, support the fact that he was probably born close by. Rebuilt during the 17th century, it was a customs house (*Almazém*) for 500 years until the 19th century when a further floor was added and the main façade rebuilt. It has now been further renovated for use as an exhibition centre and as a home for the city's archives.

Access to the Casa is limited at present to the entrance room, where scale models of ships and a few other artefacts are on display. Ask to see the painting of the marriage of João I and Philippa of Lancaster. The rest of the floor area has been given over to major excavations, in hopes of unravelling the ancient layers of history embedded in its foundations. Tantalising glimpses of this archaeological activity is the most visitors to the Casa are likely to see.

Climb up to Rua do Infante Dom Henrique, formerly Rua dos Ingleses, and the gardens of the Praça do Infante Dom Henrique with its statue of Henry in the middle. Beyond is the Mercado Ferreira Borges whilst, to the left, is the Igreja de São Francisco and the sombre frontage of the Palaçio da Bolsa (Stock Exchange) on Rua Ferreira Borges which faces the square. The external appearance of the **Igreja de São Francisco** gives nothing away of the splendour within. Founded by Dom Sancho II in 1233 and rebuilt in the 14th century, its Baroque interior ostentatiously displays the excesses of the 18th century. The elaborate gilded Rococo carvings of cherubs, vines, acanthus and flowers festoon the interior from ceiling to floor, especially notable in the Tree of Jesse on the north wall. Gold drips from every available surface almost to sensory suffocation point. A refreshing relief amidst such overpowering splendour comes in the form of a simple rose window and plain granite statue of São Francisco (St Francis). In the museum attached to the church are artefacts from the old convent and thousands of cleaned up human bones are also stored in an underground osseria.

The **Palaçio da Bolsa** next door was built on the site of the Franciscan covent belonging to Igreja de São Francisco, which burnt down in 1832. João I lodged in the convent when he came to marry Philippa of Lancaster in 1387. Constructed in neo-classical style, the Bolsa's somewhat cold and impersonal interior can only be viewed in the company of a guide. A quick glimpse into the Great Hall, with its glass domed roof and coats of arms, is possible without actually having to embark on a guided tour. The main advantage of a tour is to visit the much vaunted oval shaped 'Salon de Arabe' (Arab Room), built in pseudo-Moorish style in an effort to emulate the Alhambra in Spain. Despite the brilliant chandeliers and surfeit of gold decoration, sparkle and brightness are elusive companions in this room and fail to shake off an overall gloomy image.

Further up from the Bolsa, opposite the Mercado Ferreira Borges, is located the Instituto do Vinho do Porto (Port Wine Institute) founded in 1932 to supervise and regulate the port wine trade.

A living monument to British port wine shippers, the **Feitoria Inglesa** (Factory House of the British Association) lies further east along Rua do

Infante Dom Henrique on the corner with Rua de São João. The building was not officially opened until 11 November 1811, although it was erected between 1786–90 under the influence and guidance of the British Consul, John Whitehead. Named for the factors who belong to the association, membership is confined to firms connected with the trade since the 18th century. The forbidding colonnaded granite façade conceals an interesting interior with the main rooms located on the upper floors. An unusual addition to the Dining and Drawing Rooms is a Dessert Room, where the men retire to drink their port after a meal, with a Ballroom for more glittering occasions. This self-contained enclave houses much of interest and, although not open to the general public, access may be granted by contacting a member of the British Port Wine Shippers Association.

Retrace the route west to cross Praça do Infante Dom Henrique and along Rua São João Novo into Largo de São João Novo, in the former Jewish quarter. A 16th century church of the same name stands opposite the **Palaçio de São João Novo** (Museum of Ethnography and History), which is the main reason to visit the square. Part of Nicolau Nasoni's prolific output during the 18th century, it was built for a wealthy local magistrate and took ten years to its completion in 1733. The small museum provides an intriguing insight into the lives and customs of the Douro region from palaeolithic times. Reconstructions of a regional kitchen and wine cellar along with a wealth of artefacts make this one of the most appealing collections in Porto.

The Port Wine Story

1. British Influence

During the 13th century, the Moors were expelled from Seville thus opening up a trade route to the Mediterranean. This sparked an influx of British merchants, eager to base themselves in Porto and take advantage of the new market opportunities. Cotton, wheat, woollen cloth and Newfoundland salted cod (*bacalhau*) were the main trading items. Red Minho wines were also promoted and exported from their base at Viana do Castelo. A commercial treaty with Edward III of England, a century later, ensured continuing trade between the two countries. It was to be a further three hundred years before the wine trade began to flourish and develop though.

The Commonwealth Treaty of 1654 strengthened and revived the Anglo-Portuguese alliance sealed by the Treaty of Windsor in 1386. Through this new treaty, the British were able to enjoy extra privileges in Portugal including low taxes, the right to hold Protestant services in their homes and have their own burial-ground, the Inquisition having been instrumental in restricting Protestant religious activity.

Charles II's reaction to a French ban on the import of English cloth created the catalyst on which the wine trade was to grow and flourish. His reciprocal ban on the import of French wine, produced the effect of making Portuguese wine 'flavour of the year'. British merchants scurried around buying every available barrel of wine they could lay hands on to ship off to an eager British market.

Intrepid merchants, like Peter Bearsley, son of the founder of Taylor Fladgate and Yeatman, scoured the Upper Douro for wine and by all accounts unearthed some treasures. This sparked off a major vine planting programme in the Douro region and development of shippers' warehouses in Porto around 1678. As the wine trade began to develop in Porto, the wine merchants from Viana do Castelo prudently deserted the Minho region and moved their centre of operation to the Douro. The discovery that brandy added to wine stabilised its travelling quality is the touch of invention which gave rise to port. It also resulted in a higher alcohol content and stabilised the sweetness of the wine.

The Methuen Treaty of 1703 witnessed an upsurge in the market of Portuguese wines to England and business boomed unabated for the next 50 years. Increasing adulteration of wines by adding colourants and other additives, largely by British shippers to increase the volume of exports, prompted action from the Marquês de Pombal in 1756. To put an end to escalating malpractice, he demarcated the area for vineyards along the Douro and centralised control of the trade under the Alto Douro Wine Company.

Once the initial furore over this move died down events ticked over until Joseph James Forrester arrived in Portugal in the 1840s. A man of many parts, he devoted himself to understanding the problems of viniculture and also produced the first excellent maps of the Douro region. His untimely death by drowning in 1862 stemmed the ire of wine producers, ruffled by his criticism of their continued adulteration of the wine. Nevertheless, his observations were taken on board and strict controls exist today.

In the early 19th century, with the relaxation of certain Portuguese laws, British firms began to acquire *quintas* and farms along the Douro to use as seasonal offices. Although concerned about grape quality, they never themselves became involved in the farming and remained essentially export merchants based in Porto. Descendants of the early British merchants still live and work in Porto, have their own school and retain British customs and celebrations. They have developed their own community and lifestyle amongst the Portuguese without becoming Portuguese themselves. British names still dominate the industry along with the Portuguese, although many of these have been amalgamated and are now run by syndicates.

The story of port wine features throughout Chapter 6.

This is the area of Miragaia, once a thriving neighbourhood of seamen and merchants. A short way down the lane, off the square to the south west, is the 18th century Igreja de São Pedro de Miragaia with its tiles and gilded carvings but the main focus of interest lies in the adjacent **Chapel of the Holy Ghost**. Founded in 1443 as part of a hospital for pilots, boatswains and sailors, it houses the famous Flemish triptych of the Holy Ghost.

To see one of the country's Renaissance treasures, head back via Largo de São João Novo and the balconied and tiled houses of Rua de Belomonte to Rua das Flores and the **Igreja de Misericórdia**. Originally a 16th century foundation, the church was extensively modified in the 18th century. To see the *Fons Vitae* painting (1520), by an unknown Flemish artist, depicting Dom Manuel I, founder of the Misericórdia, and his family kneeling beneath the cross at the Crucifixion, you must apply to the church office at No. 15 next door. This is where the painting is kept. Follow Rua dos Flores up to Estação São Bento past some of the best gold and silver shops in the city.

West to the Coast

Porto's more recent hotels, the *Meridien* and *Sheraton,* are sited to the north of the city in the Boavista area. The pivotal point is the **Praça Mouzinho de Albuquerque**, or Rotunda da Boavista, in the middle of which is a huge 45m high columnar monument to the British and Portuguese victory over the French in the Peninsular War. Shoppers have plenty of choice here with the Mercado do Bom Sucesso close by and a veritable labyrinth of shops in the modern Centro Comercial de Brasília between Rua da Boavista and Rua de Julio Dinis. Not too far away either is the Porto Cricket Club off Rua do Campo Alegre, a game introduced by the British which perplexed the Portuenses and probably still does. Still further west along the same road, close by the spaghetti-like confluence of roads just north of Ponte da Arrabida and University Stadium, lies the **Jardim Botânico**. Portugal's botanic gardens enjoyed their hey-day during the glory days of the Portuguese empire, from where rare species of plants and trees were imported. Sadly, lack of money and inclination have robbed most of these gardens of their former glory but their paths provide pleasant shaded walks. Art lovers might be tempted out as far as the **Museu de Arte Moderna** on Rua de Serralves. The monthly exhibitions are administered by the Gulbenkian Foundation based in Lisbon and held in the Casa de Serralves, a 1930s *palaço*. Check with Turismo for opening dates. Even if the museum is closed whilst exhibitions are changed, entrance to the lovely gardens is free.

Avenida da Boavista runs straight as a die from the Rotunda to the coast ending at Praça de Gonçalves Zarco. On the right before reaching the sea front is Porto's newest park, Parque da Cidade. Facing the Praça on the sea edge is the mini fortress **Castelo do Queijo** or Cheese Castle. The five turreted multi-sided fort was constructed at irregular angles to better withstand bombardment. It passes an interesting ten minutes or so to cross the draw-

A view of Dom Luís bridge, Porto

bridge over the moat, wander the parapets complete with cannon and maybe have a coffee in the café/bar inside.

Up the coast is the area of **Matosinhos**. A former fishing village, it has lost much of its charm to the docks and industry at Porto de Leixões, although its waterfront restaurants still exert a pull with their reputation for good fish and shellfish. The Senhor de Matosinhos pilgrimage is more fun than it sounds and one of the liveliest festivals. Held every year during the first fortnight in June, it centres round a wooden statue of Christ on the cross which was found on the beach in the 10th century. Its present home, in the 18th century church of the same name, also known as Igreja do Senhor Bom Jesus, is the venue for the festivities.

South of the Praça de Gonçalves Zarco is the residential area of **Foz**. British residents once flocked here to bathe in the waters of the Atlantic which, in the mid 19th century, earned it a reputation as the 'Brighton of Porto'. Bathing is definitely not recommended today as this stretch of beach is unlikely to achieve blue flag status. A stroll along the promenade down to the Castelo de São João da Foz makes a restful alternative to pounding the city streets. As a change from the wide sand-coloured promenade, paths lead off through gardens and along the edge of the beach past an abundance of cafés. Sunday morning especially is shared with the locals who come here to drink coffee and read their newspapers.

The 16th century **Castelo de São João da Foz** guards the estuary at Foz do Douro (Mouth of the Douro). It was built on the site of a 13th century Benedictine monastery, the chancel of which is incorporated into the Castelo's chapel. A little further up river is the Farol de São Miguel o Anjo, the lighthouse of Saint Michael the Angel. Reputedly one of the oldest light-houses in Europe, this 16th century tower was a product of the boom time of the Discoveries. Two further seamen's chapels, Capela Senhora da Lapa and Capela Santa Catarina, lie close to the riverside in the eastuary. A fascinating insight into riverside life is possible along here but the accompanying smell of the river is an overpowering deterrent.

Excursions from Porto

A trip to the **upper Douro** is a must for visitors using Porto as a base. This can easily be arranged through a local travel agent and involves transport by train and coach along the river to visit a *quinta* where lunch is included. Independent travellers may like to travel on the Douro train as far as journey's end at **Pocinho**. Visits north to Viana do Castelo (Chapter 8), Barcelos, Braga and Guimarães (Chapter 9) can easily be accomplished in a day, including a drive east to Amarante. Vila do Conde (Chapter 9) is interesting and is the closest recommended location for sea bathing. To the south, **Espinho** is a major but not riveting resort and pollution restricts swimming until a little further down the coast. Golf enthusiasts have a chance to practise their swing at two courses in the vicinity. The *Miramar* is essentially a private members' club with nine holes but the *Oporto Golf Links* at Espinho offers 18 holes and is the oldest in Portugal (1890). The Porto to Lisbon motorway offers a chance to make the 1½ hour journey to Coimbra with comparative ease (Chapter 10) where the old university town offers a compact tour of interest with ancient Conimbriga only a further 20 minutes south.

Practical Information

Hotels and Restaurants

The constant demand for business and tourist accommodation ensures higher prices at all grades.

Hotel Infante de Sagres, Praça D. Filipa de Lencastre 62, 4000 Porto (tel. 02 200 81 01). Five-star. Central with restaurant.
Hotel Ipanema Parque, Rua de Serralves 124, 4100 Porto (tel. 02 610 41 74). Five-star. Elegant luxury, swimming pools, health club, restaurant.
Hotel Meridien Porto, Av. da Boavista 1466, 4100 Porto (tel. 02 600 19 13). Five-star. Fine dining—French and international. Well appointed.
Hotel Porto Sheraton, Av. da Boavista 1269, 4100 Porto (tel. 02 606 88 22). Five-star. Indoor pool and restaurant.
Hotel Tivoli Porto Atlântico, Rua Afonso Lopes Viera 148, 4100 Porto (tel. 02 694 941). Five-star. Swimming pools and restaurant.
Hotel Castor, Rua das Dozes Casas 17, 4000 Porto (tel. 02 570 014). Four-star. Restaurant.

Hotel Dom Henrique, Rua Geudes Azevedo 176, 4000 Porto (tel. 02 200 57 55). Four-star. Restaurant.
Grand Hotel do Porto, Rua de Santa Catarina 197, 4000 Porto (tel. 02 200 81 76). Three-star. Very central, garaging, good restaurant.
Hotel São João, Rua do Bonjardim 120, 4000 Porto (tel. 02 200 16 62). Three-star. Central hotel of character, good service and moderate price.
Albergaria Miradouro, Rua da Alegria 598, 4000 Porto (tel. 02 570 717). Four-star. Comfortable. Panoramic restaurant on top of building, Portucale, one of best in Porto.
Residencial Castelo de Santa Catarina, Rua de Santa Catarina 1347, 4000 Porto (tel. 02 495 599). Two-star. 2km north of centre in quiet off road location, pleasant tree shaded garden, parking. Moderate.
Estalagem Via Norte, Leça do Balio, Porto (tel. 02 948 02 94). Five-star, swimming pool, restaurant, close to airport.
Aleixo, Rua da Estação 216 (tel. 02 570 462). Near Campanha Station. Typical Portuguese food.
A Porta Nobre, Largo de São Francisco (tel. 02 200 11 01). Portuguese and continental cuisine. Classy and expensive.

RIBEIRA
Chez Lapin, Cais da Ribeira 40/2 (tel. 02 200 64 81). Good food. Moderate.
Don Tonho, Cais da Ribeira 13/15 (tel. 02 200 43 07). Restaurant.
Mercearia, Praça da Ribeira 33/4 (tel. 02 200 43 89). Restaurant.
Restaurante do Terreirinho, Largo do Terreirinho 7 (tel. 02 208 81 58). Behind Cais da Ribeira. Intimate atmosphere with excellent cuisine. Superb fish dishes. Good value.

Places of Interest

Museum renovation has been going on apace; check with Turismo for possible current closures.
Casa do Infante House of Henry the Navigator (tel. 02 316 025): Mon–Fri 9am–12 noon and 2–5pm.
Casa-Museu de Teixeira Lopes, Gaia: Mon–Sat 9am–12.30pm and 2–5.30pm, free.
Cathedral (Sé): 9am–12 noon and 3–5.30pm daily.
Igreja de São Francisco, Mon–Sat 9am–12.30 and 2.30–-5pm. Closed Sun and Hols.
Igreja de Santa Clara, Mon–Fri 9.30–11.30am and 3–6pm, Sat 9am–12 noon. Closed Sundays.
Museu de Arte Moderna, Casa de Serralves: Tues–Sun 2–8pm. Check with Turismo if current exhibition.
Museu do Carro Eléctrico (Tram Museum): 9am–12 noon and 2pm–5pm. Closed Mon and Hols.
Museu de Etnográfia e História: 10am–12 noon and 2–5pm. Closed Sun. Mon and Hols.

Museu Guerra Junqueiro: check if open with Turismo.

Museu Nacional de Soares dos Reis: 10am–12 noon and 2–5pm. Closed Mon and Hols. Sat and Sun free.

Museu Romântico: Tues–Thurs 10am–12.20pm and 2–6pm, Fri and Sat 10am–12.30pm and 2–6pm, Sun 2–6pm. Last admission ½ hour before closing time. Sat and Sun free. Closed Mon and Hols.

Palácio da Bolsa (tel. 02 200 44 97): (Stock Exchange) Nov–Feb. Mon–Fri 9am–5.30pm. Mar, Apr and Oct Mon–Fri 9am–5.40pm. Closed Sat, Sun and Hols. May–Sept Mon–Fri 9am–5.45pm, Sat, Sun and Hols 9am–5pm.

Solar do Vinho do Porto: Mon–Fri 11.00am–10pm. Closed 1.30–2.30pm, Sat 5–10.30pm. Closed Sun and Hols.

Torre dos Clérigos: Mon–Sat 10.30am–12 noon and 3.30–5pm, Sun 10.30 am–12 noon and 3–5pm. Closed Wednesdays.

Centro Regional de Artes Tradicionais, 37, Rua da Reboleira (tel. 02 320 076). Best place to buy local handicrafts.

Festival

Festas de São João: night of 23rd June and next day.

Tourist Offices

Praça do General Humberto Delgado (tel. 02 312 740). Mon–Fri 9am–19.00, Sat 9am–4pm. Sun 10am–1pm.

Praça Dom João I (tel. 02 371 54).

6. THE DOURO AND ITS SURROUNDS

Arising in Spain, the River Douro flows through some of the most dramatic and inhospitable country in the whole of Portugal before reaching the Atlantic at Porto. Deeply incised valleys, rugged terrain, impoverished soil from granite and schist rocks in the Alto Douro make it a most unlikely region for the birthplace of one of Europe's best known wines, port. Looking now from the heights of Ponte Dom Luís I, the high, two level bridge in Porto, the Douro is seen as a calm gently flowing river with no hint that it was once called `the river of bad navigation'. The sailors bringing down the wine in the traditional boat, *barco rabelo*, had to negotiate 200 rapids, chutes, cataracts, waterfalls and whirlpools before the river ran calm on the approach to Porto. Lives were lost including that in 1862 of Baron Forrester, one of the characters who made a unique contribution to the history of port wine. The Douro has been tamed now by a series of eight dams which can be negotiated by locks allowing boats to ply up and down the river. Nevertheless, attracted by the fame of the wine, a fund of romantic stories from the past and the lure of uncompromising scenic beauty, the Douro has been and remains the most visited region of the north. Burningly high temperatures in the summer are best avoided making spring, especially verdant with the new vine leaves, and autumn when the grapes are being harvested the best times to visit.

The River Ave, which flows close to Guimarães and enters the Atlantic at Vila Conde, marks the northern boundary dividing the Douro from the Minho. Guimarães is a little 'twixt and 'tween but is included with the southern Minho region in chapter 9. All the principal towns of the region are visited here: Vila Real, Amarante and Lamego as well as the Alvão Natural Park lying to the north of Vila Real.

Porto is a good starting place to explore the Douro, although visitors arriving from Spain and entering Portugal through Bragança can equally well enter the Douro at its eastern end. Either way, the train which runs at a fairly sedate pace along much of the Douro offers a more romantic way to view the river than driving the twisting roads. Once out of Porto, it is some 50km (30 miles) before the train joins the river to follow alongside but afterwards it is Douro scenery all the way to Pocinho, a journey which takes just over four hours on one of the faster trains (i.e. a train that does not stop quite so much).

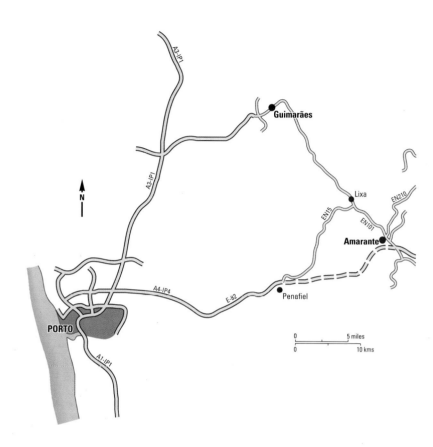

Tua station has an interesting, rustic restaurant, open at lunch time, which often attracts the people of Porto to ride out for lunch. It is around three hours on the fast early morning train which arrives in good time for lunch and still leaves time for a constitutional stroll before returning mid-afternoon.

Although it is possible to follow the Douro by car all the way out of Porto, the route is so winding that it takes an age to drive and reaching as far as Pinhão can take the whole of a day. There is a compromise faster route to this same destination which takes in the charming and elegant town of Amarante before crossing the mountains of Serra do Marão to join the Douro at Mesão Frio. From just north of Porto, a motorway toll road heads out through the typical countryside of this area — pine clad hills broken only by villages and small farming communities — towards Amarante, but is complete for the moment only as far as Penafiel. From Penafiel the road takes a northerly loop through

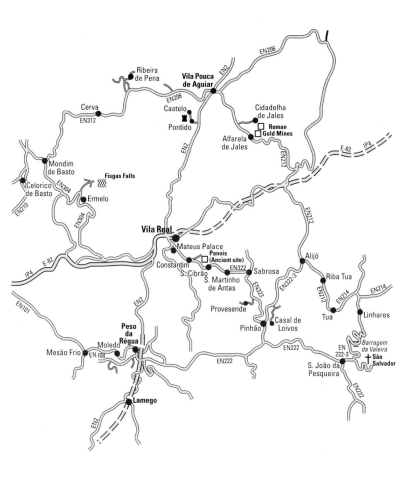

well populated areas passing plenty of eating places before it descends into Amarante.

Amarante

The historic heart of the old town of Amarante sits astride the River Tâmega and is well viewed from the new bridge. Curtained by trees, the river lazily idles around sand banks to flow through the wide arches of the old bridge, Ponte de S. Gonçales, backed by verdant mountains. White geese paddle contentedly amongst the pedalos and rowing boats watched by afternoon tea drinkers from wooden balconies overhanging the river. All the charm and elegance of the old town is captured within this one scene. The narrower part of the river where the old bridge stands today has been a crossing point for centuries, probably from Roman times although there is no trace now of the bridge they left behind. Legend relates how São Gonçalo on returning from his journey in Africa built a bridge here in 1220 which lasted until it collapsed in 1762. The fine Baroque three arched replacement was built in the reign of Maria I. An obelisk bearing a marble plaque relates how, in May 1809, the bridge was successfully defended in the Peninsular War by the Portuguese under General Silveira (who later became Count of Amarante) backed by Beresford's forces against the troops of Napoleon. The French fled in disorderly retreat into the hills.

São Gonçalo, the patron saint of Amarante, dominates much of the history of the town and exerts a strong influence on social activities to this day. His building activities did not stop at merely spanning rivers, he had the power to build bridges in relationships and gained a reputation as a matchmaker. He is now regarded as the patron saint of marriages. Curiously, Amarante's association with fertility rites is believed to reach back to pagan times and romantics are convinced that the town's name derives from 'Amar' (love) but the down-to-earth *Blue Guide* suggests Amarante is a derivation from the Latin *Ante Moranum* meaning 'in front of the Serra do Marão'. All these ancient pre-Christian fertility rites seem to have crystallised around São Gonçalo, beatified in 1561, and are celebrated in great style on his special day on the first weekend in June. On this occasion, following the ancient custom, the young men offer phallus-shaped cakes to the young women who are out in force to receive them. The festival is much more than this and celebrated in typical Portuguese style with food, wine and song and, as with many festivals in the north, fireworks.

Perhaps the most important monument in Amarante is the church and convent of **São Gonçalo** which stands by the old bridge on the north side of the river. Its construction, begun in 1540 in the reign of Dom João III, was not completed until 1620, some five kings later. A statue of São Gonçalo lodges in a niche in the impressive Renaissance style side entrance, in the first of three tiers. The loggia to the left of the doorway is embellished with statues of four of the kings who reigned during its period of construction, João III, Sebastião, Henrique and António, all from the House of Avis. Richly carved wood and gilt woodwork decorate the interior but most visitors head for the tomb of the saint to the left of the altar. The saint's influence still works and those aspiring to marriage need only touch the effigy on the tomb to be rewarded within the year. There is no record of the marriages which actually take place but the limestone São Gonçalo is getting quite worn away in places. The church has two cloisters, the second one, now invaded by the town hall, used to be the old convent. This houses a small **museum** with paintings by Portuguese painters but notably by the Cubist, Amadeo de Souza Cardoso (died 1918), a local artist who has achieved international fame.

A wander across the old bridge is irresistible and it is a great place to loiter to watch the activities on the river, although the overhanging wooded balcony of the *Salão de Cha* (tea house) on the south side of the river is an even more alluring prospect. Here you can sip tea, mentally thank Catherine of Bragança

The Barras vineyards

for introducing the habit of afternoon tea to the English, and while away time by watching the geese gaggle, the swans glide and the ducks paddle purposefully hither and thither in and out of the overhanging willow trees. A walk down **Rua 31 Janeiro**, past the tea shops, is courting temptation from the local hams, a speciality, hanging in doorways and from the array of bread on view, not to mention chocolate croissants. The market place by the river is a good place to park most days except Wednesday when the market is held. Amarante swings much of high summer under a weight of festivals in the gardens of the **Casa de Calçada** where on a Saturday evening, for the cost of the cover charge, there is enough food and drink to consume for every appetite.

Amarante is not too well endowed with accommodation but it does have a *pousada* named, as might be guessed, *Pousada de São Gonçalo* (category B) which lies just outside town on the Vila Real road, and a couple of three-star hotels. The largest of these, *Hotel Navarras*, which offers plenty of facilities including a heated indoor swimming pool, lies south of the new bridge facing the river on Rua António Carneiro.

Port Wine Country

Find the route leading over the Serra do Marrão by following the old N15 out of Amarante towards Vila Real and turning right shortly following signs to Régua. Expect slow progress along a road that twists its way through the mountains, sometimes through tall Vinho Verde vines growing up through the trees. Olive groves provide a reminder that this is still a Mediterranean country. Granite tors scattered amongst low-growing scrub announce the summit area and shortly afterwards the descent starts towards the small village of Mesão Frio on the banks of the Douro. Mesão Frio marks the start of the port wine Demarcated Region and the engaging view on the descent to this village over the neat port wine vineyards sloping down to the green waters of the river Douro is one which typifies the region and one which, like a palette of paints, has all the rich ingredients which blend effortlessly into fresh images at every bend in the river. The village of **Mesão Frio** has nothing to offer but a delightful ambience which demands of travellers at least a brief pause lest it should pass unnoticed. Once over the narrow granite bridge, the road follows alongside the north bank of the river passing through the small spa town of **Caldas de Moledo**. Its spa waters, loaded with fluorides, bicarbonates and sulphur at a very comfortable 45°C, are reputed to be good for the respiratory system, the skin, rheumatism and muscular ailments. If all that needs a little contemplation before sampling, then there is no finer place to relax than beneath the row of plane trees here which cast their shadow on the already green waters of the Douro. Peso da Régua, usually known as Régua, is reached very shortly.

The vision of high rise apartment blocks seems totally out of context with the Douro valley but this is busy, commercial **Régua** at the heart of the port wine industry and home to the head office of Casa do Douro, one of the regulatory bodies in the control of the port wine trade. A couple of ornamental square-rigged *barcos rebelos* are moored out on the river just soaking up the sun. There is no great architectural or monumental interest here but it is worth calling in the tourist office on the riverside opposite the railway station to find out which port wine lodges are open to visitors. It has three *residencials*, all rated three star, of which *Columbano* and *D. Quixote* are passed on entering Caldas de Moledo. The third, the *Imperial* lies near the railway station.

From Régua the road crosses to the south side of the river and from here there is a very short diversion to Lamego.

The Port Wine Story

2. The Vineyards

The Demarcated Region for the Douro lies some 100km (60 miles) upstream from Porto in the region known as the Alto Douro. It starts at Barqueiros and follows the river all the way to the Spanish border. A number of the tributaries of the Douro, including the Corgo, Torto, Pinhão and Tua, are included to give an area of some 3235 square kilometres in an irregular shape. The steep slopes of the Douro grow the finest grapes and it is here that most of the major port houses have their farms or *quintas*. Driving eastward from Régua, large signs mounted in the vineyards appear with regularity announcing famous names like Barros, Sandeman and Calem, and there is a fair concentration of them around Pinhão.

Characteristically, the soils are derived from the schists of Cambrian and Precambrian eras and are stony and impoverished. Add to this an inhospitable climate of cold winters and scorching hot, dry summers and it seems an unlikely region for cultivation of any sort. Vines, it seems, are the best crop, and the region is virtually devoted to this monoculture. The whole area is rugged but the steep slopes descending towards the river grow the best grapes, especially along the Douro, with the land nearest the river valued most highly. Damming the Douro raised the river level at many parts robbing the farmers of some of their most prized land. Managing the steep slopes could only be achieved in the first instance after Herculean feats of labour to produce level terraces supported by stone walls. The close packed terraces follow the contours around the hillside creating pleasing patterns which has transformed a barren landscape into something uniquely beautiful. There are some 85,000 vineyards in the Douro region and many will have at least a mile of wall but mostly much more which gives some indication of the extensive labour over many years.

Close packed on these narrow terraces, the vines are grown out along wire strainers and are never too far from the ground. The stony soil has a double benefit. Whatever moisture there is in the soil is trapped by the stones which also behave like storage heaters by absorbing the heat of the day and releasing it during the night. Irrigation is not permitted and the vines must survive on the natural rainfall which is very low throughout the summer months. When *vindima* (collecting the harvest and making the wine) does arrive, the expected yield on the traditionally grown vines is a meagre 600g per plant.

Modernisation with the help of World Bank money is slowly changing the face of the Douro. New vineyards are spaced widely enough to allow a caterpillar to drive between while earth banks and not walls are used to retain the terraces. Since caterpillars can manage steep slopes with the same ease as level ground, the rows of vines need not necessarily follow the contours but can now be planted running down towards the river. In appearance, these new vineyards are very open showing rather more bare ground than the older style and the patterns they create may not necessarily have the same regimentation along the hillside. Plant density in the new vineyards is around 3000–4000 vines per hectare compared to 5000–6000 in the old vineyards but yield per plant is higher reaching one to two kilograms.

Lamego

Set in a small fertile valley crowded by hills, Lamego does more than bask in the beauty of its surrounds, it has used it as part of its own architecture; a castle sits on one hill while the church of Nossa Senhora dos Remédios dominates another. Its spacious and peaceful location hides a population of some 10,000 farmers who, when not growing maize, melons and fruit crops in variety, are thoroughly immersed in the wine trade although not all the grapes go into the production of port. Liberated from the Moors in 1057 by Ferdinand I, Lamego's biggest claim to historical fame is that it was here that Portugal's first *Cortes* was held. Nobles, clergy and town officials met in 1143 to recognise Afonso Henriques as the first King of Portugal and to pass the Law of Succession whereby no foreigner could succeed to the throne. The coronation, it is believed, took place in the church of Almacave on the road of the same name.

The wide **Avenida Visconde Guedes Texera** is the town's main thoroughfare. At the bottom lies Turismo which dispenses maps and accommodation details but not so much information about the town. Usually, the first pilgrimage is to the town's most famous monument **N.S. dos Remédios** (Our Lady of Remedies, 1750–60) which is very reminiscent of Bom Jesus at Braga. This is reached by a stroll through the spacious Avenida Dr Alfredo de Sousa lined by cafés and *pastelarias*. Sustained by a steady stream of tourists, these shops have little need to try hard and it reflects in their service and prices. The Avenida feeds visitors directly onto the magnificent tree-shrouded **staircase** which leads up to the ultimate focal point, the church. Saints can walk but sinners are expected to climb the 650 or so stairs on their knees. Not many do but this is most likely to be seen on 8 September when the annual *romaria* is held to celebrate the saint's special day. It is a lively fair lasting several days, which mixes religious events happily with the usual feasting and dancing. The granite, white-walled, double staircase is a succession of short flights divided by landings. One of these is actually the main road crossing the steps which is a little hazardous for those making the ascent on knee. Each landing is well embellished with a selection from *azulejos*, fountains, statues and chapels. One of the *azulejos* depicting a pregnant Mary with Joseph is seen again as a painting in the museum. All this culminates in the Court of the Kings, just below the church, where the statues of the kings appear tragicomical rather than imposing. It is worth taking a little time to enjoy the staircase because the 18th century church itself may disappoint, except perhaps for the Baroque façade bounded by twin clock towers.

Lamego was a bishopric under the Suevi and its Episcopal status was restored after liberation from the Moors. The present-day cathedral, located in the Largo de Sé at the lower end of the Avenida Visconde Guedes Texera, had Romanesque beginnings but all that now remains of this is the belfry, the rest disappeared under a 16th century rebuild and 18th century renovations. Most of the remaining Gothic is seen in the handsome façade, built in 1508–15, with its triple-arched entrance. Inside, two fine organs catch the eye and the

Nossa Senhora dos Remédios, Lamego

silver frontal to the Capelo do Sacramento (Chapel of the Blessed Sacrament). Adjacent, and reached from within, is the elegant Renaissance cloister showing further evidence of Gothic influence. Built in rather grand style, the Bishop's Palace, situated in Largo de Camões close to the cathedral, now houses the regional **museum**. A selection of 18th century sedan chairs and carriages greet the visitor but these are soon replaced by furniture, church artefacts, *azulejos* and a series of 16th century Flemish tapestries depicting the Oedipus story. The most notable paintings are those by Vasco Fernandes (known as the Great Vasco, Grão Vasco) which were commissioned by the Bishop João de Madureira in 1506. All the 20 panels went missing when the cathedral was renovated in the 18th century but five were found in the Capitular house in 1881. These are the Creation of the Animals, the Annunciation, the Visitation, the Presentation in the Temple and the Circumcision.

The **castle** with its 12th century keep, reached from behind Turismo, is perhaps more impressive from a distance although its remains are kept in good order by the local boy scouts.

When Baroque façades and impressive mansions start to jade the palette, head for the fox's lair (*Raposeira*). Owned by Seagram, Raposeira make a very fine sparkling white wine and the factory is open for individual tours. Ask to be guided by Marguerita; not only does she speak excellent English but she sparkles even more than the wine and her tours usually go with plenty of fizz. Both the *demi sec* and the *brut* are sampled at the end of the tour.

Attracting a regular stream of pilgrims, Lamego has more accommodation than would otherwise be expected. *Hotel Parque*, near to N.S. dos Remédios, is only two-star but is a comfortable hotel with a good restaurant. Offering a little more comfort at more than double the price is the three-star *Albergaria do Cerrado*. Nearby are a number of manor houses in delightful country locations which are available through TURIHAB; these include the splendid *Casa de Santo António de Britiande* located at Britiande just 5km from Lamego, the *Casa dos Pingueis* standing amongst vineyards at Cambres, some 6km from Lamego, which is also the location of the 18th century *Casa dos Varais* which faces Régua and enjoys magnificent views over the Douro.

Pinhão

After this side trip to Lamego the onward route from Régua follows along the south side of the Douro which sometimes looks more like a lake than a river. Endless vines in endless rows contour the steep slopes of the winding river, famous names like Barros, Sandeman and Quinta Dona Matilde plaster the hillsides. The river is crossed again just before the next destination, Pinhão, situated at the confluence of the Pinhão and Douro rivers. Pinhão itself is small and not especially interesting although the station has some *azulejos* of note depicting scenes from the port wine story. It lies around the epicentre of the main port wine area which has given it some prominence since the arrival of the railway in 1880 and has become an important centre for despatching wine to the warehouses of Vila Nova de Gaia. The older people still insist that

---

Raposeira Sparkling Wine

The white burgundy grape, Chardonnay, one of the grapes of Champagne, and the Pinot grape were brought from France by the owners when production started in 1898. Some Portuguese varieties are also used. At harvest time great care is taken over the transport of the grapes to avoid crushing before they reach the factory. A light crushing follows to release about 65 per cent of the juice which goes on to ferment naturally without added yeast. A second crushing is used to make ordinary wine for local consumption. After the first fermentation, the wine is bottled and yeast added for the second fermentation which takes place in a cellar maintained at a constant 13°C. This stage requires around 75 days during which time the bottle is regularly rotated by hand, all three million of them, although mechanisation is now used in this rotation process which helps to complete the settling more speedily.

Removing the sediment is perhaps the most interesting part of the process. The bottle is first inverted, allowing the sediment to settle in the plastic cork, then the neck end only is passed through a freezing mixture which rapidly freezes a plug of water and sediment. This pops out and is removed as the bottle is righted leaving the wine totally clear. Sweetener is added if necessary, the bottle topped off and securely recorked.

---

the wine only becomes port wine on storage at Porto although this regulation has been relaxed in recent years. Accommodation is not too freely available in this area but a superbly restored 17th century TURIHAB manor house, *Casa de Loivos*, is close at hand. Casal de Loivos is 6km from Pinhão but in reality is perched almost directly above it. All rooms open out onto a terrace which keeps an eye on the Douro as it snakes its way through steep banks of vineyards, one of the finest viewpoints over this river. This is one of those houses which operates as TURIHAB always intended—dinner is available on request taken around a huge dining table shared with other guests and the wine list includes *Barca Velha*, one of the countries best red wines.

A Circular Tour from Pinhão

There is a short half day circular tour out of Pinhão which mixes Douro scenery and villages in a blend typical of this region. With luck it is possible to see some of the ox drawn carts in action, especially in the older villages. Head south first through Casais do Douro before climbing through terraced vineyards towards S. João de Pesqueira taking in views of the rolling hills inland. **S. João de Pesqueira** has some fine 18th century houses but it is the

Azulejo at Pinhão station

unexpected modern ones which tend to catch the eye. Follow signs through two left turns towards the *barragem* to drive through dilapidated overgrown vineyards, victims of the dreaded phylloxera and never replanted. A pointed hill littered with churches and chapels encountered on the descent towards the *barragem* is **S. Salvador do Mundo**. Pull off onto the large parking area on the right to inspect. Although it is possible to drive the narrow, difficult track to the summit, walking is the better option. The now neglected chapels are more curious than interesting but the vantage point at the summit gives a view over the Barragem de Valeira, the part of the river where, in its wild days, Baron Forrester lost his life in a boating accident.

From here the road completes its downward wind to cross the *barragem* back to the northern banks of the Douro only to zig-zag upwards away from the river through pine forested hills. Cobbled streets announce **Linhares**, a village set amidst olive groves, but it is mainly line patterns in the hills created by the vineyards that dominate the scenery. Roads in this part of the world go nowhere directly and this one weaves in and out of the valleys and over the hills, all at high level. Following signs to Tua involves a couple of left turns and a descent back towards the Douro. **Tua** has little to offer but a railway station with a restaurant and a good location by the river. The route heads away from the river again to **Alijó**, one of the largest towns in the region. Its spacious centre decorated with an *azulejoed* church and shaded by a lime tree planted in 1856. Alijó is also the location of the *pousada* named after Baron Forrester which offers stylish accommodation with the benefit of a swimming pool and a restaurant terrace. Although the town received its royal charter in 1226, the presence of old Celtic *castros* tells of much earlier occu-

Grape harvesting (vindima) on the Barras estate

pation. Alijó, and its neighbour Favaios, swamped by Douro vineyards, try to stand out from the crowd by making a remarkably good muscatel from the Moscatelo Galego grape. Beyond Alijó the road leads to a junction at **Favaios**, an old granite village with a medieval flavour, where a left turn heads back to Pinhão to complete the circuit.

The Port Wine Story

3. Regulating the growers

During troubled times in 1931, with the price of wine falling and growers close to bankruptcy, a syndicate of leading men joined forces to attempt to regulate the trade, arrest the fall in prices and promote the whole region. This new association, the Syndicated Federation of the Wine Growers of the Douro Region, was recognised in law by a decree passed by government in 1932. It is now known simply as the Casa do Douro and its base is in Régua.

The demarcation of the Douro in 1761 recognised the quality differences within the Douro region, with the better quality wine coming from the harsher Cima Corgo region east of Régua. The Casa do Douro took this a stage further by undertaking an eight year long survey of all the vineyards in the demarcated region, a register of some 96,000 properties in which each vineyard was assessed by location, nature of the land, altitude, inclination, exposure, plant density, age of vines, types of grapes and productivity. Points were awarded on an agreed scale for all these features and the vineyards classified from A downwards to F. It is on the basis of this detailed classification that farmers are paid and the amounts of port to be made in any one year decided.

Its role is now much wider and it offers technical assistance to growers, issues warranty certificates for musts and wines produced in the region, guarantees prices for unsold wine and generally regulates the region to maintain quality.

To Vila Real

Vila Real, the largest town in the Douro area, is easily reached from Pinhão. The inland route via Sabrosa has the advantage of passing the Mateus Palace on the approach to Vila Real while offering some points of interest along the way. Once away from Pinhão, there is a short worthwhile diversion into **Provesende**. It is a magnificent old village full of 18th century manor houses with impressive granite façades now sad with neglect. A pillory marks the centre and just down to the left is an old ornamental granite fountain where water issues through sculptured faces. The village of **Sabrosa**, the next major village en route, is famous as the birthplace of Magellan the navigator. Ignoring advice from the Portuguese ambassador, Magellan led the first, Spanish sponsored, expedition around the globe between 1519 and 1522 and, although killed in a skirmish in the Philippines before completing the voyage, he is remembered as the first man to circumnavigate the globe. Signs here point left for Vila Real. Vineyards relent a little to allow chestnuts to become part of the scenery. Just before Constantim, look on the right for a short diversion to the **Sanctuary of Panóais** to see the sacrificial slabs. A yellow sign directs to the site. An old man in a nearby house is often on hand to share his knowledge, all in Portuguese, and will continue quite happily even though not a word is understood by the visitors. Expect nothing but a field of granite boulders cut with troughs and inscriptions. The inscriptions date from the 3rd century venerating, amongst others, Serapis, a pre-Roman deity. Head for the large anvil shaped boulder and mount the steps cut out of the rock at the rear. This has five huge troughs some with sloping bases to assist drainage. Was it for animal sacrifice or sacred amputations? It is best to leave the imagination back home!

The Port Wine Story

4. Vindima

Vindima, collecting the harvest and making the wine, is a mixture of intensive hard work and great joy. It is not simply the realisation of a whole season's work, it is also a thanksgiving that the unpredictable natural elements which could have ruined the harvest relented once again.

Picking is still by hand so when harvest time comes around, towards the end of September, bands of pickers arrive from neighbouring villages. The women move between the rows gathering the grapes then transfer them to large wicker baskets at the end of the row. From here, the basket, now containing 50–70kg of grapes, is lifted onto the back of a man wearing a hooded sack for protection from the juices and sometimes secured around his forehead with a leather thong, or he may simply control the basket with a hooked rod to hold the top. This is carried uphill to the nearest point accessible to a vehicle. In the early days, before mechanisation, gravity was their greatest ally and everything flowed downhill towards the river. The *quinta* lay below the vineyards so the grapes were taken down to it. A split level inside the *quinta* allowed for the pressings to flow down to the lower level for vinification and finally the wine was moved down to the river to be transported to Gaia.

In the more modern vineyards, where caterpillars can reach all the rows, all the gang can concentrate on picking. When the mood is right, folk songs are taken up and sung in chorus. Food is part of the bargain, and a good meal with plenty of wine is served to the hungry workers at some part of the day.

Larger *quintas* buy grapes from smaller farmers and pay them on the basis of sugar content and weight. As a consequence of the many different micro-climates in the region, there is a whole raft of grape varieties in use, as many as 85, although of these just 15 red and eight white are used extensively. New plantings pay greater attention to grape varieties and are generally restricted to the following five: Touriga Nacional, Touriga Francesca, Tinta Barroca, Tinta Cão and Roritz.

All the grapes go for pressing where all the stalks are sifted out by the machine and the must transferred to huge concrete tanks. Fermentation is allowed to start with the aid of natural yeast present on the grape skins. It is important to agitate the must to extract maximum colour and flavour in a short time and this is achieved using the pressure generated by the escaping gases. Careful monitoring of the sugar level is essential and immediately this falls to the required level the must is run off into large vats (*tonels*) where it is then fortified with brandy to arrest the fermentation and to give a strength of 19 per cent. The young wine is wintered in the *tonels* where it also clarifies and transferred to barrels (*pipes*). Now the wine is moved down by road or train to the shipper's lodge at Vila Nova de Gaia where it is refreshed with a little more brandy to make the strength 20 per cent. The wine is then classified as wood port or vintage port and treated accordingly (see p 43).

Continuing on towards Vila Real, the **Solar de Mateus** is soon reached. Both the house and the gardens are like some period stage set but well worthy of a little time. If only the gardens are visited the charge is lower. From the entrance, a curved tree-lined avenue leads to the first view of the house. The granite and white-washed façade is instantly recognisable from the illustration on the label of the famous Mateus rosé although the wine is no longer made here, rights were sold to Sogrape some time ago. In Portugal, it requires only a king to have slept the night for a manor house or *quinta* to assume to title of a palace. Mateus, although often grandly known as a palace is just a *quinta* but a rather grand Baroque *quinta* for all that with origins stretching back to 1725. The prolific Italian architect, Nicolau Nasoni, famous for the Torre de los Clerigos which stands in the centre of Porto, was employed to construct it. A guided tour of the interior points out the rather splendid carved and vaulted chestnut ceilings. The chestnut tree is ubiquitous throughout the north and its wood is very much a local material used frequently in this type of application. Books from the 16th century are still housed in the library and there are many exhibits of merit in other rooms including Chinese porcelain, a grandfather clock from London given by King William and Queen Mary of England, 18th century four-poster beds from Brazil and some 17th century

Vila Real: Mateus Palace

still life pictures. The Holy Mother of Pleasure with her enigmatic smile presides over the private chapel. Behind this statue, the neo-classical wooden altarpiece is painted white to resemble marble while paintings adorn the ceiling, each within its own frame. The chapel is not used now except for concerts of Baroque music. In an adjacent, older chapel, only menfolk could be buried under the floor, the women being buried in the cemetery in Vila Real. Here the painted ceiling bears an inscription which reads 'the wife should love her husband and the husband his wife as much as the church'. The house is owned and lived in by the Albequerque family.

In front of the house is a large ornamental pond added in the 1930s which has a somewhat distracting sculpture of a naked lady thrown there as though no other use could be found for it. The gardens, full of neatly trimmed box hedges, sharp lines and maze-like patterns are fun but the huge tunnel, formed from clipped conifers, leading down to the vineyards has visitors staring in disbelief.

The Port Wine Story

5. The Barcos Rabelos

In the early days of the port wine trade, the dangerous and difficult River Douro provided the only means of transporting the massive volumes of wine down to Porto. A specially adapted flat bottomed boat constructed in layered wood, called a *barco rabelo*, was used for this work. To make the boat manoeuvrable in strong rapids and give it stability, it was fitted with a long oar-like rudder, called an *espadela*, which was almost the length of the boat allowing the whole crew to add their strength to help the helmsman navigate the rapids. The boat was powered with square rigged sails when needed, supported by oars which were often required for the return journey. Night time navigation was not possible so all journeys were made by day.

Crewed normally by 11 sailors, the boats carried around 45 to 50 barrels and, at one stage, bigger boats were transporting almost double that number until legislation in 1792 limited the size of the boats. The barrels were not usually full, some space was left to make sure they would float in case of an accident. Returning back up the river to Régua was just as difficult and the men would sometimes have to go ashore to pull the boat themselves or, if the terrain permitted, use oxen teams to get through the rapid sections of the river. By 1940, there were hundreds of the boats navigating the river.

Vila Real

With a population reaching 14,000, Vila Real is one of the largest towns in the region belonging, administratively, to the Trás-os-Montes. The old part sits on top of an easily defended bluff in a huge loop of the River Corgo. Geographically, it is isolated from the west by a near continuous chain of mountains of which the immediate ones are Serra do Marrão and Serra de Alvão. Although there is evidence of early settlement in the area, it was depopulated throughout the battles between the Barbarians and the Moors. It was only resettled around the beginning of the12th century and received a royal charter in 1289 from the hands of Dom Dinis.

Although Vila Real is a lively, bustling industrial centre, much of the character of the older part of town has been preserved around the central tree-lined boulevard of **Avenida Carvalho Araújo**. Much of the rest of the town is an uninteresting sprawl of suburbs. Turismo is located on the Avenida in the former Palace of the Dukes of Vila Real which is fronted by four attractive Manueline windows. Almost opposite but a little to the south is the Gothic Igreja de São Domingo, now raised to the status of cathedral, which has some modern stained glass windows but little else to detain. Further south down the avenue on the same side as the cathedral is the 15th century house where the navigator Diogo Cão was born. Diogo Cão was commissioned by King João II to explore the west coast of Africa and he was the first European to set foot on African soil south of the equator (1482) where he established friendly relations with local rulers. Not to be missed is a stroll down the avenue, through the **square with the Pelourhino** (pillory), towards the 14th century chapel of São Dinis (S. Bras), not this time to see the church especially, but for the dramatic views down into the gorge. The old town walls hardly seem necessary for the defence of the town with the protection afforded by the River Corgo, which flows all around this promontory, and its steep banks.

Pontido Castle, Jales Gold Mine and Alvão Nature Park

One of the best excursions out of Vila Real explores the area to the north and visits a castle, old gold mines and the Alvão Nature Park. There are hardly any access roads to this Nature Park but the route described here explores some of the best known parts. A full day is enough to accomplish this tour of 144km (90 miles) but it could be a very long day if all the suggested side trips are included. Head out of Vila Real on the Chaves road with the intention of reaching as far as Vila Pouca de Aguar. The route follows the Corgo valley offering spectacular views of the Serra de Alvão for much of the way but there is an extra cragginess in the hilltops around Vilarrinho da Samarda where time and the elements have not yet mellowed the younger granite. Turn left for **Pontido** and the castle. From here it is a short drive along a single track road through woodland well-sprinkled with chestnut trees to the centre of Pontido where a *Castelo* sign points to the right. The road, now cobbled, remains

The Port Wine Story

6. Historical Characters

Marquês de Pombal: born in Lisbon on 13 May 1699 as Sebastião José de Carvalho e Melo, he rose to power as adviser to the young King José and, acting by exercising royal prerogative without assuming personal power, he managed to establish an oppressive and dictatorial rule throughout the country. His contribution to the protection and development of the wine trade was second to none. After the Methuen Treaty of 1703, which limited the duties on Portuguese wines to two thirds of that paid on French wines, the market for port in England expanded significantly. To meet the demand, inferior wines were disguised with colourants, extra brandy and other additives by which port began to lose its good name and the trade began to fail. This is when the Marquês de Pombal intervened and set up a powerful company in 1756 charged with the task of defining the area from where the wine could be drawn so creating the world's first Demarcated wine region. The region was marked out with 201 megaliths made of granite bearing the word *feitoria* (factory), a number and the date. In 1761 a further 134 megaliths were added bringing the total to 335. Some of these '*Pombalinas*' are still around either in their original positions or now incorporated into buildings. The company was also given powers to check and maintain standards. Pombal's edicts were by no means universally popular since some luckless neighbouring areas not within the region had their vines rooted out. Protests in Porto over the formation of the Douro wine company led to 17 hangings. Ultimately, these moves to re-establish the industry were successful in ensuring the lasting fame of port wine.

Baron Forrester: Joseph James Forrester was born in Hull on 21 May 1809 and arrived in Portugal as a young man in 1830 to work for his uncle, a merchant in Porto. He took a great interest in preserving the quality of the wine from the Douro region. He had a boat built rather like a *rabelo* and spent many years travelling the river and mapping out the area in very great detail. It was this work which earned him the title of Baron, the first time such an honour had been bestowed on a foreigner. Ironically, he died in a boating accident on the river in 1862. Out boating as a guest of D. Antónia Adelaide Ferreira, trouble at the rapids known as Cachão da Valeira led to the boat capsizing and the death of three people including Baron Forrester, dragged down, it is said, by the weight of gold in his belt. Antónia was saved by her dress which ballooned out to provide buoyancy.

D. Antónia Adelaide Ferreira: she was born in 1810 into one of the rich and powerful port wine families. She married her first cousin and had two children by him. Only after her husband's death did the power and strength of D. Antónia manifest itself when she became administrator of a major agricultural holding on the Douro. Her work on expanding the estates and her devotion to charity work brought her such great esteem that the Duke of Saldanha decided that his son should marry D. Antónia's 11-year-old daughter, Maria. Although honoured, D. Antónia would not agree which angered the Duke of Saldanha into plotting a kidnap. Catching wind of this, D. Antónia and Maria disguised themselves as country women and fled via Spain to England. Maria later married the Count of Azambuja and D. Antónia herself married her secretary, Francisco José da Silva Torres. Returning to Portugal she continued to manage her estates. In one particular year, a glut forced prices down so D. Antónia obligingly bought all the surplus wine to help the farmers. Phylloxera struck the very next season causing widespread destruction of the vineyards and leaving the Ferreiras sitting on a huge profit. She helped to re-establish the vineyards, paid for the construction of roads and railways and improved access to her own 23 farms. Antónia was widowed again in 1880 but carried on with her charity work, donating funds for the construction of hospitals in Régua, Vila Real, Moncorvo and Lamego and creating many scholarships before she died in 1896.

narrow but good and quickly leads to the upper village where the footpath off to the castle is accessed from the track on the left immediately before the old village is entered. Steeped in a straw and dung medieval atmosphere, the old granite village blends itself unobtrusively into the background. The well-crafted granite structures standing on granite mushrooms seen in this village are *espig-ueiros*, used for storing maize (see the feature on p 101). There is only one way to the castle, on foot, and the route starts under the trellis marked by an orange disk. Agility and footwear with good grip are essential for this short walk and scramble to reach Castelo da Pena de Aguiar. The approach requires a crouched walk at one point through a low passage formed by giant boulders before entering the castle through an arched doorway. Welded onto a rocky summit, little remains of the castle except for a few walls, but the ambience and sense of isolation is reward enough, as is the very private satisfaction of finding it!

Heading north again on the main road, **Vila Pouca de Aguiar** is soon reached. Located in a wide fertile valley between the Serra do Alvão to the west and the Serra de Padrela to the east, Vila Pouca de Aguiar lives on vegetables and cereals. There is little reason to stop except for refreshments or to look at the local pottery or linen. There are choices to be made from here. This tour continues with a left turn heading next for Mondim de Basto, but for the curious there is a side trip off right along the N212 to see the old **Jales gold mines**. It is a 32km (20 mile) return trip but, in truth, there is not too much to see since the old open cast sites are now recognised only as lakes, at least for much of the year. Gold was mined by the Romans in Três Minas and Campo de Jales from 21 BC to AD 211 so the whole area is scattered with relics from that period including 18 Roman forts.

The left turn in Vila Pouca de Aguiar is at a major junction in the centre and signposted Mondim de Basto, 29km. Very shortly the road climbs on to the narrowest of corniches on the mountain side and offers a bird's-eye view of a cultivated valley bottom. One of the forestry activities, resin collecting, may be noticed on the next long downhill wind. Gone are the old terracotta pots; these have been replaced with polythene bags stapled to the tree, sometimes in ranks of two or three, and are mostly full of milky white resin. Sitting in a valley bottom is the village of **Cerva** with population enough to warrant a church, cafés and a market. The switchback ride continues as the road climbs back to the heights through the village of **Asnela** where women still wash clothes on the stone slabs by the fountain, not an unusual sight in many parts of the north. A swarm of modern developments announces Mondim de Basto set beside the Tâmega river.

There are perhaps two reasons to stop in **Mondim de Basto**, one is to visit the Turismo, for which turn right at the first roundabout, and the second is to visit the exhibition in the offices of the Alvão Nature Park showing some of the natural features of this region. Walkers will eschew both those reasons with their focus clearly set on reaching the summit of **Monte Farinha**, the highest peak in the region, which lies to the east of the town. Mountain peaks are not always easy to identify but this one is a symmetrical cone with the church of Senhora da Graça perched firmly on top and easy to pick out. There is a path up from Campos, found on the Vilar de Ferreiros road, and near the top this path flirts with and crosses a track which originates on the Cerva road which may be used on the return to make a round trip. If a guide is needed, try 1 September when thousands make the trip for annual pilgrimage. There is more good walking out along the Cabril valley starting from the campsite just south of town. Diners will probably have none of this and settle for the roast sirloin of veal which is a local speciality.

The final leg of this tour samples the full flavour of **Alvão Nature Park** and visits the typical village of Ermelo and the Fisgas waterfalls before heading back to Vila Real. Once out of Mondim de Basto, the route starts to wind its way to higher levels through heath covered slopes, detouring around valleys whilst cutting through two mountain ranges, Serra do Marão to the south and Serra de Alvão to the north. Granite changes to schist as the road follows the mountainside to reveal scenery on a grand scale. There is a shady picnic area with tables on the right overlooking a river just before Ermelo is reached. Immediately beyond, before crossing the bridge, take the road on the left to visit the **waterfalls of Fisgas**.

This road, narrow but good, climbs through pines to reach a small hamlet where it continues to the right to reach, after 4km (2½ miles), the viewpoint for the waterfalls. A narrow gorge with a precipitous drop separates the viewpoint from the falls so the view remains fairly distant but clear enough.

Alvão Nature Park

Alvão Nature Park occupies an area of 7220 hectares of high ground, mainly covering the hydrographic basin of the Olo River which flows into the Tamega. It lies principally on the western slopes of the Serra de Alvão which act as a condensation barrier to the mass of humid air from the Atlantic providing ideal conditions for lush vegetative growth in contrast to the drier eastern region. Granite predominates in the upper regions, and is separated from the lower schists in some parts by a much harder quarzite barrier.

Lamas de Olo, at 1000m (3280ft) is one of the highest villages in the region and owes its existence to an island of schist within the extensive upland granite which provides an area of viable farm land. Only a mere 8km away and 550m (1800ft) lower, Ermelo also farms on schist in a similar style using the lands close to the village intensively and the outer communal land extensively. The drop in height between these two villages provides the dramatic backdrop for the Fisgas water-falls which can be approached from Ermelo.

There is no easy circuit to explore the park, the only option is to drive around the perimeter and make incursions to visit some of the older villages, like the two mentioned, where typical rural architecture and an old way of life prevail. The route between Mondim de Basto followed in the tour described here visits Ermelo, the waterfalls at Fisgas and gives a good overview of typical scenery.

Vine festooned **Ermelo,** with its typical rural architecture, requires another short diversion from the main road, this time to the left. From here the road leads upwards once again for the final mountain pass before dropping down towards Vila Real.

Practical Information

Accommodation and Restaurants

Manor houses and *quintas* which have been restored to provide tourist accommodation are indicated by TH (TURIHAB), TR (Turismo Rural) or AT (Agroturismo) according to which scheme they belong. See the introduction for further details.

AMARANTE
Hotel Amaranto, Murtas-Madelena (tel. 055 422 106). Medium sized three-star hotel with restaurant, facilities for disabled.
Hotel Navarras, Rua António Carneiro (tel. 055 431 036). Three-star hotel

with good facilities including indoor and outdoor swimming pools and restaurant.

Casa de Pascoaes, S. João de Gatão (TH) (tel. 055 422 595). Next to the River Tâmega, manor house of some style with four rooms.

LAMEGO

Albergaria do Cerrado, Lugar do Cerrado (tel. 054 63 154) Four-star accommodation, 30 rooms but limited facilities.

Hotel do Parque, Parque Nossa Senhora dos Remédios (tel. 054 65 203). Well situated two-star hotel provides a standard of accommodation above its grade, restaurant.

Quinta da Timpeira, Lugar da Timpeira (TR) (tel. 054 62 811). Located just north of Lamego in a vineyard, five rooms.

Quinta de Marrocos, Valigem (AT) (tel. 054 23 012). Near to Regua, south of River Douro on Pinhão road. 17th century house surrounded by vineyards and overlooking river, five rooms and swimming pool.

Quinta de Santo António de Britiande (TH) (tel. 054 699 346). Manor house with four rooms just 5km (3 miles) south of Lamego.

Casa dos Pinguéis, Cambres (AT) (tel. 054 23 251). Typical Douro house set amidst vineyards 6km (3¾ miles) north of Lamego, three rooms.

Casa dos Varais, Cambres (TH) (tel. 054 23 251). 18th century manor house overlooking River Douro, three rooms.

Lamego sees a steady flood of pilgrims and accordingly, although there are plenty of restaurants, they are fairly uninspiring and expensive. **Hotel Parque** is reasonable otherwise try:

Combinada, Rua de Olaria. Cosy and not too expensive.

PINHÃO

Pousada do Barrão de Forrester, Alijó (tel. 059 959 215). Around 16km (10 miles) outside Pinhão, this pousada offers 11 rooms in modern building. Swimming pool, tennis and restaurant which offers the best food in this locality.

Casa de Casal de Loivos, Casal de Loivos (TH) (tel. 054 72 149). Superb position overlooking Douro, excellent standard of accommodation and service. Evening meals on request, seven rooms and swimming pool.

VILA REAL

Hotel Mira Corgo, Av. 1 de Maio, 76–78 (tel. 059 25 001). Fairly large three-star hotel with indoor pool and covered parking but no restaurant.

Casa Agrícola da Levada, Timpeira (TH) (tel. 059 322 190). Fine house on farm estate very close to Vila Real, four rooms. Breed wild boar, make own bread, honey and sausage.

Espadeiro, Av. Almeida Lucena (tel. 059 23 153). Good regional cooking and regarded as the best restaurant in town, moderate.

Places of Interest

LAMEGO
Municipal Museum. Open 10am–12.30pm and 2–5pm, closed Monday and holidays.

VILA REAL
Solar de Mateus. Open 9am–1pm and 2–6pm, guided tours
Sanctuary of Panóis. Open site.

Tourist Offices

Amarante: Rua Cândido dos Reis (tel. 055 432 259).
Lamego: Av. Visconde Guedes Teixeira (tel. 054 62 005).
Mesão Frio: Travessa da Cerca (tel. 054 99 200).
Mondim de Basto: Rua Comendador Alfredo Alves de Carvalho (tel. 055 381 479).
Pinhão: Largo da Estação (tel. 054 72 883).
Vila Real, Avenida Carvalho Araújo (tel. 059 22819).

7. TRÁS-OS-MONTES

Trás-os-Montes, geographically isolated from the west by the mountains of Marão, Alvão and Gerês, cut off from the south by the River Douro and bordered on the north and east by Spain, has developed an individuality which makes it distinctly different to other regions in the north. Climate and geology have played their part too. Cut off from Atlantic influences, its climate is both drier and hotter in summer and significantly colder in winter, especially up in the north-eastern region which is often called the *Terra Fria* (the cold lands) as distinct from the *Terra Quente* (the warm lands) of the southern parts, especially the valleys of the Douro and its tributaries, Corgo, Tua and Sabor which cut deeply into the province. Vines are not an economic proposition for the Terra Fria and their place is taken with grain crops. This alone creates different images, paints the landscape in different hues and presents a different lifestyle from other northern regions. Poor roads and communications in general left Trás-os-Montes as a backwater over the centuries where villages lived in isolation connected only by donkey trails to major centres. This last decade has seen the road system extended to these outlying villages leaving now only a tiny handful in the remoter parts of the Montesinho Natural Park still isolated. The region has little industry and lives by the land. It remains one of the poorest areas of Europe where education in the villages has been almost entirely practical, learning to farm and learning to survive. Oxen are the beasts of labour in some parts, mules in others, but these animals draw the ploughs, drag squealing wooden-wheeled wagons and pull their weight wherever strength is needed. But change is taking place quickly now. A partly-finished major new road crossing the territory diago-nally provides good access from Vila Real to Bragança and will, shortly, be extended eastward to Zamora in Spain providing a motorway link all the way from Porto. Farming subsidies are bringing in mechanised power, much needed wealth and a faster tempo to life. There are still windows in Trás-os-Montes through which travellers can look on to an elemental medieval lifestyle but modernisation is moving apace and these windows will soon be forever closed.

Although sitting in the extreme north-east corner, Bragança is a good base for exploring the region. It is close to the Montesinho Natural Park, which hides some of the fascinating old villages, and excursions can easily be mounted to the most far flung places of interest, like Miranda do Douro.

Until the southern section of the new road is complete, the N15 takes the strain of whatever traffic is moving on from Vila Real to Bragança and it is not usually too heavy. If granite pigs are reason enough for a break, divert left into the bustling farm town of Murça. In the gardens there stands a roughly sculptured granite boar, known as a *berrões* or *porco*, of pre-Roman origins. This is one of the more famous of a number of similar sculptures in Trás-os-Montes, including one in Bragança. The age, origins and purpose of these pigs remain a mystery but they are thought to date back well over two millennium and have a religious significance (see the feature below). The one in Bragança is particularly curious since it is pierced by a pillory.

Celtic Pigs and Medieval Pillories

In this part of Portugal history is written in great tablets of granite. There is no monument more intriguing than the **granite pigs** which are found particularly in the Trás-os-Montes region. The Celts, it seems, were superstitious people who believed that spirits were everywhere, in trees, unusual rock shapes, springs and in animals. It was not a question of mythical animals but real animals encountered in everyday life, maybe animals they hunted and respected. This may have been the case with the wild boar, once prolific in the mountains of this region, which they identified with power and strength, endowed with mythical spirits and associated with the Celtic goddess Diana Arduinna. Celtic deities were bewildering in their number, without organisation and with the majority probably very local but, curiously, Diana was also the Roman goddess of the hunt. The boar achieved some significance with the Celts in other regions indicated by relics found elsewhere. A bronze shield found in England was embellished with a stylised rendering of a boar and a Celtic helmet found in Hungary was adorned by a bronze boar.

A **pillory**, or *pelourinho*, in granite adorns almost every town and village throughout Portugal. It symbolised the right granted to the town to dispense justice and was accordingly built near to the centre of authority, the church, monastery or town hall. Where it was used for justice, the unfortunate criminal was chained either to the cross at the top or to hooks provided for whatever punishment was to be meted out. Most were built from the 13th century onwards and many moved away in design from the strictly functional to an expression of art. Pillories are seen in a wide variety of designs, even with twisted columns, and many bear personal motifs or sometimes a coat of arms. Some of the pillories seen in the northern villages, like the one in Soajo, look older than medieval and here the mysterious smiling face on the Soajo pillory may have some other symbolism.

Inside Bragança castle

Olive groves soften the landscape for a time on continuing along the N15 across the fertile Tua valley where peach, apple, cherry and almond also grow. **Mirandela**, on the sandy banks of the Tua, takes full advantage of these farming opportunities as the bustling market suggests but the town itself offers little to persuade a passing visitor to linger. The wide **bridge** spanning 17 arches built in the 15th century on Roman foundations is the main attraction, but dominating the town is the **Palace of the Tavoras**, now the town hall. The Tavoras were a powerful family for a period after the birth of the Portuguese state but their fortunes declined after 1587 when they accompanied King Sebastião on his ill-fated attack on the Moors in Morocco. The building has a fine whitewashed façade but nothing of interest within. Mirandela really comes to life and lets its hair down during the festival of Nossa Senhora da Amparo which takes place on the first Monday in August but the period of the festival starts before and extends beyond.

The IP4, the section of new road from Mirandela to Bragança, makes for speedier progress. There is a small diversion for the curious to **Romeu**, just off the motorway. It is a recently renovated village which supposedly represents typical architecture of the region. The village is too neat and lacks the muck and straw atmosphere of ordinary working villages but it is the home of one of the region's best known restaurants, *Maria Rita*.

Bragança

Bragança has long since spilt beyond its mellow defensive walls which guarded the old city against a once powerful Castilian neighbour. Now it is an expanding modern city with an industrial sector, a far cry from its Celtic origins as Brigantia. Located amongst rolling hills at an altitude of 660m (2165ft) and commanding a good strategic position on a low promontory, Julius Caesar regarded it as a valuable guard post along his military highway so promptly fortified it and named the stronghold Juliobriga. It became a battleground for centuries between the Christians and the Moors. Granted a royal franchise by King Sancho I in 1187, the castle was rebuilt strong enough to withstand a siege by King Alfonso IX of León just over a decade later. John of Gaunt, Duke of Lancaster, and King João I passed through before the Anglo-Portuguese attack on León in 1387. Even though it was cast in this provincial backwater, Bragança still found its way into the heart of Portuguese history and it started with the line of Dukes. The very first Duke of Bragança was Afonso, the love child of King João I from his affair with Inês Pires. The title was not bestowed until 1442, by which time Afonso was into old age. It was the start of a rich and powerful family which in 1640 ascended to the throne and provided the country's rulers down to the 20th century.

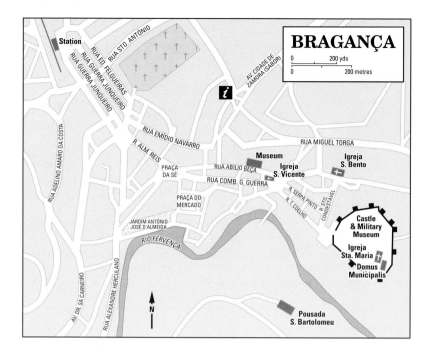

The Town

At the heart of the town, but not the centre, is the *citadela* with its fortified walls which still look remarkably sturdy and likely to last another century or so. Inside the walls is a village of small red-roofed white-painted houses with steps and verandahs, a living community of families with children and chickens, plants in pots and corner shops. Mounting the steps to walk the wide castle walls opens up panoramic views, not just of the surrounding countryside, including the Montesinho Natural Park to the north, but over the whole of Bragança which has spread in a narrow area westward away from the castle and is bounded to the south by the River Fervença. Dominant within the walls is the tall castle keep, the **Torre de Menagem**, which was built in 1187, strengthened and reinforced by João I and again by Afonso V in the 15th century and renovated in 1928. It now houses the military museum and is full of swords, pistols and muskets with enough reality to stimulate the imagination of one young boy we saw who danced and skipped around locked in a deadly sword fight with an equally skilled opponent, all with simulated sound effects, but given his choice of sword from the display he would not even have been able to lift it! It is a particularly fine collection gathered from the Spanish and Napoleonic wars through to the World Wars of the 20th century.

Immediately outside the castle walls but within the old town walls is the 16th century church of **Santa Maria** which is entered through an elaborate door flanked by twisted columns. Look for the best part which is the painting of the Assumption on the barrel vaulted ceiling. Hidden behind the church and accessed by a narrow passage is the remarkable and beautiful **Domus Municipalis**, a Romanesque civic building with five unequal sides. Meetings to decide land rights and disputes took place in the arcaded first floor whilst below is a cistern now grilled for protection. At the side of the keep is the *pelourinho* which arises from a granite *porco*, similar to the one seen in Murça. A bit the worse for wear now, this pig is held together by an iron band! For the romantic there is also the **Torre de Princesa** to inspect, but only from the outside. History and legend have narrated many tales of love and passion for this particular tower. Dona Sancha, sister of the first king, is believed to have taken refuge here while grieving over the infidelities of her powerful husband Fernão Mendes, and some beautiful Moorish princess was imprisoned here as punishment for her love affair with a Christian after rejecting her father's chosen bridegroom. Legend these may be, but the drama of the Spanish Dona Leonor is real enough. Leonor was locked up by her jealous husband Dom Jaime, fourth Duke of Bragança, who suspected her of infidelity. The tale has a sad ending since both Dona Leonor and her lover were later murdered by the Duke in Vila Viçosa.

For the best overview of the *citadela*, head south along Rua Alexandre Herculano to cross the river then turn at the first roundabout following signs to the *pousada*. The viewpoint is a little way past the *pousada* but from here the whole structure of the *citadela* is easily appreciated and captured on film.

Descending out of the old town walls and turning right leads to **Igreja São Bento** where the Renaissance doorway seems to be a gathering place for locals but inside it is eyes up again for the painted 18th century barrel-vaulted painted ceiling showing Father, Son and Holy Ghost flanked by Mary and Peter in mellow but clear colours. The painting is given a perspective of depth by the inclusion of windows and columns. There is one other church worth a visit, that of **São Vincente**, found in the square of the same name when descending towards the town centre from São Bento. This is where, in 1354, the young prince Dom Pedro is supposed to have clandestinely married Inês de Castro in defiance of his father, another tragic love story from the rich tapestry of Portuguese history and one which is featured in Chapter 10. The Baroque carved and gilded altarpiece brightens the gloom somewhat but the figure of Christ depicted in the act of ascension through the ceiling is as subtle as a nightmare. Just a little way down Rua Abilio Beça from São Vincente is the former bishop's palace which now houses the **museum** at present under restoration. Exhibits normally include archaeological remains from the Iron Age, regional tools, coins, church artefacts, Indo-Portuguese furniture and paintings. To complete the exploration of this area, there is some interesting ambling around the side streets near the castle and in the market area. For the rest of Bragança, it is all modern houses, main roads and moving traffic.

Pombal in Montesinho Natural Park

Montesinho Natural Park

On the doorstep of Bragança is the **Montesinho Natural Park** which will absorb as much time as can be spared without ever revealing all its faces. The features which make up the landscape are not extraordinary, they are rolling upland hills, tree-lined valleys, Galego-Bragançan sheep, Mirandian cattle and acres of grain fields, and yet they combine and recombine around every bend to present a timeless landscape of elemental beauty. Hidden away in nooks and crannies are the villages which live in an age long since past where traditional architecture, lifestyle and farming techniques are little changed from medieval days. Many of those migrants who were forced to leave in search of work and were successful in finding fortunes elsewhere are now returning to their former villages with the money to build new homes. These new houses are not built in traditional style, they follow French and German style homes and are totally inappropiate here.

Most of the villages in the park are now connected by a surfaced road but often on branch lines rather than circuits, which makes for a lot of driving to explore large areas of the park. Although the roads are narrow they are generally good but not for those in haste.

If only one tour into the park is possible then perhaps it should be to Rio do Onor situated on the border with Spain. The access road is from the N218 which leaves Bragança to the east. Only one of the park's villages is passed en route, **Varge**, which sits astride the Rio Igrejas and is full of modern white houses.

Montesinho Natural Park

This nature park covers the upland areas of Serra da Coroa and Serra do Montesinho lying between Bragança and the Spanish border to the north. Designated a Natural Park in 1979, it is one of the largest protected areas in Portugal covering 750 square km of rounded uplands and intersecting valleys which shelter and hide some 92 small villages providing homes for a total population of 9000. The altitude range is from 440m (1440ft) to 1486m (4875ft). Habitation can be traced back for thousands of years through archaeological remains and through village names of Germanic origin, like Fresulfe and Sernande, bestowed by the Visigoth settlers. Later, with the emergence of the new Portuguese nation, the monarchy attempted to populate the kingdom by land grants to nobles and to the Church and also by the creation of a system of collective tenures where geographical considerations made this necessary. Here, in the park, those communal customs are still observed.

Schist is the dominant geology but granite can also be found as well as small areas of basic rocks including limestone. The traditional architecture involves local materials and the older houses built of schist with slate roofs are typical, as are the communally-owned water mills and *pombals*. **Pombals** are fascinating structures, unique to the region, which were built to house pigeons in the days when they were bred for food. These white-painted, horseshoe-shaped structures are constructed to a uniform size and design, and they adorn the landscape in the same way as a little white church in Greece. Part of the remit of the park authorities is to assist in the reconstruction and conservation of structures like these to preserve the traditional way of life in the park as well as promoting the development of local home-made products and crafts. Tourism too has a role to play in stabilising the local economy but without it becoming an intrusive force and disturbing the balance of normal rural activities.

Although the region seems fairly extensively farmed, there are still vast areas which lie totally undisturbed, making this an outstandingly important refuge for wildlife. The Iberian wolf, the royal eagle and the black stork are prized inhabitants but the list of fauna is much longer and includes the otter, marten, water-mole, roe deer, red deer, wild boar, rabbit, hare and the horned viper. The flora, too, is equally diverse, from rich woodlands of chestnut, holm oak, pine, ash and birch to a wide range of species at lower levels. Some of the more interesting plant species include:

Adjuga reptens	*Asphodelus albus*
Allium vineale	*Campanula rapunculus*
Arbutus unedo	*Campanula transtagana*

Cistus ladanifer	Geum sylvaticum
Cistus laurifolius	Hyacinthoides hispanica
Cistus populifolius	Iris pseudacorus
Cistus psilosepalus	Jasione montana
Cistus salvifolius	Linaria triornithophora
Clematis vitalba	Lithospermum officinale
Crocus carpentanus	Mattiola fruticolosa
Dactylorhiza maculata	Merendera pyrenaica
Daphne gnidium	Muscari comosum
Dianthus larifolius	Narcissus asturiensis
Doronicum pardalianches	Narcissus bulbocodium
Epipactis helleborine	Narcissus triandrus
Erica australis	Ononis spinosa
Erica cinerea	Orchis coriophora
Erica tetralix	Orchis mascula ssp olbiensis
Erica umbellata	Orchis morio ssp champagneuxii
Erysimum linifolium	Origanum virens
Erythronium dens-canis	Paradisea lusitanica
Gagea nevadensis	Polygala microphylla
Gagea saxatilis	Romulea bulbocodium
Genista anglica	Scilla autumnalis
Genista florida	Serapia lingua
Genista micrantha	Viola arvensis
Geranium dissectum	Viola bubanii
Geranium lucidum	Viola parvula

There is self-catering accommodation available within the park, so far in seven converted traditional houses (*Casa Abrigo*) but most of these are remotely situated and reached along tracks which are best suited to four-wheeled-drive vehicles — ideal for a genuine away-from-it-all holiday. More accessible is a well-equipped camp site for caravans and tents just within the park's southern boundary. Further details of the Natural Park and the accommodation is available from the park office, detailed below.

From here the soft green landscape is lost to low scrubland which persists until **Rio de Onor** is reached. Nothing moves quickly in Rio de Onor, even the dogs sleeping on the cobbled roads are too lazy to bark or even move when the cows are herded past. Locals wash clothes in the river as a matter of course or in a specially constructed pool with running water. The narrow streets are crowded with houses, washing draped from their upper balconies reached by outside steps. It is a medieval atmosphere which changes a little when the boundary marker is crossed indicating Spain to one side and

Portugal the other. The cobbled road smoothes out to a concrete surface, the houses are brighter and more modern but the communal life of the people spanning these two countries continues as it always has. Understanding each other in their own mixed dialect, called *Rionorês*, they share land — the patchwork of crops in the fields show it — flocks and facilities. Contrary to what some maps may show, the return to Bragança is by the outward route.

Perhaps more typical village life and park scenery is encountered in another short foray into the park which starts along the Chaves road before the village of Vinhais. Head north to **Paçó** through a landscape of cultivated fields scattered with chestnut, oak and birch and, here and there, a single or a group of *pombals*. Tightly clustered villages barely reveal their character and busy life without exploration on foot although Paçó itself is one that can be missed. Bullock- or mule-drawn carts are most active in the spring when the enriched winter litter is being used to fertilise the fields or in the autumn when there are crops to collect. **Santo Cruz**, a mixture of old and new, is worth a diversion as is chestnut engulfed **Fresulfe**.

The road to **Dine** runs out before the village is reached so there is little option but to explore on foot. Also surrounded by chestnut, Dine rises onto two hills with most of the village nestling between. Although not too many grapes are grown, every village seems equipped with its own still, which is brought out in the autumn to convert the wine into *aguardente* ready to ward off the cold winters. Rolling hills yield more villages in delightful pastoral settings, like **Monfreita**, but other villages are too small to pass as anything but hamlets. The road back through Terrosa and Espinhosela leads past the *Ceto Verde campsite* before reaching the main road back to Bragança.

East of Bragança

Out to the east of Bragança, on the banks of the Douro, lies Miranda do Douro and, a little further south, Mogadouro and both are worth a visit. A circular tour out of Bragança takes in both these towns, a host of smaller villages, spectacular landscapes and requires only around 210km (132 miles) of driving. The N218 heading eastward out of Bragança leads all the way to Miranda do Douro. *Pombals* enhance the scenery to the north almost on leaving Bragança and there is a fine perspective of the town lying south too. Egyptian vultures soar over a wild undulating countryside which offers views almost as far as the eye can see long before Outeiro is reached.

Outeiro has a large church and a castle on a hill from the days when defending the border was of the utmost importance. The only battle now is in reaching the castellated remains. There is a choice of ways here, the main road leads off to the left but heading right via Argozela takes in Vimiosa before the N218 is rejoined.

Hotchpotch **Argozela** has cobbled roads, horses and donkeys harnessed together on the plough, jumbled new and old houses and a population which seems to be all old ladies in black wearing identical thick, crocheted woollen

Rio de Onor

shawls. **Vimiosa** has less character but it does have a 17th century church, Igreja Matriz, with an unusual cruciform window and the Torre de Atalaia. Little remains of the tower now but the hill on which it sits offers a good viewpoint. There is one good reason for stopping awhile, the town is famous for its freshwater lobsters! Approaching Miranda, it is the castle and the cathedral which dominate the view.

Miranda do Douro

Perched above a craggy gorge of the Douro, fortified Miranda do Douro spent much of its former life keeping a fearful eye on Spain in difficult times whilst growing prosperous from cross border trade in others, especially under the rule of the powerful Távora family. Now it is settled times again so the new road across the hydroelectric dam brings in waves of fresh invasions of Spaniards almost daily, all happy to spend, spend, spend and pesetas are acceptable currency. Its population has grown in recent years and the town now spills outside the old citadel.

Like many of the border towns, it has something of a turbulent and sometimes violent history. Known as Sapontia by the Romans, it became Mir-Hândul when the Moors pushed out the Visigoths in AD 716. Later, in the 11th century, the Moors themselves were ousted and in 1136 it received its first town charter from King Afonso Henriques. The town was walled and the castle built by King Dinis in the 13th century. Relatively soon afterwards, the Castilians coveted the town as an access point into Portugal and occupied it from the second half of the 14th century until it was recovered by King João I before the end of that century. A settled existence for a while allowed Miranda to prosper and become the most important centre of culture and religion in Trás-os-Montes. The town was raised to a bishopric in 1545 and shortly afterwards built a cathedral but, in 1782, the see transferred to Bragança.

One of those tragic events of war which is written poignantly into history books occurred in May 1762, in the Seven Years War, when the city was besieged by Franco-Spanish troops. A shell landed in the castle arsenal igniting the gunpowder and blowing up most of the castle, part of the town walls and killing 400 but the cathedral remained undamaged.

Like a number of the remote northern towns, Miranda, and especially the villages around, has its own dialect, *Mirandês*, which blends Latin with old Portuguese, Galician and Spanish with a smattering of Hebrew words. In the early days of the kingdom, Miranda was home to a large community of Jews until they went underground or fled in the face of the Inquisition.

The Town

Unless it is an exceptionally busy day, there is usually parking in the Largo do Castelo within the town walls which is handily situated for a tour around the old town. The excellent folk museum, the **Museu da Terra de Miranda**, in the old town square has to be the first port of call. Shuttles, weaving gear and spinning sticks start the exhibition of Mirandês culture which includes medieval lamps, religious artefacts from the 16th–18th centuries, two huge carved and painted wooden candlesticks, Roman stele and ceramics, fragments of pre-Roman pottery, a barely recognisable granite pig (*Barroã Iberica*), pistols, bedroom furniture, notes and coins, watermill artefacts and a room devoted to figures wearing local ritual masks and dancing gear. There is a chance to see here the thick brown woollen capes, often hooded and hand embroidered, for which the region is famous. Buttoned gaiters are made of the same material. It is one of the finest museums of its kind, full of curiosities and giving a colourful insight into traditions of the region.

Rua da Costanilha, down to the right beside the museum, has 15th century houses with granite doorways, now all neatly whitewashed. Straight on from the square leads to the **cathedral** which stands in the corner of the old town nearest the dam and looking over the ravine. Started in 1552, just seven years after Pope Paul III created a diocese here, it was built by a Spaniard, Francisco Velázquez, to the designs of the Tomar architect, Gonçalo do Torralva, and completed around 1576. The carved and gilded retable on the high altar is by the Spaniard Gregório Fernandes with more than 50 images in relief. In the south transept, contained in a glass case, is a curious clothed figure smartly turned out in a top hat; this is Menino Jesus da Cartolina or Baby Jesus in a Top Hat. This statue is much revered in the town where the locals make clothes for him in the fashion of the 17th century. Legend relates that in the battle to expel the Spaniards in 1711, a little boy with sword in hand rushed out to lead the Portuguese and give them courage. After the battle, which the

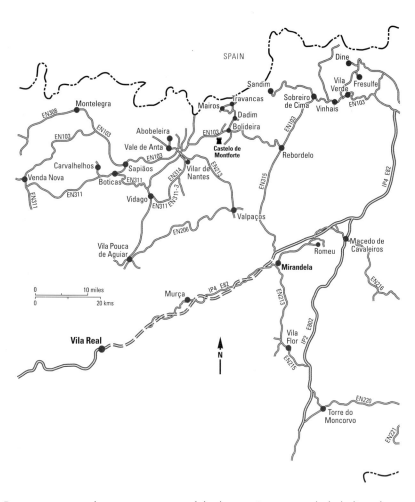

Portuguese won, there was no trace of the boy so it was popularly believed that their inspired leader was none other than the boy Jesus. Behind the cathedral stood the 16th century bishop's palace which was destroyed by fire in 1706 leaving a rather fine arcade which still stands.

Near the cathedral are a number of **craft shops** where typical capes and waistcoats made from brown woollen cloth can be bought as well as wicker-work or tin work like a long spouted conical-shaped olive oil pourer which no kitchen can manage without. Strong in individuality and folklore, this region is also famous for its dances, especially the stick dance of the *pauliteiros* performed by men in white shirts and aprons with decorated black shawls and flower decked hats. Danced to the music of bagpipes, cymbals and drums, it represents a ritualised sword dance. Other folk dances include

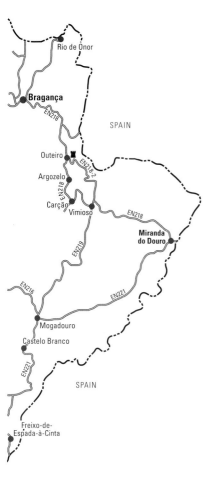

the *Geribalda,* which is a round dance, and the *Mira-me Miguel,* a square dance. The time to see all these dances performed is during the festivals, especially the *Festes da Santa Bárbara* which takes place on the Sunday after 15 August.

Outside the walls, but on the edge of the gorge overlooking the Douro, is the *pousada* of Santa Catarina whose 12 balconied rooms overlook the huge dam. Apart from hotel restaurants, the place to try the local speciality, *posta à Mirandesa,* a thick slice of beef braised in an iron pot, with perhaps melon and smoked ham for starters, is *O Mirandês* in Largo da Meagem.

The onward road towards Mogadouro is uncharacteristically straight and flat for this part of the world leading through extensive fields of cereal, at least for the first part. Once through Brunhosinho, the mountains of the Serra do Mogadouro start to rise in the distance and there is a return to more typical landscapes.

Mogadouro

Hedged roads lead into Mogadouro, a small, lethargic frontier town which sleeps comfortably in the shadow of its 12th century castle. Built by Dom Dinis on earlier Roman foundations, it was promptly handed to the care of the Knights Templar until they were suppressed by Pope Clement V and evolved in Portugal to become the Order of Christ. Later it became the stronghold of the powerful Távora family until they were crushed by Pombal. Now its rugged remains perch on a rocky hilltop looking forlorn and neglected, the keep door firmly closed against visitors; but the views once enjoyed by the old castle guards are still there to be appreciated.

Below the castle, in the square, stands the old granite pillory which has functional arms, long enough to suspend miscreants for flogging. If the town residents do ever stir themselves, it is probably to attend the 16th century Igreja Matriz to meditate on the 18th century carved and gilded woodwork.

113

Espinhosela, Montesinho Natural Park

Via Freixo de Espada à Cinta

For a longer tour which adds on around 140km (90 miles), the N221 can be followed down to Freixo de Espada à Cinta, the N220 to Torre de Moncorvo and from there head for Mirandela and the fast road back to Bragança taking in Vila Flor along the way. **Freixo de Espada à Cinta** brims with *Manueline houses*, said to be the finest collection in Portugal and monuments such as the Torre de Galo. This is the place to buy silk, too, for it is one of the main silkworm breeding centres in the region. **Torre de Moncorvo** is a medieval town now with only vestiges of its ancient walls. Its claim to fame is its parish church, the largest but not the prettiest in Trás-os-Montes, which was started in 1544 and took 100 years to complete. **Vila Flor**'s natural attributes at least impressed Dom Dinis who promptly named it the town of flowers, granted it a royal charter and built walls around it. Now only the south gate remains named after Dom Dinis. Fascinating amongst its monuments, mainly churches, is the old Roman fountain.

The Return to Bragança

If leaving out the extended tour to Freixo de Espada à Cinta, follow the N216 towards Marcedo de Cavaleiros to join the fast IP4 back to Bragança. Once out of Mogadouro, the scenery becomes mountainous for a time and the route winds around fertile valleys looked over by barren mountain peaks. Olive groves abut more olive groves on the way down to cross the River Sabor after which cork oaks start to populate the landscape. Once stripped of cork, these trees become distinctive by their wine red trunks allowing the eye to pick out every single one even when travelling at speed. Easy for the eye to pick out too are the huge storks' nests lodged in the tree tops. The road flirts with the mountains of Serra de Bornes before Macedo de Cavaleiros is reached. It is a modern town which was granted town status as recently as 1863. If there is a reason to stop, it is only for the handicrafts which include weaving, lace quilts and chestnut wickerwork. From here the IP4 is soon reached for a quick return to Bragança.

West of Bragança

Chaves, in western Trás-os-Montes, is a useful gateway for passing between the Peneda-Gerês and Trás-os-Montes and a good base for exploring the immediate area. The almost direct N103 west out of Bragança is a scenic route spiced with rustic villages and rural scenes from an age long since past in other parts of Europe. Soft green wooded valleys and rolling hills of the Montesinho Natural Park dominate the scenery to the north until **Vinhais** is reached. Huddled on a hilltop looking down onto the River Tuela, Vinhais was founded by King Sancho II in the 13th century as a border post. Its castle has long since decayed and remnants include some walls and part of a tower. Old houses with overhanging balconies, corn drying on the footpath, chickens running with the children add colour to the old part of town within the castle walls. Shortly after departing Vinhais there is a last glimpse of a *pombal*, endemic to this very small corner of Portugal, before the road heads south to detour around a gorge at Rebordelo. Each part of the north seems to have its preferred beast of burden, strong oxen predominate in the Douro, donkeys and mules are more common in Trás-os-Montes and cows are used in much of the Minho. Crossing the border from mule to cow country, it should have been no surprise to see a cart drawn by a mixed team, a cow and mule harnessed together.

Once the descent starts towards Chaves, watch out for the sign to **Castelo de Monteforte** which is a short diversion along a rough track. The castle sits atop a rocky rise which commands views the whole way to the Spanish border. From early origins, perhaps starting as a hilltop settlement fortified by the Romans, it was rebuilt by Dom Afonso Henriques after being taken from the Moors in 1139. Further restoration was carried out by Dom Afonso III after it sustained damage in a battle against the Leónese. Dom Dinis significantly reinforced the castle by the addition of a keep and three other towers but endless local wars inflicted damage necessitating further repairs through the years. During the reign of Don João I, the borough became a sanctuary for fugitives by royal assent with the proviso that the fugitives were neither traitors nor guilty of fraud. From the 18th century, its inhabitants declined and now it is neither a borough nor a parish and all that remains are the high walls and keep of this robust structure.

Castles in Portugal

For a country which has been a battleground over millennia, castles are firmly woven into the fabric and history of this country. Social organisation in the form of *castros* (fortified hilltop settlements) appeared with the Celts around 700–600 BC and many of these have been discovered in the north, particularly around the Minho where excavations have revealed whole fortified villages, or *citânias*. Two very fine examples are those at Briteiros, near Braga, and the newly excavated site at Viana do Castelo. The Romans too adopted and strengthened some of the *castros*. More conquerors in the form of the Visigoths and the Moors underlined the need for strongholds, especially in the north. By the 11th century Portugal was emerging as a nation and many of the earlier forts and castles, particularly those strategically placed near their borders and along the coast, were fortified to the best standards of the day. Spurred on by the fear of Castilian domination, the pace of castle renovation and rebuilding markedly quickened with the arrival of the energetic Dom Dinis to the throne towards the end of the 13th century. Castle after castle was built or rebuilt and towns fortified in a broad defensive belt around borders most under threat and his son Dom Afonso IV carried on the same strategy. Modification and modernisation of castles carried on through to the 18th and 19th centuries.

Central to a castle was a principal defensive tower, a keep, which was the ultimate defensive position. It was also used as an emergency or even permanent residence and often contained the public treasury, placed there for safety. Military appointments sometimes went to a local nobleman who was appointed the *alcaide* (captain) which often became hereditary. If the nobleman was particularly powerful and landed then the appointment might become *alcaide-mor* (captain major). The *alcaide* was responsible for the management and maintenance of this and other fortifications in the region, for enlisting men, collecting rent, taxes and fines as well as paying a tribute to the king.

Outside the keep lay the garrison protected by the castle walls or ramparts, although the ramparts now means the top of the wall, or the path around the top encircling the enclosure. This was an essential element for providing sentries with a high and commanding viewpoint, allowing access to towers and offering a protected firing position down on the enemy. The thickness of the walls determined the width of the ramparts but where good width was provided it allowed easy and quicker access for archers to assume position and for the movement of defensive engines. Access was normally by stone steps set against the wall. Where the walls were thinner, the ramparts were often constructed of wood rather like a long platform. The introduction of cannons in the 16th century necessitated some changes in design leading to thicker walls, wider ramparts with access by wide ramps rather than steps.

Towers were also built into the castle walls as buttresses or simply as defence for long stretches of wall. From the 12th century, towers were predominantly square but prismatic angle towers offering a greater range of firing positions started to appear in the 14th century. Angled towers suffered a distinct weakness, destruction of a corner by the enemy led to the collapse of two adjacent walls seriously weakening defences. Recognition of this weakness led to the building of cylindrical corner towers around the 15th and 16th centuries. Walls were castellated for the protection of the sentries or archers but the battlements acquired various forms, typically square or chamfered in Portugal, and sometimes included arrow slits. From the 14th century onwards, the merlons were widened and the spaces between often made with a downward slope to assist the launching of stones or boiling liquid onto the enemy. Later, when cannons arrived, these spaces were adapted and shaped for guns or special embrasures were incorporated in the parapet.

Strongly constructed balconies were often used as an element of vertical defence and they are mostly seen typically at a high position on the keep or sometimes on the castle walls. They were often provided with a hole in the floor through which boiling liquids could be poured. Brackets, or corbels, supported the balconies which themselves became a decorative element. A later development was the bartizan, a small enclosed tower built at the angle of the castle walls although it was more frequently used on forts which lacked a keep or a tall tower. The bartizan provided a sheltered and protected lookout point for a sentry, usually just big enough to enclose a standing soldier. Architects had a field day with bartizans and many amongst the varied designs are decorative and attractive while still wholly practical.

Doors or gateways into the castle called for special defensive precautions often resulting in two offset entrances with a space or courtyard between them which could be used to trap and attack intruders. Ironwork, plate and bars were used to strengthen the doors against attack by battering rams and later an iron portcullis was introduced. Drawbridges too were part of the defensive system which was used from the Middle Ages onwards.

Gradually, when artillery had firmly replaced archers, the castle evolved into a fortress of simpler design but which was more suited to modern weapons. The high tower was no longer appropriate. Now bastions were built into the angles of the fortress walls allowing fire to the flanks along the face of the main fortress wall.

Northern Portugal is rich in castle remains, some still in good shape, others in sad decay but all have experienced the thick of battle. Their mute stones could tell of heroic deeds, of death and starvation but, mute or not, they tell a tale of survival, of the emergence of a nation and their own redundancy.

Chaves

Old Chaves is entered once the Tamega river is crossed. It was settled more than 2000 years ago, before the Romans started tramping through it whilst passing between Braga and Astoria. The hot springs here, emerging at an incredible 73°C, probably worked wonders for their sore feet. Flavius Vespasian, Emperor of Rome, was truly impressed so, in AD 78, he named the settlement Aqua Flavia. Not too long afterwards, Emperor Trajan, who probably detested getting his feet cold and wet again crossing the river, worked out that 18 arches would span the river nicely so set about building the 90m (300ft) bridge in AD 98 which was finished around six years later. The bridge is still named after him but two of his arches became redundant later and were built over. After the Romans, the Vandals set about vandalising the town and the Suevi followed rebuilding. Next it was the turn of the Moors to occupy and rebuild the town after 713 until the Leónese came on a mission of liberation in 888 only to lose it back to the Moors. It finally fell into the hands of the Christians and Dom Afonso III rebuilt the castle and turned it into a fortified town surrounded by walls but the persistent Moors recaptured the town for a time in 1129. Recognising the defensive importance of Chaves, that irrepressible castle builder Dom Dinis was along to add a monumental keep and a new belt of walls in the late 13th century/early 14th century. Chaves was never far from the theatre of war during this period and the King of León occupied the town for a number of years in the late 14th century. Eventually, governorship passed into the hands of Dom Afonso, Count of Barcelos, who later became the first Duke of Bragança. There are several explanations of the modern name Chaves, which means 'keys', but it probably arises from Aqua Flavia which became popularly Flavias and eventually corrupted to Chaves.

The Town

Old Chaves today huddles around narrow streets in a compact area close to the river. Its military significance which left it a legacy of two fortresses and a castle has slipped into history and the town is content to serve as a market centre for this fertile region. Both the fortresses lie on the eastern side of town and are not open to the public. The **castle**, at the heart of the old town and now surrounded by colourful gardens, is a good place to start a tour. Notable on this castle are the number of balconies introduced for vertical defence, especially along the top of the crenellated keep, the Torre de Menagem, which houses a small military museum concentrating on material from the latter two centuries. Below the castle to the west is the **spa** whose waters, loaded with carbonates and fluorides, emerge steamingly hot at 73°C (164°F) and are said to cure rheumatism, and muscular and skeletal problems. Close to the keep to the south, in the Praça de Camões, is the town's **Museu da Região Flaviense** housed in the former 15th century palace of the dukes of Bragança which exhibits a lot of granite of Celtic and Roman origins, some Roman pottery and relics of the Stone and Bronze ages. It is strangely disappointing in view of the long history of the town. There is much to be enjoyed in the ambience of the old narrow streets, especially those with wooden painted verandahs. If the attractive façade of the Baroque **Igreja da Misericódia** is tempting then there are some fine *azulejo* panels inside depicting New Testament scenes.

Chaves boasts the best cured ham in the country but trout, veal steaks and roast kid are also amongst the specialities on offer. In town, *Hotel Trajano* serves good ham and trout, and restaurant *Carvalho* is well recommended but some of the best restaurants lie out of town like the one at **Bairro do Retornado** found by heading out of the town along Avenida Nuno Alvares.

To Boticas and Montelegre

Black pottery features amongst the craft items on sale in Chaves, alongside baskets, rugs and blankets, but it is only a short excursion to see where it is made in the village of **Vilar de Nantes**, and there is no cheaper place to buy it. Equally this village can be incorporated in a larger tour of 100km (60 miles) covering a westerly circuit which includes Boticas and Montelgre. Leave Chaves by crossing the Tamega and taking the N2 towards Vila Real. Look on the left shortly for the road to Vilar de Nantes and drive through the village until just past the centre. At the sight of visitors, the potters are usually on hand to issue invitations inside. The secret of this black pottery is in the reduction firing achieved by using burning brushwood and covering the pots with soil and ashes to exclude oxygen. When the pots are brought out from the ashes they have a pewter-like cast. Although the pots are on the crude side, they do have a certain charm. Opposite the potters is the basket maker equally keen to demonstrate the cutting of chestnut wood into strips ready for basket making.

Continue down the Vila Real road but turn right for **Boticas** where the sign indicates. This is the place to drink '*vinhos mortos*', wine of the dead. In order to protect their wine stocks from the French during the Peninsular War at the beginning of the 19th century, the villagers buried the wine in the ground only to find later that it had actually improved in quality. Delighted with this discovery, it has become common practice to bury the wine to assist maturation. Head for a local bar to sample this speciality but keep expectations down to earth! For a more refreshing drink, head out west to nearby **Carvalhelhos**. It is a spa town which provides drinking water widely appreciated throughout the whole of the country. The carbonated, or *com gas*, is particularly sweet and refreshing and makes a good drink any time of the day. Close to the spa is a very comfortable *estalagem* which provides an ideal base to explore the area, especially the villages of Serra do Barrosa. There is nothing to see in the town but the 2800 year old Iron Age hill fort is well worth a visit. Access is by the track close to the *estalagem* signed '*Castro*'. The wall encircling the hilltop provides a walkway and an overview of the circular huts now reduced to small walls. Unusually, there are dwellings outside the walls but this may have been the work of the Romans who converted the *castro* into a centre for mining a tin ore, cassiterite.

To proceed on to Montelegre, return towards Boticas and pick up the road heading north through Beça which shortly joins the N103. **Montelegre** is a busy market town but at its heart lies a 13th century castle now reduced to the keep and three towers with some adjoining walls. From uncertain beginnings, the town received its first charter on 9 June 1273 from the hands of Dom Afonso III and this day is celebrated as a municipal holiday even now. Dom Dinis had a hand in some castle renovations as did his son, Dom Manuel I. The town stands at an altitude of 966m (3800ft) and the castle sits proudly on a hill but the keep is particularly tall at 28m (107ft) which must have provided a commanding look out post to watch for the enemy approaching from Spain over the Serra do Larouco.

The easiest way back to Chaves is along the N103 and when virtually back in town divert the short distance west to Vale de Anta and ask for directions to **Abobeleira**. Here, in a granite outcrop, lies the prehistoric rock which bears simplistic carvings of the human figure and axe heads. Granite boulders seem to have achieved some fame in the Chaves area; there is also the well-known rocking boulder, **Pedra da Bolideira**, which lies well to the north east of Chaves. It is located close to the Spanish border and is reached by turning north along a track from the Chaves–Bragança road at Bolideira following signs to Travancas.

Practical Information

Accommodation and Restaurants

BRAGANÇA
Pousada de São Bartolomeu, Estrada do Turismo. Built in 1959 with 15 rooms and one suite, commanding view of castle.
Hotel Bragança, Av. Sá Carneiro (tel. 073 22 578). Centrally located and comfortably furnished three-star hotel with 42 rooms and restaurant.
Residential São Roque, Zona da Estacada, lote 26/27 (tel. 073 22 427). Good, inexpensive accommodation, three-star.
Moinho do Caniço, Junta ao Rio Castrelos/Baceiro (tel. 073 23 577). Superbly converted water mill in quiet position by river around 10km (6⅓ miles) outside Bragança. Delightfully rustic but with modern comforts and two bedrooms, one en suite. Vital to book ahead.
Restaurant Solar Bragançano, Praça da Sé (tel. 23875). Highly regarded, interesting menu and prices reasonable.
Arco de Noe, Rua 25 de Abril (tel. 073 22 759). Fish figures strongly on the menu, reasonable.

CARVALHELHOS
Estalagem de Carvalhelhos (tel. 076 42 116). Quietly located *estalagem* providing a good standard of accommodation. The spring water of the same name from the nearby plant tastes better here than anywhere else! Very good restaurant at moderate price.

CHAVES
Hotel Aquae Flaviae, Praça do Brazil (tel. 076 26 711). Relatively new, this four-star hotel is the best in town with good regional restaurant and outdoor pool.
Estalagem Santiago, Rua do Olival (tel. 076 22 545). Moderate size (30 rooms) but with limited facilities.
Hotel de Chaves, Rua 25 de Abril (tel. 076 21 118). A touch of faded glory, one-star but good and cheap.
Quinta da Mata, Estrada de Valpaços (AT) (tel. 076 23 385). 17th century manor house surrounded by thick woodland just 3km (2 miles) outside Chaves with five rooms.
Quinta do Lombo (AT) (tel. 076 21 404). Rustic stone house close to Chaves, Six rooms.
Restaurant Carvalho, Largo das Caldas (tel. 076 21 727). Good regional restaurant.

MIRANDA DO DOURO
Pousada de Santa Catarina (tel. 073 42 255). Located overlooking a dam on the River Douro, nine rooms and three suites, good restaurant.
Restaurant o Mirandês, Largo de Meagem.

MIRANDELA
Hotel Mira Tua, Rua da Republica (tel. 078 22 403).

Places of Interest

BRAGANÇA
Military musem in castle keep. Open 9–11.45am and 2–4.45pm, closed Mondays and holidays.
Museu Do Abade de Bacal, Rua Abilio Beça. Has been closed for restoration, check with Turismo.

CHAVES
Military Museum, Torre de Menagem. Open 9am–12.30pm and 2–4.30pm, closed Mondays and holidays.
Museu da Região Flaviense, Praça de Camões. Open 9am–12.30pm and 2–4.30pm, closed Mondays and holidays.

MIRANDA DO DOURO
Museu da Terra in historic centre. Folk museum, open 10am–12.15pm and 2–4.45pm, closed Mondays and holidays.

Montesinho Natural Park. Park office at Bairro Salvador Nunes Teixeira, lote 5, Bragança (tel. 073 28 734). Has leaflets on flora and fauna and details of eight restored houses to let in the park, all fairly remote and self-catering.

Golf
Vidago, near Chaves (tel. 076 97 106): nine hole course, par 33 course, with caddies and trolleys for hire. Tennis courts also available.

Doorstep crocheting in Rio de Onor

Tourist Offices

Boticas: Rua 5 de Outubru (tel. 076 42 353).
Bragança: Av. Cidade de Zamoua (tel. 073 381 273).
Chaves: Terreiro da Cavalaria (tel. 076 333 029).
Miranda do Douro: Largo do Menino Jesus da Cartolina (tel. 073 41 132).
Mirandela: Biblioteca Municipal (tel. 078 23 381).
Montalegre: Praça do Municipio (tel. 076 52 255).

8. THE ALTO MINHO

Alto Minho lies above Braga stretching up to the Minho river itself and is an area of great natural beauty. It is a tale of two halves. Inland, against the Spanish border, lies the wild, rugged mountains of Serra da Peneda and Serra do Gerês which together are protected as the Peneda-Gerês National Park, the country's only National Park. The rest of the northern Minho is a sea of rich, vibrant green—green from the lush vegetation thriving in its rich granitic soils overlaid by vinho verde vines which grow in every available field, along every available hedge and in every available corner. Often called the Costa Verde, the green coast, it lives up to its name all year around but especially in spring when the newly emerged vine leaves lend an additional vibrancy. Central to the region is the Rio Lima flowing gently through a wide fertile valley. And the Romans were right, this is Lethe, the mythical River of Forgetfulness. Anyone crossing its banks to wander into the beauty of the countryside will forget all thoughts of homeland forever. It is known that the Romans did cross the river, but it is less certain that they ever returned to Rome.

Viana do Castelo, the region's administrative capital lying at the mouth of the River Lima, offers a seaside resort close to beaches which is convenient for exploring the Lima valley. Two inland towns full of character, Ponte de Lima and Ponte da Barca, lie on the banks of the river and either provides an excellent base for exploring the whole of this northern region, including a large section of the National Park. Arising in the high mountains of Spain, the clean and sparkling waters of the Lima have over aeons of time deposited fluvial sand banks along its lower reaches, conveniently so at Ponte de Lima and Ponte da Barca, which provide safe areas for sun bathing or bathing in the waters of the river. For the southern range of the park, Serra do Gerês, most head for Caldas do Gerês to use as a base but there is very limited access to the mountains from here and a short stay is all that is needed.

After Porto and the Douro, the Minho is probably the second most popular northern region, especially in high season. On a fly-drive holiday, it is reached within the hour from Porto airport while travellers arriving by car mostly enter via Lindoso in the National Park. Bragança is another popular entry point, then travelling westwards through Chaves to reach the area. This chapter picks up this route at Chaves and describes places and events along the way to a base in Ponte de Lima. All other areas of the region are described as tours out of this base.

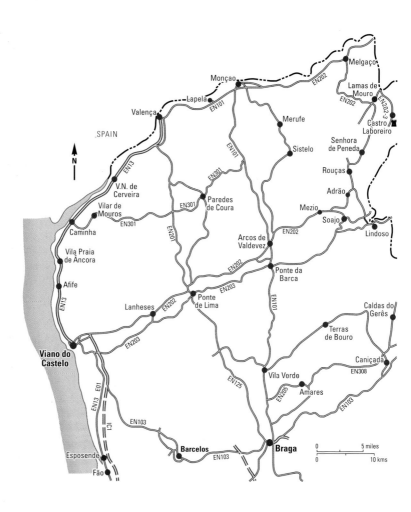

For the intrepid, there is a new road, the EN311, not on all maps which leads from Boticas through the Serra do Barrosa to emerge at Venda Nova, otherwise the EN103 leads a slightly more erratic course westwards arriving at the same town by a slightly longer route. The EN103 offers some lakeside views over the Barragem de Alto Rabagão along the way, although both routes are very scenic. Wooded slopes, pretty villages, green pastures, lakeside views and high mountains provide scenery on a dramatic scale beyond Venda Nova. Once past the dam at the end of the Barragem de Venda Nova, more drama unfolds as the depth of the gorge reveals itself backed by a distant vista of mountains. At least the road sits comfortably on a broad

SPAIN

Portela do Homem

EN308-1

EN103

Louredo

Venda
Nova

corniche, wide enough to dispel vertiginous fears for most. A remarkable tapestry of mountain life slowly unfolds, women carrying goods on their heads, houses clinging to hillsides, vines growing up trees and all ribboned along a road which winds and twists, climbs and falls. Once through Louredo, prepare to leave the Braga road by following signs initially to Caniçada, then continue to cross the dam at the end of the Barragem de Salamonde and head up the narrow valley leading to Caldas do Gerês.

Buried within a deep, narrow valley, **Caldas do Gerês** earned its popularity as a spa town first with the Romans but more recently in the 18th century and many of the hotels date from the turn of this century. Its spa waters are good and warm, at 47°C (116°F), loaded with bicarbonate, sodium fluoride and thiosulphate and are alkaline enough to be an effective detergent for washing clothes. Efficacy is claimed for improving circulation, the digestive tract and the metabolism. The town has an out-door swimming pool, tennis courts, souvenir shops and plenty of cafés but it is a difficult place to escape from, except along the line of the valley. One short excursion by car leads further up the valley to **Portela do Homen**, the Spanish border with its collection of old Roman mile stones and to one of the few walking opportunities in the region. The walk starts immediately before the bridge crossing the River Homen along an old paved route which once served some wolfram mines at Carris, now disused. Although the old mine workings provide a focal point, any turning point can be elected since the walk returns by the same route.

Leave Caldas do Gerês by heading back down the valley to continue on to Ponte de Lima via Amares. Roads wind and twist in this part of Portugal without ever going in a straight line but, from Amares, cut over through vine-laden countryside to join the EN 101 to Ponte da Barca and after Vila Verde turn left to head across to the Ponte de Lima road.

Peneda-Gerês National Park

Ponte de Lima

Ponte de Lima perhaps may not offer too much in the way of monuments but it is a town of considerable charm and ambience. It sits largely on the south bank of the River Lima which is spanned here by an old **bridge** which started life under the Romans to help them on their way between Braga and Astorga. It was rebuilt in the Middle Ages after silting and meandering pushed and widened the river bed to the south. The remains of six broad Roman arches are seen on the north side, now over dry land, whilst it is believed that three of the 14th century arches lie buried under the Praça de Camões on the south side. Now some 15 broad arches span the river separated by 13 narrow arches, built above the buttressed supports, which relieve the flood pressure after periods of heavy winter rain. A tower once stood guarding the entrance on the north side which is remembered now only in the name of the church standing close by, Igreja de Santo António da Velha Torre (Old Tower). Nearby, a grassy picnic site with granite tables offers a quiet retreat. A new bridge to the west carries the flow of modern traffic leaving the old bridge in the care of pedestrians, horses, cows and the occasional goat.

As the town emerged as an important centre of trade around the 14th century, Dom Pedro ordered fortifications to be built around the town which included towers and gateways. By the 19th century, most of the walls were in a poor state so they were demolished but there are still a few remnants left to see near **Torre de Cadeia**. This tower is the most westerly of the two towers standing near the river; the other is **Torre de São Paulo**. It was built in 1511 and formerly used as a prison but now houses a display of local crafts and is the place to buy a complete local costume.

Most of the activities in town take place by the riverside, either taking coffee in the **Praça de Camões** overlooking the fountain designed by the 16th century artist, João Lopes, or strolling in the deep shade provided by the long avenue of plane trees alongside the river. The eagerly awaited event is the **market** held every second Monday. It covers the wide sands mainly to the west of the old bridge, although most of the cattle are to the east, and it spills forward into the nearby streets and towards the municipal market. Canvas appears by the acre and everything is on sale from pigs to wine presses and cow carts and from shoes to bread and fruit. Perhaps the most fascinating part is the area reserved for the locals who stand in lines leaving just enough space for the shopper to pass between and inspect the home grown produce displayed in bags or baskets at their feet.

The municipal market opens daily selling fish, meat, fruit and vegetables. Although the town has a selection of restaurants, none is of great reputation. *Beco das Selos*, in the street of the same name, offers good food from a limited menu at a modest price. *Tulha*, on Rua Formosa, with a more extensive menu, is worth a visit as is *O Brasão*. Those intent on dining with a view might try *Santa Margarida* perched on a hill just to the south of town. Wherever is chosen, make sure that *Ponte de Lima Loureiro* is on the wine list as it is one of the best Vinhos Verdes.

Vinho Verde Wines

Although the name translates to 'green wines', it is a reference to age rather than colour for they are at their very best when young and fresh. In fact twice as much red as white is made but this is almost entirely for local consumption since outsiders regard the white as markedly superior. Both are slightly sparkling which was once produced by a secondary fermentation but commercial production now employs a quick carbonation with carbon dioxide gas. The white wine is light, crisp, fresh and acidic showing marked variation region to region. Ponte de Lima make some of the finest and particularly recommended is their Loureiro. In contrast the red is fairly aggressive and rough but the locals drink little else.

The demarcated region covers a large area in the north-west of the country from the western Douro up to the Minho river and eastwards towards the Basto region. So large and diverse is the area that it is divided into six sub-regions:

Amarante: famous for its red Gatão and whites from Lixa.
Basto: is the most mountainous region and it produces highly acidic wines.
Braga: the largest sub-region covering the soft rolling hills of central Minho. Mostly associated with aromatic grape varieties.

Lima: the Loureiro grape has its natural habitat here and the wines produced are of superior quality. The very best vineyards are alongside the river.

Penafiel: has average conditions which favour the Azal variety.

Moncão: benefits from good conditions along the banks of the Minho.

Vinho Verde vines are mostly grown in granitic soils which are short of nitrogen and phosphorus so constant work is required by the farmers to maintain good fertility. Some parts of the Douro also produce these wines but grown on shale soils. Climatically, the vines rarely suffer extremes of temperatures, winters are mild with only short cold spells and summers rarely have the intense temperatures experienced along the Alto Douro. Humidity is often high arising from a high winter rainfall and moist Atlantic sea breezes which causes problems with disease.

Patterns of agriculture changed in the 16th and 17th centuries following the successful introduction of maize from America. So important did this crop become that the vines were pushed to the edge of the field and grown taller to make space for the maize. Granite posts holding strainer wires are used to support the vine, sometimes forming pergolas so that crops can still be grown in the space below. More spectacular is the hanging tree method where usually four vines are planted around the base of a tree and allowed to spread rampantly and colonise the tree. The biggest difficulty created for the farmer by these various growing techniques is in the labour required to complete the annual prune.

Some of the favoured white grape varieties include:

Alvarinho: this is a typical low yielding Moncão variety but it makes a high alcohol wine.

Azal: used around Amarante but ripening is slow and it requires favourable conditions.

Avesso: a high quality grape which produces aromatic wines and does best on the margins of the Douro.

Loureiro: this is a good quality, very productive grape which is used throughout but it does best in the Lima region. Capable of producing wines with a good alcohol content.

Paderna: this is an old variety which is used exclusively in blends.

Harvesting takes place from the second half of September into October when the grapes are normally collected in small tubs for transport to the factory. Sugar content is measured at the factory gate and the grape batches separated accordingly. As usual, the farmers are paid on quantity and sugar content. Natural yeasts present on the fruit were normally used in the fermentation but times are changing and a selected yeast is now being added after sulphur dioxide sterilisation of the must.

Gold filigree is a speciality of the region, especially Viana do Castelo, but there are two good gold shops in Ponte de Lima which are a little cheaper and both in Praça de Camões, the square at the entrance to the old bridge. Matos is particularly favoured and shoppers looking for second hand (*segunda mãu*) bargains make a point of visiting the day after market day when often a good deal of gold is traded in.

Peneda-Gerês National Park

Exploring the Peneda-Gerês National Park is not especially easy as so much of it is impenetrable by car. Walkers have a better chance, especially if armed with *Landscapes of Portugal: Costa Verde* (same authors) which describes a selection of walks mostly in the park region. The following two tours give a good flavour of the scenery and insight into the unique way of life in this part of northern Portugal (see also p 137).

This first tour which visits Ponte da Barca, Arcos de Valdevez, Soajo and Lindoso does not require too much driving but it is laced with interest and may easily fill a day. Cross the new bridge from Ponte de Lima to head inland along the north side of the river to head directly to Arcos de Valdevez. It is a scenic run through vine-laden countryside with occasional glimpses of the river. Slow-moving cow carts are a particular hazard along these narrow roads, especially in spring, but their numbers are declining now with increasing modernisation. **Arcos de Valdevez** is a quaint town which is intimately bound around the River Vez, a tributary of the Lima. Most of the town hides in a labyrinth of narrow streets rising up the hill to the west and there are perhaps two reasons to enter the maze, the first is to view the Manueline pillory bearing the coat of arms of Dom Manuel I and the second is to take lunch at *O Lagar*. If it is time just for coffee and cakes with a stroll, stay down by the river to enjoy the parkland there before finding the *pastelaria*. No self-respecting town is complete in this part of the world, it seems, without a picturesque arched bridge and Arcos is no exception.

The onward route leads across the bridge picking up signs, first to Sistelo and then to Soajo. Steadily increasing elevation improves the views which become more interesting once the National Park is entered at **Mezio**. By the junction here is a neolithic granite burial chamber, a dolmen, constructed of giant slabs of granite and thought to be of Celtic origin. Steep terracing graces the hillsides on the approach to **Soajo**, a village which lives by farming in the old traditional way. To explore the centre of the village, leave the car and follow the signs to Casa do Adrão on foot to reach the square with the old granite pillory carved with a smiling face. Wandering the narrow streets reveals facets of the daily life otherwise unnoticed but life is changing with a small but increasing number of tourists visiting. Before leaving the village, turn left into the road with the sign indicating '*Espigueiros*', the granite-built maize stores. This is not the largest collection of **espigueiros** in the vicinity, Lindoso has more, but the grouping here, ringed around an area of roughly level granite, is easily the most photogenic. Granite is shaped, cut and jointed

Espigueiros, granite-built maize stores, at Soajo

with apparently the same ease as wood to make structures which have already lasted for two centuries. Perched on granite mushrooms, to keep the rodents at bay, and with slotted sides and a heavy stone roof, they provide airy conditions ideal for the purpose of *espigas* (maize) storage. Just to make sure that prayers for their safe storage are answered, each *espigueiros* bears at least one but usually two crosses. The open space in the centre of this group is used as a winnowing area when the harvest is brought in, usually in September. Sorting the maize is a communal affair often with a festive air and there is a special custom which ensures the willing participation of all teenagers. Any young man who is fortunate enough to uncover a rare red cob amongst the yellow maize can claim a kiss from the girl of his choice.

The road on from Soajo to Lindoso follows contours around the hillside with views down into a now rugged Lima valley rippled with terraces and soon towards the *barragem* at Lindoso. **Cunhas,** pasted to the hillside, seems a forgotten village accustomed to seeing visitors passing by on their way to Lindoso. The route leads in descent to the valley bottom, across the dam wall before climbing back to join the improved road which leads to the left into Spain. **Lindoso,** which takes its name from *lindo* meaning beautiful, lies to the right and is reached along a side road. It is usually easy to park below the castle. South below the castle lies a large but untidy collection of *espigueiros* which is best viewed from the well-preserved castle walls. Built sometime in the 13th century, Lindoso **castle** was strengthened by Dom Dinis to guard this pass between Portugal and Spain. The Araújo family were appointed governors and it remained in their control from the 14th to the 16th century. It was

The castle at Lindoso

captured by the Spanish in 1662 but recovered from them two years later. Further modifications in the 16th and 17th centuries leaves now a remarkable monument to military architecture which shows many of the features employed over a span of four centuries. The drawbridge is down now to welcome visitors into the castle interior where the splendid keep houses a small information office and occasional exhibitions of art. The old oven once used by the Araújo family has been restored. Outside, the walls are accessible and offer panoramic views over the bleak and hostile border country. Of interest in the castle architecture are the corner bartizans and the barbette, the fortified placements for the canons below the main inner wall.

The route back towards Ponte da Barca follows along the line of the scenic Lima valley with the option of a side trip to one of the more isolated villages in the park. For this take the road signed to **Ambos-os-Rios** and Ermida with the latter as the intended destination. Nervous drivers should travel no further than the first village for beyond the narrow surfaced road climbs into the hills along a slender corniche which some might find disturbing. **Ermida** village is just one large farmyard without shops which relies on self-sufficiency and daily visits from itinerant sales vans.

Ponte da Barca

Ponte da Barca is the place to buy a wheel barrow or a cement mixer. It is a busy, active little town not embracing the river but strung along the nearby main road which is the focus of all day-to-day activities. There is plenty of parking space down by the 15th century bridge which gracefully spans the river here. This is where the bustling market is held every second Wednesday, alternating with Arcos de Valdevez. Boats provided a ferry service before the bridge was built and these aristocratic lands were known as Terras da Nóbrega but this changed at some time to Bridge of the Boat (Ponte da Barca). Its ribbon development arose from its need to serve travellers along the pilgrim routes to Santiago and to Orense in Spain. Now it is rich in 16th and 17th century granite mansions with some equally fine churches. For peace and quiet, head down to the riverside parkland area with its restaurant and other facilities which is ideal for relaxing, perhaps swimming in the river or just taking a quiet stroll. Ponte da Barca is an ideal base for exploring both the Peneda-Gerês National Park and the whole of northern Minho. Much of the accommodation is in manor houses under TURIHAB control and it has fine restaurants in *Veranda do Lima,* facing the market area by the river, and *Marisqueira,* opposite the wine co-operative on the Braga road.

Stay on the south side of the river to head back to Ponte de Lima. The scenic pastoral Lima valley, dripping green with vines, is perhaps more alluring here than seen along the northern route. **Bravães**, not too far out of Ponte da Barca, has an especially fine Romanesque church, São Salvador, built at the end of the 11th century by a local nobleman. The church is a small rectangular granite building but its sheer simplicity endows it with a special reverence. Of particular interest are its two finely sculptured doorways with animal carvings.

The Story of Maize

In the turbulent history of northern Portugal, no force surpassed that of the introduction of maize from America in the 16th century. It was a quiet earthquake which revolutionised life in the countryside bringing in a new viable crop which became instrumental in sustaining a farming existence in the countryside and in particular in the mountains. Space had to be made for it. On the lower levels, vines were pushed to the edge of the field and grown taller whilst, in the mountains, cattle were pushed off their grazing fields. Seasonal migration became a way of life where the cattle were taken up to the high mountain pastures in summer, often on a communal basis, with shepherds looking after all the cattle but rotating the responsibility according to their proportion of animals in the communal herd. Stone huts built igloo style, **abrigos**, used for shelter, dot the higher pastures and are very often accessed by stoutly-made granite trails. Some of these huts are still used today. Terracing provided new ground for maize and many of the steep-sided sheltered valleys are spectacularly terraced from floor to ceiling.

Espigueiros, used for maize storage, are sometimes located on communal ground, as at Soajo and Lindoso, but many of the villages at lower levels with more space have private ones in the gardens. Whilst the basic design prevails, they are not all made from solid granite and some have slatted wooden sides or are made largely of wood. There is one other design less commonly seen called **canastros** made in an open basket weave from wicker and often with a thatched roof.

Whilst some of the maize is used for animal food, a large proportion is ground into flour to make **broa**, a delicious heavy brown bread which is extremely popular throughout the maize growing regions in the north. It usually forms part of the breadbasket on a restaurant table and is sold in the shops either as whole loaves or as a piece cut to instruction. Baked in a hot oven, *broa* turns out with a crusty outside and a moist, chewy inside.

There is one link of the maize story still to unfold, the conversion of the maize into flour. Streams, rivulets and watercourses running down the granite mountainsides provided the perfect answer, free energy. In and around the villages by the streams are **watermills** by the hundreds but hardly recognisable as such. In appearance they look like any small granite building and the only real clue is that the water flows beside or beneath. One small stream can supply a whole line of watermills with power and typical is the stream above Soajo which serves a good number of mills. High technology has no place here, but the mills can function continuously without supervision and the technique is simplicity itself. A hopper feeds the corn onto the mill wheels and the rate of flow is determined by the angle of the hopper feed which is adjusted by a length of wire hooked onto one of a vertical line of nails above. The lower the nail chosen, the steeper the slope of the feed and vice versa. The problem of maintaining a constant feed is overcome by another simple but ingenious device. A wooden stick, standing through a small hoop, is allowed to bounce on the rotating mill wheel. The constant bouncing of the stick continually nudges the hopper feed to maintain a steady flow of corn to the wheel.

Nothing is wasted in the annual cycle of maize. The stalks are gathered in the fields and stooked together, often under trees to keep dry, and used for winter litter in the cow sheds. Maize is a greedy crop which needs a constant supply of fertiliser. Trampled under the animals' feet, the maize stalks are crushed, mixed with the droppings and so converted into ready-made fertiliser to spread back on the fields. Cow carts are active in bringing in the stalks to the farm in autumn and winter then active again taking out the manure in spring.

The Church of São Salvador at Bravães

To Melgaço and Moncão

A second, longer tour penetrates a little deeper into the National Park, to Castro Laboreiro via Serra da Peneda, and returns along the Minho calling in at Melgaço and Moncão before returning inland through Sistelo for more dramatic mountain scenery. It is a full day with 220km (137 miles) of driving in prospect and plenty to see.

The route out follows that described in the earlier National Park tour, along the north of the river to Arcos de Valdevez and through there to pick up the Soajo signs. Once past Mezio, look out for the road off to the left plastered with signs which include Branda do Murça (6km) and Lamas do Mouro (31km) but does not mention the intended destination, Peneda. It starts as a forest road through pine with some chestnut and cypress trees but extensive views suddenly open out left, over the Lima valley. From here, too, the extensive cultivation on the terraces above Soajo can be appreciated. Ruined houses in local stone of the now deserted **Branda de Bordença** blend so well into the landscape that it is easily missed, especially with the distant mountain peaks starting to make a distracting presence. The road loops revealing **Adrão** down below one moment then across the valley the next, where your eyes have difficulty picking out the old granite houses against the mountainside. Immediately beyond this point is a road off right which leads back to Soajo but the way here is straight ahead into yet more dramatic scenery, especially when the viewpoint is reached overlooking Tibo. Surrounded by green fields, **Tibo** straggles in a narrow but fertile oasis at the confluence of two valleys, whilst **Rouças** is in view to the left. Looking ahead into the valley east of north, the white façade of Senhora da Peneda is just visible. From here the road winds down through Rouças before heading back towards Peneda. Strong images prevail — clustered villages, *espigueiros*, green terraced fields, stooks of maize stalks, stark barren hillsides, inviting old trails leading to high pastures, huge granite tors — and the senses are not spared until **Peneda** is reached. The road actually passes above the village and the access is from the north end.

In the middle of this wilderness is the amazing church of **Senhora da Peneda**, which is built along similar lines to the better known church of Bom Jesus. Starting from the south, steps lead up past 14 chapels each of which contains a tableau portraying a major event in the story of Christ, from birth to crucifixion and resurrection. An ornate staircase embellished with statues completes the approach to the church which is built beneath a towering rock face. Twin bell towers flank the granite and white façade. Inside is bright and airy, departing from the traditional, especially the altarpiece which is borrowed Classical Greece with gilded Ionic columns in simulated marble. Cafés are on hand and on Sunday, when there are more visitors around, one or two market stalls appear; busier still are 7 and 8 September when the annual *romaria* is held.

A right turn at Lamas de Mouro leads to the ancient settlement of **Castro Laboreira** with an 11th century castle. The village is strongly associated with a large breed of dog bred originally to protect the village from marauding wolves in winter, but this breed is in danger of extinction and measures are in hand to ensure its continuity. Do not expect to fall over the **castle**, it is so well tucked away that it requires insider knowledge to find it. Drive above the village to a small roundabout and turn left, almost immediately the road bends to the right. Drive a few yards down here and park opposite a distinct footpath on the left. Be warned that at least some agility is required for an exciting 20-minute walk to the castle. Vertigo sufferers may be unhappy in places, although hand rails are there to give assurance at difficult parts. The sharp peak which hides the castle is easily seen but offers no hint of the castle. Granite tors weather into all sorts of shapes and there is an excellent granite tortoise here seen on the right shortly after the start. Crude steps and footholds over boulders help in parts as the path is easily followed to enter the castle through a narrow arched doorway. Built by Afonso Henriques, Portugal's first king in the 12th century, it was partially destroyed when lightning struck the gunpowder store. The spacious interior is divided by a central wall with an arched doorway to the lower section. It is a great place to picnic with excellent views over the surrounding countryside and over a surprisingly large number of small, red-roofed hamlets. If a restaurant now calls, there is a choice of the *Miradouro do Castelo* on the roundabout, which is popular on Sunday with the Portuguese, or the smaller da *Serra*.

For **Melgaço**, first head back to Lamas do Mouro and bear right. Modern developments in Melgaço dampen first impressions but a sight of the **castle keep** guides to the historic centre at the heart of the town. Some fortification may have been in place since Roman times, certainly the Moors were here for a time in the 9th century and are believed to have built a castle which was later ruined. More certain history starts when Dom Afonso Henriques granted a franchise around 1181 and ordered a castle to be built in this strategic border town. The castle was damaged by Leónese invaders in the early 13th century but restored again by Dom Sancho II and later, Dom Dinis ordered a second set of walls around the town which have now largely disappeared. A third line of walls constructed in the 17th century have also suffered demolition so that little remains.

Tales of fearless women feature strongly in the history of the border towns along the Minho and the most frequently told story here relates to the time when the Castilians had possession of the castle and were being held under siege by Dom João I and John of Gaunt. After 52 days, the deadlock was broken when a woman fighting for the Castilians, A Renegada (the renegade), heard that the loyal Inês Nigra was fighting for the Portuguese and challenged her to single combat with the outcome to decide the fate of the castle. Combat details get rather embroidered but Inês Nigra won and the Castilians surrendered.

Wandering the old town towards the castle leads past the 13th century Romanesque **Igreja Matriz**, not dissimilar to the church at Bravães, which has a griffin-type animal displaying a strong set of dentures carved above the door. The keep of the castle stands isolated in a walled enclosure and below lies a terrace with seating and cafés.

Peneda-Gerês National Park

Other areas of natural beauty in Portugal are preserved as Natural Parks but this area is especially important and since 1971 has been protected as a National Park. It covers an area of 72,000 hectares (278 square miles) encompassing principally the two mountain ranges which give the park its name, but squeezed in between these are the Serra do Soajo and Serra Amarela. There are a great many peaks over 1300m (4265ft) including Cornos da Fonte Fria at 1456m (4777ft), Nervosa at 1545m (5069ft) and Borrageiro at 1433m (4702ft).

Even though 15,000 people live in 114 villages in the park and traces of occupation reach back to the Iron Age, there are still vast areas which are little influenced by the effects of human exploitation. The rural environment housing the villages roughly follows the perimeter of the park and penetrates a few of the valleys and it is in this area where recreational facilities are being developed and tourism encouraged into the park. Difficulty of access and remoteness protects the rest of the region and there are no plans to change that.

Essentially a granite region, Europe's last wilderness offers a vast array of climates and micro-climates which has aided colonisation by plants with different origins. Species more commonly associated with the Mediterranean, the Continent or the Atlantic can all be found in the area whilst others have taken refuge here and can be found nowhere else, like the purple *Iris boissieri*. Although bears have not wandered these parts since 1650 and the last wild goat was recorded in 1890, the park is still home to a good range of species including wolf, boar, fox, deer, skunk, otter, wild cat, marten, royal eagle, falcon and a host of other bird species. Wild ponies still wander the park, and this is one of the few mammals that the casual visitor is likely to see.

The villages themselves are a treasure trove of cultural heritage where old traditions and an unchanging way of life are still preserved.

Monção, on the banks of the Minho, is the next port of call. The EN 202 running alongside the Minho has been much improved in recent years and a by-pass now exists around Monção which is still missing off most maps. This new road does not directly connect up with the Sistelo road which is the intended route back but it is accessible from the old road, as detailed shortly. Monção is another fortified border settlement saved from the Castilians by the wiles of a woman. In the siege of 1368, when the Portuguese were nearing the point of starvation, Deu-la-Deu Martins scraped together the last of the flour to bake a basket of bread which she threw over the castle walls to the Spanish attackers telling them that there was plenty more. The bluff worked. Disheartened and believing they had failed, the Spanish lifted their siege and the town was spared. Little cakes named after her are on sale in honour of the event and her statue stands in the large square, with a pensive expression, her back to Spain and her bread basket empty.

The walk along the northern ramparts gives views over the Minho river into Galicia and here a plaque bearing a poem by João Verde arouses awareness of the sensitivity of this closeness.

> Seeing them so close
> Galicia and the Minho
> They are like two courting lovers
> Separated by the river
> Almost since they were born.
> So let them court
> Since their parents
> Will not consent to marriage.

Monção prides itself on its food, offering salmon, lamprey, *cozido à Portuguesa* and roast kid with rice, but the only wine to drink here is the local vinho verde from the alvarinho grape.

On leaving Monção, take the old road back in the direction of Melgaço and look for the turn off right to Merufe and Sistelo. Fork right shortly to cross the by-pass over a bridge (the left fork leads down to the new road with no option to cross directly over). Once this far it is only a question of following the road and enjoying the scenery all the way back to Arcos de Valdevez. Vertiginously steep hillsides around Sistelo, patterned with terraces from top to bottom, present a spectacular sight unrivalled anywhere in the north.

Paredes de Coura offers a short side trip out of Ponte de Lima for yet more spectacular views of steeply terraced hillsides. There lies much to be discovered in this little-explored part of the Minho which most visitors tend to drive around rather than through. The *albergaria* at Paredes de Coura, with its clean modern lines, is a good base, and with good restaurants in town like *O Conselheiro,* offering trout fresh from the River Coura, it has all the necessary comforts.

Viana do Castelo

Viana do Castelo lies only 30 minutes' drive out of Ponte de Lima and can be reached either along the north bank of the Lima or the south. Arguably, the southern route is the more scenic, at least until Lanheses; beyond that industry, then urbanisation creep in to diminish the countryside. Once it was necessary to queue to cross the old Eiffel bridge which carries both the road and the railway across the river but a new road bridge further upstream has relieved all traffic problems. Town parking is never easy but the best option here is to head down to the riverside where the pay car park is normally shunned by the locals leaving plenty of space for visitors.

Tibo, Peneda-Gerês National Park

Backed by a wooded mountain and overlooked by Santa Luzia, Viana do Castelo earns its description of elegant, at least in the old part. The biggest disappointment is the front on the river estuary which has seagulls but lacks atmosphere and looks over to a busy port and heavy industry on the other side.

There has been life around these parts at least since Celtic times as the *citânia* of Santa Luzia suggests. Under the Romans it was known as Diana, which was eventually corrupted to Viana. History only starts to solidify in 1258 when Viana do Castelo was granted a royal charter by Dom Afonso III. Providing a good sheltered port in the estuary of the River Lima, it prospered on its maritime trade and through involvement in Portugal's great age of discoveries. Its sons joined the ranks of explorers. Gança Velho from Viana settled the Azores and João Velho was involved with the Congo discoveries. Thanks to another Viana explorer, João Alvares Fagundes, who mapped out the banks of Newfoundland for the Portuguese cod fishermen, the *bacalhau* trade became a new source of prosperity and the trade net widened to include England, Europe and Russia. By the 16th century, a British community had settled in the town exporting wines back home but they were expelled by the Spanish in 1580 although they were back by 1700 setting up a British Factory and becoming involved with the export of port wine. They moved to Porto later when Douro wines grew in importance and when the harbour at Viana started to silt up. Brazilian gold and sugar brought a new wave of prosperity in the 18th century.

The Town

A legacy of the prosperity from the 16th century onwards is an unusually large number of Manueline and Renaissance buildings and the best place to start a walkabout is the tourist office, housed in the old hospital, in the Praça de Erva off the central boulevard. Armed with a town plan, head for the **Praça da República**, a lovely open square surrounded by elegant buildings which is perhaps one of the best features of the town. Central to the square is the tiered **Chafariz fountain** built in 1554 by the celebrated stone mason, João Lopes. Water cascades from below an armillary sphere over graduated basins skilfully carved with birds and leaves with such pleasing effect that the style has been much copied throughout the country. Behind, at the head of the square, is the 16th century **Paços do Concelho**, the old town hall, with its Gothic arches and now restored. Bread was once sold from beneath these arches whilst the town hall meeting room lies above, reached by outside stairs. To the north side of the town hall, the three storeyed 16th century **Misericórdia church** presents an interesting façade with caryatids stoically supporting the upper two balconies. It started life as an almshouse or hospice in the 16th century and the adjoining church was rebuilt in the 18th century. The nave has some fine *azulejos* showing scenes from the Bible painted by Policarpo de Oliveira Bernades and there is more of his work in the museum.

Rua de Sacadura leads south from the square to the **cathedral** which was built in the 15th century originally as the parish church. Romanesque square towers and Gallic styles combine in the H-shaped façade which guard a Gothic door with carved figures on the surrounding mouldings. The municipal **museum** is housed in the 18th century Palacete Barbosa Maciel in Largo de São Domingo to the west of the main boulevard. There is some fine glazed 18th pottery on display notably from Coimbra but also from Viana itself, exquisite Indo-Portuguese furniture and some hunting scenes in *azulejos* painted by Policarpo de Oliveira Bernardes.

Out west lies **Castelo São Tiago da Barra** which started out only as the Torre da Roqueta built by the people of the town soon after receiving royal recognition in 1258; this and the town walls were said to have taken over a century to complete. The town walls were pulled down when the main boulevard leading to the railway station was built. In the early 16th century, with Viana growing into a major trading port, Dom Manuel ordered that the tower and castle be rebuilt and later the same century, with a growing threat from pirates, Dom Sebastião and Philip I ordered further modifications. The projecting ravelins in front of the main walls were built in the early 18th century. Now the castle has been restored and many of the buildings inside house municipal offices, including the administration of tourism, but access to the castle remains for the public.

There is no immediate town beach but there are regular ferries across the river mouth to the excellent **Cabedelo beach** facing the sea. Surfers pray for wind and are often rewarded with fine Atlantic surfing conditions. Yachts are served by a new marina operated by the port authority which is located on the north bank just before the old iron bridge of Gustav Eiffel fame.

Viana offers a number of traditional eating places but the one to visit at a weekend is *Os Três Potes* housed in the town's first public bakery, although booking is normally essential. Typical regional food is offered amongst swinging gourds and shaded lamps in a set menu which includes wine and entertainment by a group of local folk singers who are good exponents of the Portuguese raucous style of singing. Behind the old town hall is *Cozinha da Malheiras* which is a little more expensive but offers a good menu and good food. Towards the other end of the scale in cost is *Atrio,* which is nearer the new marina. It is a traditional eating place where the quality of the food takes precedence over the surroundings, the local red wine from the barrel is worth a try too.

There is a municipal **market hall** which is open mornings for the sale of meat, fish, fruit and vegetables and a weekly open air market on Fridays held in the open space near the fishing harbour. Souvenir hunters might look at the gold and silver filigree work for which the town is famous, embroidered table cloths and bread basket liners to hold individual cobs as well as ceramics and copper work.

A special event in Viana takes place on the Friday nearest 20 August for the **festival of Nossa Senhora de Agónia**. In solemn processions through flower decked and decorated streets, images of Our Lady of Agony are carried to the church of the same name on the western edge of town. The mood lightens later as festivities get into full swing, with singers and dancers moving into action and fireworks starting to explode.

On the mountain behind Viana is the church of **Santa Luzia** and a recently excavated *citânia*. A road leads up to the top of the mountain but there is also a funicular on a regular 30 minute service which starts from behind the railway station. The easiest way on foot is to go into the main railway station, turn right along the platform, cross the track, climb the steps and the funicular entrance is across the road. Cold, uninviting Santa Luzia, completed in 1926, sits uncomfortably on the hill top and rarely receives good comment but it at least offers an excellent viewpoint down over Viana do Castelo and the Lima river mouth. Above the church lies the ancient *citânia* which is Celtic in origin but is believed to have been taken over by the Romans and developed further. It is provided with unsightly walkways above the extensive ruins which at least allow a good overview of the many houses.

The road north out of Viana do Castelo follows along the Minho linking a line of fortified border towns. **Afife** is worth a stop on the way for its two excellent sandy beaches, both are a short diversion off the main road. The first, backed by steep dunes, is served by a seasonal café whilst the second, a little further north, has the advantage of *Restaurant Praia* which is particularly popular with the locals for Sunday lunch. Further north still lies the ancient fishing village of **Vila Praia de Âncora** at the estuary of the River Âncora and the best thing about it is the long sandy beach on the south of the river estuary and the cheap fish restaurants.

Caminha

Watery Caminha, further up the coast, lies at the confluence of two rivers, the broad graceful River Minho and the smaller River Coura. As an important sea port before the 16th century, it was troubled by pirates and the **fort at Insua** was built on an offshore islet for protection and for the safety of an earlier monastic settlement. Dom Afonso III rebuilt and strengthened an older fortification in the 13th century which was further enhanced by both Dom Manuel I early in the 16th century and soon afterwards by Philip II. Visiting the castle is possible on a Sunday when local fishermen run trips out from the sands at Foz de Minho.

With the growing importance of Viana do Castelo as a port in the 16th century, trade ebbed away from Caminha and it is left with a legacy of old town walls, charming medieval streets and a number of architecturally fine buildings from the period of its prosperity.

The place to drink coffee and enjoy the atmosphere is in the 14th century square of **Largo do Terreiro** sporting a fountain similar to Viana's. It is overlooked by a clock tower which started life in the 11th century, still with its original base, and the 17th century town hall. The gateway through the tower leads to the parish church, **Igreja Matriz**, which was stoutly constructed as part of the town's defences in the 15th century although the tower is from the following century. Renaissance carvings with sea motifs decorate two doorways and, if it is open, look for the carved wooden panels on the ceiling with their distinctly Moorish flavour. The gargoyle on the north wall might raise a smile too.

A little further upriver lies the small walled town of **Vila Nova de Ceveira**. The river was once fordable here, which the French tried to do in 1809; but the castle was built to prevent such invasion as the brave garrison successfully did on that occasion. History fails to detail the early history of the castle but Dom Dinis recognised the strategic importance of the town and ordered further strengthening of the fort which also included building walls around the town. Now the castle provides a historic and elegant setting for the *Pousada Dom Dinis* which also has a restaurant. The town offers a quiet retreat with a tree-lined promenade by the river and the chance to slip over to Spain using the ferry service to Goyan.

Valença do Minho

The pearl of the Minho is historic Valença do Minho, still firmly enclosed within impregnable 17th century walls and looking out over the river keeping a fearful eye open for invaders from Spain. How times have changed, the eye still watches but the fear now is that the Spanish will not come. They storm the castle daily bringing with them buckets of pesetas which they trade in for bags of corks, ormolu clocks and candlesticks, linen, ceramics and goods of all description which they take home by the sackful. Prices here are marked in both currencies.

View of the Lima valley from Paço de Calheiros, one of the TURIHAB manor houses

Modern developments outside the old town walls offer little of interest so visitors generally head straight for the historic centre entering through an entrance in the old walls to find plenty of parking space. A jumble of narrow shopping streets colourfully decked with displays spreading onto the pavements tempts browsers to wander deeper into the disorientating maze of this fortress within a fortress. Although a castle existed here from fairly early times, and was constantly enlarged and updated, it was in the 17th century, during a vital war to restore Portugal's independence, that the present fort started to take shape. With the growing importance of artillery warfare, the fort was built with projecting angular ravelins outside the main walls which presented different angles of fire and allowed for the protection of the curtain walls themselves.

A walk out to the north along the mossy ramparts gives good views of the Minho and the bridge across the river which carries road, rail and pedestrians to Tuy on the Spanish side. At this viewpoint is the modern *Pousada de São Tetónio*. Largo Bom Jesus lies in the southern part of the fortress and here the restaurant/café of the same name offers outside dining with good food; but for a more traditional menu try nearby *Restaurant Baluarte*.

The next major town along the Minho is Monção, already visited; before Monção is a short diversion down to **Lapela** on the edge of the river. Lapela has a tower which was part of the chain of defence along this northern boundary and used for sending warning messages in times of danger. Now it is buried amongst the narrow streets and granite houses of this small village,

143

surrounded by free range chickens and hens, supporting stacks of firewood ready for the winter months and looked over by a battered *espigueiro*. Pastoral eloquence lies just a little further on, down by the green banks of the riverside, where herons fish on the slow-moving Minho and where a picnic can last a very long time.

Options for returning to Ponte de Lima from here are fairly numerous: the EN101 from Monção leads through attractive countryside to Arcos de Valdevez; heading back past Valença offers the opportunity of returning via winding country roads through Paredes de Coura, with sight of some spectacular hillside terracing around Rendulfe; or you could return almost as far as Caminha and take the road through Vilar de Mouros which is famous for its Romanesque bridge and watermills.

Practical Information

Accommodation and Restaurants

This area has a greater number of *quintas* and manor houses than anywhere else in the country and these offer the best standard of accommodation in the region. Only a very limited selection is listed and they are mostly in TURIHAB (TH); see introduction for details and phone number.

ARCOS DE VALDEVEZ
Residencial Dom António, Rua Dr Germano de Amorin (tel. 058 521 010). Acceptable accommodation in pleasant three-star *residencial*.
Restaurant O Lagar, Rua Dr Vaz Guedes (tel. 058 66 002). Small, typical restaurant, limited menu but good food and very reasonable.

MONCÃO
Albergaria Atlântico, Rua General Pimenta de Castro, 15 (tel. 051 652 355). Small four-star *albergaria* with restaurant.

PAREDES
Albergaria Paredes de Coura, Rua Dr Narciso Alves da Cunha (tel. 055 92 450). Handily situated on edge of town, small four-star hotel with restaurant.
Restaurant O Conselheiro, Rua Conselheiro Miguel Dantas (tel. 055 783 298). Serves fresh trout from River Coura.

PONTE DA BARCA
Quinta da Prova (TH). A collection of five cottages scattered on farm estate overlooking River Lima. Three suitable for four people and two for couples.
Casa da Agrela (TH). Three rooms in an attractive granite and white manor house, swimming pool.
Restaurant Bar do Rio, Praia Fluvial (tel. 058 42 582). Seasonal restaurant with good location down on the riverside beach.
Veranda do Lima, Campo do Corro (tel. 058 43 469). A little pretentious but

good food and moderately priced.

A Marisqueira, Rua das Maceiras (tel. 058 42 514). Mainly fish, good portions, locally popular and very reasonable.

PONTE DE LIMA

Albergaria Império do Minho, Centro Ibérico-Av. 5 de Outubru (tel. 058 741 158). Well situated by River Lima and close to the centre, comfortable well furnished rooms. Facilities include swimming pool and restaurant.

Paço de Calheiros, Calheiros (TH). Grand palace just outside Ponte de Lima, excellent terrace with views over the Lima valley.

Quinta do Rei, Estorãos (TH). Around 6km to the west of Ponte de Lima, manor house divided into two nicely furnished apartments taking three and four people.

Moinho de Estorãos, Estorãos (TH). Delightfully-converted water mill providing an apartment for two people, same location as above.

Casa do Tamanqueiro, Estorãos (TH). House for four people, two double bedrooms and wonderful traditional kitchen with log fire. Location near the Quinta do Rei, see above.

Restaurant Tulha, Rua Formosa (tel. 058 942 879). Typical restaurant, moderate prices.

O Brasão, Rua Formosa (tel. 058 941890). Pleasant restaurant offering good food, moderate.

Beco das Selas, Beco das Selas (tel. 058 943 576). Small restaurant with limited menu but food is good and prices reasonable.

Santa Monte Madelena, Monte (tel. 058 943 941 239). Superb view from top of the hill south of town while dining on good regional dishes, prices not over the top.

SOAJO

Casa do Adro, Soajo (TH) (tel. 053 973 477). Out in the wilds in this small rustic village, just three rooms.

Espigueiro do Soajo (tel. 058 67 136). Bar/restaurant serving good regional dishes.

VALENÇA DO MINHO

Pousada de São Teotónio (tel. 051 824 920). Located in the old castle overlooking river, 16 rooms in elegant setting. The restaurant here offers the best eating in town.

Hotel Lara, Lugar de S. Sebastião (tel. 051 824 348). Passable three-star hotel.

VIANA DO CASTELO

Hotel Parque, Praça da Galiza (tel. 058 828 605). Large four-star hotel, restaurant and swimming pool.

Hotel Viana Sol, Largo Vasco da Gama (tel. 058 823 401). Comfortable three-star hotel, good standard of accommodation and centrally situated.

Casa dos Costa Barros, Rua de S. Pedro, 22 (TH) (tel. 058 823 705). Located in the historic centre, 16th century house with Manueline windows, 10 rooms.

Quinta do Paço d'Anha, Vila Nove de Anha (tel. 058 322 459). Four apartments on farming estate which produces and bottles vinho verde wine; just 3km (approx. 2 miles) outside town.

Os Três Potes, Beco dos Fornos (tel. 058 829 928). Typical restaurant in old bakehouse which is worth visiting on Saturday (set meal) when a group of folk singers and dancers are in action.

Cozinha da Malheiras, Rua Gago Coutinho (tel. 058 823 680). Good food but on the expensive side.

Viana's, Rua Frei Bartolomeu dos Mártires (tel. 058 823 032). Unpretentious, limited menu but best food in town and cheap.

VILA NOVA DE CERVEIRA

Pousada Dom Dinis (tel. 051 795 601). Located in the historic centre overlooking ramparts, 26 rooms.

Places of Interest

LINDOSO

Castle. Open 9.30am–12 noon and 1.30–5pm, closed Mondays and holidays.

Peneda-Gerês National Park.

PONTE DE LIMA

Fortnightly fair held on a Monday.

VIANA DO CASTELO

Igreja Santa Luzia for the views.

Citânia de Santa Luzia. Open 9am–12noon and 2–6pm, closed Mondays and holidays.

Museu Municipal, Largo de S. Domingos. Open 9.30am–12 noon and 2–5pm, closed Mondays and holidays.

Tourist Offices:

Arcos de Valdevez: Av. Marginal (tel. 058 66 001).
Caminha: Rua Ricardo Joaquim Sousa (tel. 058 921 952).
Caldas do Gerês: Av. Manuel Ferreira da Costa (tel. 053 391 133).
Melgaço: Loja Nova (tel. 051 42 440).
Monção: Largo do Loreto (tel. 051 652 757).
Paredes de Coura: Largo Visconde de Mozelos (tel. 051 783 592).
Ponte de Lima: Praça da Republica (tel. 058 942 335).
Ponte da Barca: Largo da Misericódia (tel. 058 42 899).
Valença do Minho: Av. de Espanha (tel. 051 23 374).
Viana do Castelo: Rua do Hospital Velho (tel. 058 822 620).
Vila Praia de Áncora: Av. Ramos Pereira (tel. 058 911 384).

9. THE SOUTHERN MINHO

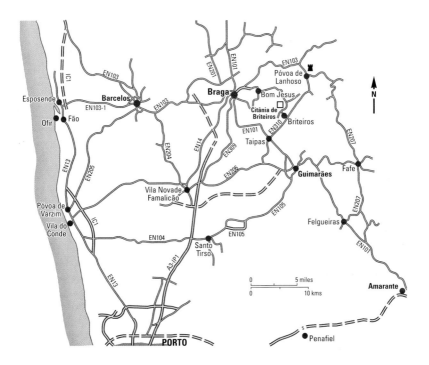

Here lies the cradle of the nation, the heartland of ancient Portugal which bristles with historic towns like Guimarães, Braga and Barcelos. These towns bustle with activity, hint at modernity and harbour what little industry there is in the north outside Porto, whilst the surrounding agricultural land belongs to an earlier age where people still farm small plots in the traditional way and still grow vinho verde vines. Bordering the region to the west is the Costa Verde, lapped and often lashed by the cool Atlantic which has perhaps prevented the development of significant seaside resorts in spite of having some good stretches of beach. Bathing from the coast north of Porto up to Póvoa de Varzim is generally avoided by the locals because of pollution and frequent oil spillage arising in Porto.

Braga

A good if winding road leads down from Ponte de Lima directly into busy Braga. Street parking away from the centre is possible but a multi-storey car park just south of Avenida Central is very convenient.

First in the queue for heaven, and once a major employer of religious architects, Braga boasts churches by the dozen and is the seat of the powerful Primate of Portugal. Its ecclesiastical pre-eminence declined in the 18th century when the patriarchate passed to the capital, Lisbon, so Braga turned to a new god, money, or so it seems. Industry and commerce have grown to prominence now but visitors at Easter time, witnessing the series of spectacular if sometimes solemn celebrations when hundreds of barefoot and hooded penitents march the streets by torch light, will be left in no doubt about the depth of religious feeling which still remains.

Celtic settlers calling the town Bracara were amongst the earliest inhabitants followed by the Romans who dedicated this town to their emperor and named it Bracara Augusta. With its convenient position in the heart of fertile farm land, it became the capital of Galicia, the region from north of the Douro to Cantabria, and a communication centre with no fewer than five important roads. Ousting the Romans in 411, the Suevi made it their capital until it fell to Theodore II just 45 years later. Two synods held in Braga in 563 and 572 commenced the conversion of the Visigoths from Arianism to Catholicism and marked the beginnings of the ascendancy of the church. From around 730 it was conquered and destroyed by the Moors after which it passed into the shadow of history until it was retaken by the Castilians in the 11th century. The see was restored in 1070, not entirely to the pleasure of Santiago. Diego Gelmirez, bishop of Santiago, anxious not to be under the power of Braga, took unilateral action in 1103 when he went there and carried off the relics of St Victor and St Fructuosus. Seeking approval from Rome, the superiority of Braga over all sees in the western peninsula as far south as Coimbra was confirmed.

The Town

Shop-lined **Avenida Central**, headed by the Torre de Menagem, is the location of Turismo and a good place to start a tour. Walking westwards leads past an assortment of street venders, offering anything from tights to roasted chestnuts, into pedestrianised Rua do Souto towards the cathedral. This is the place to buy religious artefacts of all descriptions; shops here selling anything from a simple candle to a wax replica of some part of the body. **Largo de Paço**, on the right, housing a castellated Baroque fountain from 1723, is the courtyard of the archbishop's palace which now houses an important public library and some parts of the university. Just beyond, on the left, is Braga's main attraction for visitors, the cathedral.

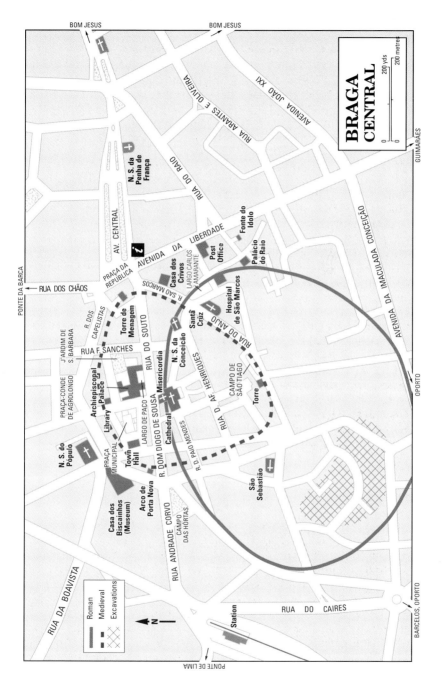

BOM JESUS

BOM JESUS

BRAGA
CENTRAL

200 yds
200 metres

GUIMARÃES

AVENIDA JOÃO XXI

RUA ARANTES E OLIVEIRA

RUA DO RAIO

AV. CENTRAL

N. S. da Penha de França

Fonte do Idolo

AVENIDA DA IMACULADA CONCEIÇÃO

AVENIDA   DA   LIBERDADE

Post Office

Palácio do Raio

PONTE DA BARCA

RUA DOS CHÃOS

PRAÇA DA REPÚBLICA

Casa dos Crivos

LARGO CARLOS AMARANTE

Hospital de São Marcos

R. SÃO MARCOS

Santa Cruz

OPORTO

R. DOS CAPELISTAS

Torre de Menagem

RUA F. SANCHES

RUA DO SOUTO

N. S. da Conceição

RUA DO ANJO

JARDIM DE S. BARBARA

PRAÇA-CONDE DE AGROLONGO

Archiepiscopal Palace

Library

LARGO DE PAÇO

Misericordia

Cathedral

CAMPO DE SÃO TIAGO

Torre

N. S. do Pópulo

PRAÇA MUNICIPAL

Town Hall

R. DOM DIOGO DE SOUSA

R. D. PAIO MENDES

RUA D. AF. HENRIQUES

Casa dos Biscainhos (Museum)

Arco de Porta Nova

CAMPO DAS HÓRTAS

São Sebastião

OPORTO

RUA ANDRADE CORVO

RUA DA BOAVISTA

Roman
Medieval
Excavations

N

BARCELOS, OPORTO

Station

RUA   DO   CAIRES

PONTE DE LIMA

149

The portico of the Misericórdia, Braga

Starting life about 1100 as a Romanesque structure and financed by Henry of Burgundy and his wife Dona Teresa, the **cathedral** has been almost constantly modified with the introduction of Gothic, Baroque and Renaissance styles. This confusion of styles might rob the cathedral of a sense of grandeur but it lends an added interest to inspecting the individual parts which are often quite beautiful. The entrance from this road leads first into the 18th century cloisters which has to the south the important Gothic **Capela dos Reis** (Chapel of the Kings) which contains the tombs of the founders, Dom Henry of Burgundy and his wife Dona Teresa, parents of Afonso Henriques, the first king of Portugal. Here also is the mummified body of Archbishop Lourenço Vicente who fought in the battle of Aljubarrota to help defeat the Castilians. At the eastern end of the courtyard is the **Capela da Glória** with the beautifully carved 14th century tomb of Archbishop Gonçalo Pereira which was commissioned in his own lifetime. Next to this is **Capela de São Geraldo** lined with blue *azulejos*. The entrance to the west leads into the gloomy and somewhat disorientating interior.

If the cathedral proper, tastelessly modernised in the 17th century, seems uninteresting, the exuberant gilt Baroque organs certainly catch the eye. Lighting a candle here is a novel experience — they are electric and require a coin in the slot. It is strange that the candles are all red. A fee is asked for entrance to the **treasury museum** but it contains an extraordinarily diverse and rich collection of religious objects presented without much organisation. Perhaps the earliest piece on display is a 10th century Hispano-Arab casket in ivory, the 11th century offers a chalice and a Byzantine cross and later centuries seem to explode with gold and silver plate, embroidered mitres, valuable paintings, a working 17th century organ and a staggering 8.5kg

(19lb) silver receptacle encrusted with 450 precious stones which belonged in the 18th century to the Archbishop Gaspar de Bragança.

An exit through the west door into Rua D. Paio Mendes provides the opportunity to look at the main façade of the cathedral with its square flanking bell towers. The arching over the main door, sheltered now by a late Gothic porch added in 1532, is one of only two remaining Romanesque features.

Braga's **museum** is housed in the elegant 16th century Casa dos Biscainhos mansion on the street of the same name. The house itself provides some delights including a passageway in the façade to allow coaches the convenience of driving directly through to reach the stables incorporated in the main house. A series of rooms furnished with period furniture, some with painted ceilings and some with *azulejos*, display silver and porcelain whilst the ground floor offers artefacts from the recent Roman excavations. The site of the excavations lies close to the museum but it is not open to the general public and there is little to see through the fencing.

In spite of the large number of churches and buildings in Braga, there are only a few worth visiting and those for their different architectural appeal. These include the Renaissance-style **Misericórdia** next to the cathedral, with its portico built in 1562 and fine carving inside; the 17th century Baroque church of **Santa Cruz** in Largos Carlos Amarante, with Rococo ornamentation and a fine Baroque organ; and the 18th century **town hall** in Praça Municipal, which has a highly regarded 18th century Baroque façade.

Looking beyond the ornate votive candles, which are big business in Braga, there is some interesting shopping for local crafts including wicker baskets and straw hats. Home spun items from locally grown flax include quilts and damask bedspreads, while the artistic ox-yolks made by the wood workers are hard to carry away unless a miniature is found. There is a choice of restaurants for trying out some of the town's gastronomic specialities. For roast kid try the family-run *Inácio* in Campo das Hortas, which offers good food including *bacalhau* dishes and the pork and maize dumplings, *rojões à Minhota*.

Bom Jesus

Braga's main attraction for pilgrims is the curious and intriguing church of Bom Jesus which sits on a hill outside town. It is reached by taking the dual carriageway leading eastwards out of Braga and turning left at the sign for *elevador* and restaurant to climb the hill. At busy times, it is more convenient to park at the bottom of the hill in the car park and picnic area on the left soon after turning into this road. This area is located below the main, highly ornate, double staircase of the church which only reveals its glories to those on foot, and the best perspectives are enjoyed when climbing upwards. True penitents will be on their knees but for others there is a water-operated funicular on hand so options are to ride up and walk down or vice versa or, of course, walk both ways. The gain in elevation from this point is 285m (935ft) which is worth bearing in mind, particularly in hot weather.

Architecture in Portugal

Influenced perhaps by their early history or simply reflecting the nature of the people, Portuguese buildings often have the solidity of Roman construction. Stable rectangular forms have their clean lines emphasised by a neat facing of white plaster which leaves the bare stone of the aperture frames and structural members free. Portuguese architects have always preferred horizontal structures so that most buildings are of no great height and have not shown any inclination towards curves and domes. Even in the Romanesque churches of the north, the curved apse is often ignored in favour of a square wall. The oval plan used by church architects of Germany, Austria and Italy in the 17th and 18th centuries was almost completely ignored although Nasoni built the 18th century Clérigos church in Porto to this plan. Domes, too, are rare in Portugal and barrel-vaulted roofs are by no means common.

In total contrast to this simplicity of line and style, the Portuguese found great delight and demonstrated extraordinary creative talent at surface decoration. This is evident in the decorative sculptures on the Romanesque churches where doorways are often decorated with carvings. A fine example is the Romanesque church at Bravães near Ponte da Barca which has a very ornate portal with monkeys climbing a column alongside other figures and a griffin carved over the south door. The Manueline, Baroque and Rococo periods provided opportunities for expanding this art which was fully embraced by the sculptors, stonemasons and wood carvers of the time.

This same genius for surface decoration spread inside the church, especially to the retable behind the altar which evolved into a highly carved and usually gilded piece of woodwork often embellished with cherubs and vine leaves. Uniquely Portuguese, this style developed until sometimes the whole church interior was entirely covered in carved and gilded wood.

Gothic architecture, which brings together a number of elements like the pointed arch, the principle of the flying buttress as half arches or half tunnel vaults and generally more slender elements, was introduced to Portugal by the Cistercians and the most outstanding early example is the abbey of St Maria Alcobaça (1178–1252). Gothic architecture only really found support towards the end of the 16th century and reached full expression in the Monastery of Batalha. Good examples in the northern region include the church of São Domingos at Guimarães, although there are plenty of Gothic cloisters which were added to many churches and cathedrals.

The Manueline style, which developed out of late Gothic, sprang from the great riches pouring into the country and it represents Portugal's unique contribution to the world's architecture. Its peak coincided roughly with the reign of Dom Manuel (1495–1521) after whom the style was named but not until much later. Apart from lavish surface decoration, the style also involved some transformation of structural members with a particular passion for twisted columns and ribs. There was no great uniformity within the style and it sometimes borrowed ideas, like sea motifs, and other effects like Mudéjar which evolved in Spain from Christian architects absorbing Muslim influences. Most of the finest examples of Manueline occur south of Coimbra with Jerónimos monastery at Belém and the Convent of Christ at Tomar famous for its carved stone frames of twisted tree trunks, coral, knots and ropes.

Preoccupied with the Manueline style, the influence of the Italian Renaissance was late in reaching Portugal—it creeps in around 1530 at the earliest. French architects working in Portugal were the first practitioners in this return to the harmony, stability and poise of the Greco-Roman style which extended to statues, portals, retables, tombs and whole chapels. Amongst the most elegant and harmonious of the early works is the chapel of São Pedro in the old cathedral at Coimbra (1537). From the middle of the 16th century, Portuguese architecture responded to changes arising in Italy and evolved the Mannerist style. This involved a shift away from the basic classical proportions to characteristic distortion and exaggeration to present an ideal of beauty opposed to a representation.

The Baroque style in architecture developed in the 17th century and was initially resisted in Portugal. This style is characterised by exuberant decoration, expansive curvaceous form, a delight in large-scale and sweeping vistas, preferring depth over plane as, for example, in the Baroque staircase at Bom Jesus near Braga. It was gold and diamonds from Brazil and the munificence of João V which attracted foreign craftsmen to Portugal and stimulated architectural advances. Complex surface ornamentation was not neglected and the Portuguese took to wood carving with particular enthusiasm and retables emerged with twisted chestnut columns decorated with theatrically gilded grape vines and birds.

The first truly Baroque church is Santa Engrácia in Lisbon which was not actually completed until 1966 whilst the most extravagant project launched by João V was the huge complex of Mafra Palace, near Sintra. A movement away from the dark and ponderous Baroque to the lightness and colour of Rococo represented the dying phase of this style of architecture which faded around the middle of the 18th century.

The church of Bom Jesus

Starting from the car park at the bottom, the way follows a mosaic zig-zag ascending path lined with chapels each with a tableau depicting scenes from the life of Christ, like the Last Supper and the Crucifixion, until the staircase proper is reached. This rising and receding double granite and white **staircase** leading up to the double-towered church is classic Baroque. The steps were started by Rodrigo Moura Teles, archbishop of Braga, in 1723, and each landing was subsequently adorned with wall fountains representing the five senses, commencing with sight on the first landing. Hearing, smell, taste and touch follow in succession, and each landing is also adorned with statues. This is followed by the stairway of the Virtues, Faith, Hope and Charity each represented by fountains surrounded by granite biblical figures. The church itself, built by Carlos Luís Ferreira Amarante between 1748 and 1811 on the site of an earlier sanctuary, is of neo-classical design and based on the Latin cross but has little of special interest.

Well-tended and neat gardens around the church provide a relaxing retreat, except at weekends when the Portuguese themselves visit in force. The views from this vantage point on Mount Espinho take in the hills of the Peneda-Gerês National Park to the north and out to the Atlantic coast in the west. Snack bars and hotels add their touch of commercialism but the hotels here are recommended over those in Braga itself.

For those still in a religious mood, there is a short excursion (4km/2½ miles) south east from here to the **sanctuary** on **Mount Sameiro** which is the second most important in Portugal after Fátima and attracts thousands of pilgrims annually. It began only in the last century with the erection of a cross followed later by a chapel. The views score more points than the church.

Festivals

Not a summer weekend passes without a festival taking place somewhere in Portugal. These festivals are deeply bound up with religion and are usually held to celebrate a saint's day (*a festas*) or a religious pilgrimage (*a romario*). In addition there are some popular festivals, like music festivals, but even these may have a religious connection.

Every village in the country has at least one celebration to look forward to in the season, while bigger villages and towns may have several. Months are spent planning the events, and organising committees work hard to raise money to decorate the village and the route of the procession. On the day, the villagers gather for mass then walk in procession carrying images of their patron saint often to music provided by the local brass band. Do not for one moment think that these are entirely solemn occasions for once the church procession is over, the folks let their hair down and really go to town, especially in the evening. Often dressed in local costume, the villagers dance and drink the evening away to music blared through speakers from brass bands or from groups of folk singers. Some of the larger ones are attended by street vendors and travelling fun fairs which help to create a lively market atmosphere. Fire crackers add to the noise as celebrations move towards a climax.

Apart from these local celebrations, there are also big events in the calendar, like Easter and May Day, which are celebrated nationally. Some dates to look for include:

March/April
Easter is celebrated everywhere but one of the bigger processions is held in Braga.

May
Festas da Cruzes, 2 and 3 May at Barcelos.
Festival of Our Lady of the Roses, early May, Vila Franca do Lima.

June
Festa de São Gonçalo; 1st weekend, Amarante.
Feira de São João: celebrated on 23–24 June in towns up and down the country but especially in Porto and Braga.
Festas de São Pedro: 28–29 June, Póvoa de Varzim and Vila Real.

August
Festas Gualterianas in honour of St Walter: 1st Sunday, Guimarães.
Festas de Santa Barbara: Sunday after 15 August, Miranda do Douro.
N. S. da Agonia Romaria: Friday nearest to 20 August in Viana do Castelo.

September
Festas de N. S. dos Remédios: end of August to middle of September, Lamego.
Feiras Novas: 20 September, Ponte de Lima.

Citânia de Briteiros

Citânia de Briteiros, a fortified Celto-Iberian settlement and one of the north's most important historical sites, lies only a short run from Bom Jesus. Start out along the Póvoa de Lanhoso road then pick up signs for Briteiros to enjoy a pleasant rural run through curtains of vines, eucalyptus, pines and cultivation. This complex Iron Age site which sprawls over a hillside was occupied from around 300 BC and seems to have been one of the last strongholds to hold out against the Roman invaders until about 20 BC, although the site may have been occupied later. Well-directed routes and a map received on entry allow visitors to wander around to inspect the remains of Celtic round, elliptical and rectangular houses, water conduits, bathing houses and streets all within fortified walls. Excavation was started in 1883 by Dr Francisco Martins

Sarmento, an archaeologist from Guimarães, and most of the finds are now contained in the museum named after him in Guimarães. Two round houses reconstructed by Martins Sarmento help to bring the ruins to life but their authenticity is now questioned.

Póvoa de Lanhoso

Nearby, Póvoa de Lanhoso boasts one of the smallest castles in Portugal on one of the biggest mounds. It is kept locked up but if the nearby restaurant is open the key is usually available. Twin towers guard the entrance and inside there is a small keep and a garrison courtyard. As a fortification it is believed to have started life under the Romans to guard their route between Braga and Asturga but it was built up to its present form in the Middle Ages. Tragic stories seem to attach themselves to romantic castles. Rodrigo Gonçalves Pereira, a former commander of the castle, was inflamed with jealousy at the belief that his wife was having an affair so he set fire to the castle residence while his wife was inside with, he believed, her lover. The castle was abandoned in the 17th century and bought by a wealthy business man who had visions of building a sanctuary on the hill with shrines and chapels, but it had no lasting appeal to the pilgrims.

Guimarães

It is only a short drive from here to Guimarães, the birthplace of the Portuguese nation. Surrounded by green wooded hills but hemmed in now by urban development, historic Guimarães is where the Portuguese go to discover their roots as a nation and where visitors of all nationalities share the deep sense of history.

Do not be seduced by counter claims from Lisbon (1109) or Viseu (1106), according to tradition Afonso Henriques, the first King of Portugal, was born in Guimarães in the year 1110. Other dates are sometimes quoted because there was no registry of births at that time, not even for nobles. Before he was born, his father, Henry of Burgundy, had been granted the County of Portucale by Alfonso VI, king of Castile, on marriage to Alfonso's illegitimate daughter, Teresa. With the ambition of emancipating the territory, Henry settled at Guimarães with his wife and strengthened the defences by building seven towers around an existing central tower. This latter tower and a circle of walls had been constructed two centuries earlier by the powerful Galician Countess Mumadona to protect the town of Vimaranes, as it was then known. In accordance with her husband's dying wishes, she had built a monastery where Nossa Senhora da Oliveira now stands, around which Guimarães developed.

Henriques succeeded his father around the age of five with his mother acting as regent. Teresa's struggles to maintain the independence of Portucale failed when her armies yielded and she was forced to accept Galician dominance under Alfonso VII. With growing strength of character and stature,

Largo da Oliveira, Guimarães

Afonso Henriques rebelled against his mother's regency and dispatched her and her Galician lover into exile. He emerged with great honour on defeating the Moors in the battle of Ourique in 1139 and from then on was recognised as king although he was not formally crowned until 1143.

The Town

Forget the urban surrounds, all the interest in Guimarães lies in the heart of the city. Early development took place between the monastery in the south and the castle to the north creating a peanut shell-like area full of old squares, cobbles, houses and churches. It was once surrounded by medieval walls of which a part still remain on the east side of the town, along Avenida Albert Sampaio. Appended now to the south are the wide, gardened boulevards of **Largo de República do Brasil** and Alameda de Liberdade. The former of these is perhaps a good place to start a tour if only to see the imposing façade of the 18th century **Igreja dos Santos Passos** which guards the southern end. Regarded as one of the most beautiful in the city, it is in Baroque style with a bowed front flanked by slender towers.

A walk along the boulevard leads into the opposite narrow side street and into the spacious medieval **Largo da Oliveira** surrounding an olive tree. Here, wrought iron balconies garlanded with flowers and decked with washing look down from tall, elegant white-washed houses onto sun umbrellas shading café tables, and a cobbled square where children play safe from traffic. Standing in the square, in front of **Nossa Senhora da Oliveira** (Our Lady of the Olive Tree) is a Gothic canopy sheltering a **cross**. The cross and the olive tree are linked by a story which stretches back to the early 14th century. At that time, an olive

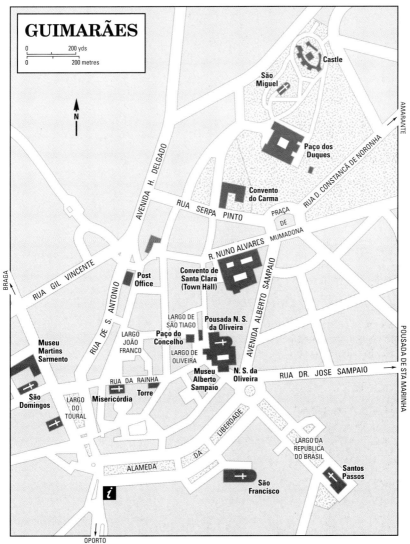

GUIMARÃES

0   200 yds
0   200 metres

N

Castle

São Miguel

AMARANTE

Paço dos Duques

RUA D. CONSTANÇÂ DE NORONHA

Convento do Carma

AVENIDA H. DELGADO

RUA SERPA PINTO

PRAÇA DE MUMADONA

R. NUNO ALVARES

RUA GIL VICENTE

BRAGA

Post Office

Convento de Santa Clara (Town Hall)

AVENIDA ALBERTO SAMPAIO

RUA DE S. ANTONIO

LARGO DE SÃO TIAGO

LARGO JOÃO FRANCO

Paço do Concelho

Pousada N. S. da Oliveira

LARGO DE OLIVEIRA

Museu Martins Sarmento

Museu Alberto Sampaio

N. S. da Oliveira

RUA DR. JOSE SAMPAIO

POUSADA DE STA MARINHA

RUA DA RAINHA

Torre

São Domingos

LARGO DO TOURAL

Misericórdia

LIBERDADE

ALAMEDA

DA

LARGO DA REPUBLICA DO BRASIL

Santos Passos

São Francisco

i

OPORTO

tree, which had previously provided oil to light the lamp guarding the martyred saint at the monastery of São Torcato, was dug up and brought to this square in Guimarães. The tree withered but was left in place until 1342 when Pedro Esteves chanced along on 8 September and had a cross erected nearby. Three days later the withered olive tree suddenly sprouted green leaves and burst into healthy growth. It is the same cross which is now protected by the canopy while the square and the church were renamed after the olive tree. One murky night in 1870 the olive was vandalised and, after a rather lengthy deliberation, the tree was eventually replaced in 1985.

The church itself, a national monument, was constructed by Henry of Burgundy on the foundations of a monastery built in the 9th century by the Countess Mumadona. Later additions and modifications, and there were many, include the west portal and a window, now blind, commissioned by Dom João I after the Battle of Aljubarrota. The tower with the quadrangular base was originally 13th century but was rebuilt in Manueline style including battlements at the start of the 16th century. A chapel inside the tower contains the remains of Pedro Esteves and his wife, Isabel Pinheiro.

Azulejos

The Portuguese fascination with surface decoration extends to *azulejos*, coloured ceramic tiles, which are inescapable throughout the country. They are not unique to Portugal, it is just that the Portuguese have a passion for them and use them imaginatively in a whole variety of ways from simple patterns to creating large scenes or even documentaries to decorate churches, water fountains, railway stations, palaces, public buildings and house fronts.

This love affair started around the 15th century, inspired by tiles with a geometric pattern imported from Seville. Home production of essentially blue tiles started and the patterns were established in firing by separating the colour with rivulets of linseed oil or by ridges of clay. In the 16th century, the Italian majolica technique was introduced by which the clay tile was covered by a white enamel which could be painted onto directly. This greater freedom allowed the Portuguese to introduce a design element to create patterns and by the 17th century coloured tiles, chiefly dark blue, yellow, green and white, were used to make up either geometric, carpet or tapestry designs, often based on a module of four tiles. Exotic designs with animals, fishes and flower motifs made an appearance too but the polychrome fashion waned with the appearance of Delft blue. Europe had been captivated by the imported blue and white Chinese porcelain and the Dutch responded by developing a delicate blue and white tile which quickly found favour in Portugal.

Towards the end of the 17th century, narrative tiles made their appearance telling a story of events in life like harvesting grapes, fishing or hunting and these increased in size and realism to become very popular. Tile painting rapidly became recognised as an art form, both in its creation and use as a complement to architecture to enliven interiors. One of the recognised masters, António de Oliveira Bernardes (1684–1732), together with his son Policarpo set up a school in Lisbon which rapidly became influential in the development of this art. A number of beautiful works in the first half of the 18th century are often assigned with authority to the Bernardes but the works of Terço can be seen in the Church of Terço in Barcelos (1713) and of Policarpo on the walls of the Misericórdia in Viana do Castelo (1720). Quite a number of artists became well known but one outstanding craftsman remains unknown to this day apart from his initials, P.M.P., which adorn his works.

Blue and white tiles dominated throughout this period but by the mid 18th century, polychromy returned to favour at more or less the same time as an earthquake shattered much of Lisbon. During the rebuilding phase, when the demand for tiles was high, a large number of factories opened but not all of these maintained the previous high standards. The use of *azulejos* for the exterior decoration of church façades and house walls was imported in the 19th century when the royal family and other emigrants returned from Brazil where they had moved to escape the French invasion. One of the best places to trace the history and development of *azulejos* is in the Museum of *azulejos* in Lisbon.

Adjacent to this church, surrounding the cloisters to the south, is the **museum of Alberto Sampaio** which is full of treasures taken as booty from the Castilians by Dom João I, including a silver altar which was offered to Our Lady as a thanksgiving after victory at Aljubarrota and a leather coat said to have been worn by Dom João I himself.

To find the ducal palace and the castle, leave Largo da Oliveira from centre north to enjoy first the ambience of Praça de Santiago before heading out to the east to enter the delightful, medieval **Rua de Santa Maria**. This was one of the first streets to link Mumadona's monastery in the lower part of town with the castle and is lined with attractive granite houses. Higher up, shortly after passing beneath the house which arches over the street, is the 16th century convent of Santa Clara, now the town hall, set back behind a square with seats and a fountain. Further along to the right, the building with all the curious tall brick chimneys, is the **Ducal Palace**, or the Palace of the Dukes of Bragança to use its full title. Little seems to be known about the early history of this building, although suggestions are that it was built by the first Duke of Bragança in the 15th century. It was allowed to fall into ruin before it was rebuilt by the architect Rogério de Azevedo, starting in 1937, as an official residence for the head of state. Since its official opening in 1959, the building has not drawn too much good comment but the combination of graceful Gothic windows and castellated walls in mellow granite topped by 39 tall brick factory chimneys raises a few eyebrows. Rarely now is it used for state affairs but it does house a museum. The waiting room is decked with tapestries illustrating Portugal's conquests in North Africa but these are copies of the originals now in Spain. Much of the furniture is Portuguese 17th century but the ornaments include Chinese porcelain. If conversation in the

Guimarães castle

dining room ever flagged, the ceiling resembling an upturned boat would have offered a good talking point.

From here it is but a short walk through wooded parkland to the tranquil setting of the **castle**. No longer now a killing field as it was in the 10th century when the Moors and other tribes ravaged the northern villages which persuaded Mumadona of the need for a defensive tower and walls. A decisive battle which was to secure independence for Portucale and enter the annals of history took place not exactly here but close by. This was the Battle of São Mamede in 1128 in which the young Afonso Henriques decisively defeated the Galician forces of his mother, Teresa. Guimarães castle did not see action until 1322 when the future Afonso IV, in an insurrection against his father, Dom Dinis, stormed the castle but failed to conquer it thanks to valiant resistance by the commander; then again, 50 years later, when three weeks of siege by Henry II and his Castilian troops backed by the French failed. It came closest to defeat in 1836 when an alderman proposed that the stones of the castle be used to pave the streets of the town. The proposal was defeated by the slenderest of margins, one vote. In 1910 it was declared a national monument and eight years of restoration work started in 1932.

Now the restored 10th century Torre de Managem and the surrounding eight towers, the inspiration behind the Portuguese coat of arms, looks like an imposing stage set, but it is one which the public can wander around and enjoy. Just below the castle is the 12th century Romanesque church of **São Miguel do Castelo** in which, according to tradition, Afonso Henriques, the first King of Portugal was christened. Inside, the floor is covered by the gravestones of Portuguese nobles.

The Rio Cávado, Barcelos

One of Guimarães' finest museums is the **Martins Sarmento museum** set up originally in the old Convento de São Domingos in 1888 to display finds from Citânia de Briteiros and named after the archaeologist who carried out the first excavations. It is found just west of the old centre, on Rua de Paio Galvão and, for some reason, does not receive too many visitors so there is usually a guide on hand to lead individual tours. The museum is crowded with fragments from Citânia de Briteiros and from another nearby site, Castro Sabrosa, as well as a numismatic collection. Larger exhibits are housed outside in the beautiful cloisters of the old convent and include Roman columns and stelae, two headless Lusitanian warriors in granite holding their shields before them and the huge granite Colossus of Pedralva standing about 3m (10ft) high which was found in 1876 by Martins Sarmento in Monte de Picos in Pedralva. Experts cannot agree whether this granite statue is pre-Roman or from a much later date. The other item of particular interest is the Pedro Formosa, which is thought to be the granite front of a crematorium.

Guimarães is a good base for exploring the southern Minho, it is close to Porto and there are interesting tours on hand without the need to travel too far. It has a high quality central hotel in *Hotel Guimarães,* with an excellent restaurant open to non-residents; two *pousadas, Pousada da Oliveira* in the old square in the centre of town and *Pousada de Santa Marinha da Costa* which is housed in a 12th century monastery on the Penhas hill. The latter is worth a visit just to enjoy the views or to dine at the *pousada* which has possibly the best restaurant around. There are also a number of houses in the TURIHAB scheme in the surrounding area, including the comfortable *Casa de Sezim* set amidst its own vineyards which produces one of the most respected vinho verde wines.

As often seems the case with the larger towns in the north, in Guimarães there is a wide choice of eating places but good ones are harder to find. *Casa do Arco*, near the town hall, is worth seeking out, the restaurant of *Hotel Guimarães*, is recommended and, a little lower priced but still good, is the *Mumadona* at the northern end of Rua de Santa Maria.

Barcelos

The easiest route from Guimarães to Barcelos tumbles through countryside busy with hamlets and villages each, like the other, with swarming vines. Vila Nova de Familicão is where the road turns to run more directly north and Barcelos is entered through Barcelinhos on the south side of the River Cavado. **Barcelos** is an attractive ancient town which stirs to life every Thursday with the arrival on Campo da República of the largest outdoor **market** in Portugal. It teems with colour and activity and is the place to buy just about everything, from a new cow cart complete with double ox-yolk to an extra large size bra of a particular robust nature and, of course, Barcelos cocks in all sizes.

Barcelos is noted for being the centre of a handicraft region and much of it finds its way on to the market including linen, baskets, straw hats, distaffs and spindles and regional pottery, both decorative and practical. There is little now to match the imaginative figurative work of the late Rosa Ramalho but granddaughter Rosie carries on the family tradition and her works are available in the medieval crenallated Torre de Porta Nova, a relic of earlier town fortifications, which is now the turismo and craft centre.

Tourist interest in Barcelos revolves around the huge **market square** and the old centre down towards the river. **Igreja do Terço**, alongside Campo da República, the former church of the Benedictine sisters, attracts attention for the remarkable 18th century *azulejos* by António de Oliveira Bernardes depicting the life of St Benedict. Another much visited church around this large square is the octagonal church of **Bom Jesus** (also known as the Templo do Nossa Senhor da Cruz), overlooking neat and colourful gardens, which is laid out on a Greek cross ground plan inside and freely decorated with *azulejos*.

Most remnants of the old city are found down by the river which is the location of the **archaeological museum** in the grounds of the old ducal palace. Now in ruins after the great Lisbon earthquake of 1755, the palace once belonged to Afonso, the natural son of Dom João I by his lover Inês Pires, who became the immensely rich and powerful eighth Duke of Barcelos and much later, towards the end of his life, the first Duke of Bragança. *Azulejos* tiled panels on the wall picture the palace when it was built and again at a later date; otherwise all the exhibits in this rough and tumble of an open museum are in granite from Roman stones to coats of arms and includes the famous 14th century Cruzeiro do Senhor do Galo which is finely carved with figures of the man himself, of the pilgrim St James and a cockerel. Looking down from the terrace here gives a good view of the **medieval bridge** over the River Cavado where townswomen still wash and dry clothes along the river banks.

The Legend of the Barcelos Cock

Legends, like myths, sometimes take on an air of romanticism and sometimes mysticism but rarely do they embrace earthly incredulity and survive as this one has. There are several variations to this legend but the theme is constant. It concerns a particular crime which happened in the town some centuries ago. The finger of suspicion pointed at a poor Galician pilgrim who strongly protested his innocence throughout but was found guilty and sentenced to hang. As a last wish before his execution, he asked to be taken into the presence of the judge to plead his cause. The judge, who was in the midst of entertaining guests to dinner, agreed to see the condemned man. Once again he pleaded his innocence and, in one last act of desperation, he pointed to the roasted chicken on the table and said 'If I am innocent, the cock will crow'. This brought peals of laughter from the guests but miraculously the cock stood up and crowed. The man was allowed to go free but years later he returned to Barcelos to build the monument of San Tiago and the cross, Cruzeiro do Senhor do Galo, associated with this legend which is now in the archaeological museum.

Unfortunately, a garish version of the Barcelos cock has been adopted as a national symbol from which there is no escape in any corner of the country.

Barcelos has plenty of restaurants but less in the way of accommodation. Providing the best facilities in town is the *Albergaria Condes de Barcelos* but for a touch of real elegance, try the *Quinta do Convento da Franqueira* at Pereira just south of Barcelos. With only two guest rooms in this elevated former convent, built in 1563 with stones from the castle of Faria, visitors have the run of a charming lounge, card room and gardens. Expect eating places like the very reasonable *Bagoeira*, within easy reach of the market, to be busy on a Thursday which might also be true of *Muralha* near Turismo. Possibly, thanks to the market, Barcelos has an unusually large number of restaurants so there is plenty of choice and room to experiment.

A fast road leads from Barcelos out west to reach the coast at **Esposende**. This resort has the support of the Portuguese but lacks international appeal. The beach at the inlet to the estuary, guarded by a small fortress, is of good quality sand although the best beaches and dunes are just south of the estuary at Fão. This whole stretch of beach, 18km (11¼ miles) centred on Esposende, is designated for protection to preserve the dune environment while tourism developments will be limited to a very narrow strip. The following section of the road south towards Porto is lined with market stalls selling whatever fresh vegetables are in season creating a market atmosphere, especially on a Sunday. **Póvoa de**

Barcelos has the largest outdoor market in Portugal

Varzim manages to combine graceless industry and high-rise apartment blocks with a popular resort which boasts, at nearby Estela, a modern 18-hole golf course opened in 1990. The pink *Grand Hotel* and casino look incongruous and uncomfortable amidst the surrounding sea of concrete. Still in the heart of town is the old fisherman's quarter, Bairro dos Pescadores, where daily auctions take place to sell off the day's catch.

Vila do Conde

The last stop on the way back to Porto is the charming estuary town of Vila do Conde which offers a complete contrast to Póvoa de Varzim. A prominent fort guards the mouth of the River Ave and rocks below are greatly favoured by local fishermen while the bathers head for the stretch of sand to the south. The town, once famous for its shipyards and fishing before the river silted up, lies just a little inland and is perhaps more famous now for its **lace-making** and there are plenty of examples to be seen in the handicraft centre attached to the Turismo. It is also possible to visit the school of lace-making which occupies the former Convent of Carmo, near the old boat building area.

Dominating the town is the **Convent of Santa Clara** which was once fed water from a source 5km (3 miles) away by a graceful aqueduct of which only a few 18th century arches remain. The convent was founded in 1318 by Afonso Sanches, illegitimate son of Dom Dinis, and more or less rebuilt in 1777 only to fall into disuse within the following century. Now it is a reform school but the church is still open for visitors. Gothic in style, the granite church boasts fine wood carving which includes the ceiling whilst, over to the left, the chapel of Conception contains the tombs of the founders, Afonso Sanches, and his wife, Dona Teresa Martins, and two of their children who died in infancy. There are some illuminated manuscripts behind glass which, when we were there, a young guide from the nearby school showed no hesitation in opening to turn pages.

Two highlights in the annual calendar take place throughout summer, the first is the festival of St John which takes place on 23 and 24 June when, apart from the usual partying, there is a candlelit procession to the beach with the lace makers leading the rest of the town's population. The second is a craft fair during the last week of July and the first of August which is one of the finest in Portugal.

From Vila do Conde, it is only a short drive back to the airport or into Porto itself.

Practical Information

Hotels and Restaurants

See the introduction for details of TURIHAB (TH).

BARCELOS

Albergaria Condes de Barcelos, Av. Alcaide de Faria (tel. 053 810 061). Best place in town and reasonable.

Quinta do Convento da Franqueira, Pereira (TH) (tel. 053 831 606). 16th century former convent set amongst vineyards, with two rooms and large lounge.

Quinta de Santa Comba, Lugar de Crujães (TH) (tel. 053 832 101). Situated on farm estate about 5km (3 miles) south of Barcelos, six rooms, lounge and kitchen.

Restaurant Casa dos Arcos, Rua Duques de Bragança (tel. 053 811 975). Small restaurant with good local reputation and not expensive.

Restaurant Bagoeira, Av. Dr Sidsnio Pais, (tel. 053 811 177). Popular restaurant, especially on market days.

BRAGA

Most visitors prefer to stay at nearby Bom Jesus away from the heat and pollution of the town and only hotels in that region are listed.

Hotel Sopete Elevador, Parque de Bom Jesus do Monte (tel. 053 675 548). Offers genteel four-star accommodation, good views of the gardens surrounding Bom Jesus and a good restaurant.

Hotel Sopete Parque, Parque de Bom Jesus do Monte (tel. 053 676 548). Another four-star hotel, recently renovated in original style, no restaurant but close to the above hotel.

Hotel Sul Americano, Parque de Bom Jesus do Monte (tel. 053 676 548). A much cheaper alternative to above hotels while still offering a good standard.

Castelo do Bom Jesus (TH) (tel. 053 676 566). Splendid 18th century house set in 10 hectares of parkland, 10 rooms with good facilities including swimming pool and tennis.

Restaurant Inácio, Campo das Hortas, 4 (tel. 053 613 235). Rustic, family run restaurant on the expensive side but well regarded.

Abade de Priscos, Praça Mouzinho de Alberquerque (tel. 053 76 650). Small family run restaurant with limited menu but food is good and prices reasonable.

Casa Pimenta, Praça Conde de Agrolonga, 74 (tel. 053 22 119). Good typical restaurant.

GUIMARÃES

Hotel Guimarães, Rua Eduardo Almeida (tel. 053 515 888). Best hotel in town with plenty of facilities including squash courts and a pool. The restaurant, too, is one of the best in town.

Pousada Nossa Senhora de Oliveira (tel. 053 514 157). Right in the heart of historic Guimarães, offers 10 rooms and six suites.

Pousada de Santa Marinha (tel. 053 514 453). Opened only in 1985, this *pousada* is beautifully located in a converted 12th century monastery on the slopes of Penha, just outside town. With 51 rooms, it is also one of the largest *pousadas*.

Albergaria das Palmeiros, Rua Gil Vincente (tel. 053 410 324). Offers the best reasonably priced accommodation in town, restaurant and pool.

Casa de Sezim (TH) (tel. 053 523 196). Quietly located just 4km (2½ miles) outside town, this estate produces a remarkably good vinho verde. Charming accommodation, six rooms.

Restaurant Casa do Arco, Rua da Santa Maria. Typical restaurant, reasonably priced.

El Rei, Praça de São Tiago, 20 (tel. 053 419 096). Intimate restaurant, moderately priced.

Mumadona, Rua Serpa Pinto, 268 (tel. 053 414 791). Popular eating place and very reasonable.

VILA DO CONDE
Estalagem do Brasão, Av. Dr João Canavarro 9 (tel. 052 642 016). Handy for the airport.

Places of Interest

BARCELOS
Outdoor market held every Thursday.
Museu Archeological on site of ruined Ducal Palace, open access.

BRAGA
Cathedral.
Sacred Art Museum (in cathedral). Open 10am–12.15pm and 2pm–5.30pm.
Casa dos Biscainhos Museum. Open 10am–12 noon and 2–5pm, closed Mondays and holidays.
Citânia de Briteiros. Open 9am–5pm in winter and till dusk in summer.

GUIMARÃES
Museu Martins Samento. Open 9.30am–12noon and 2–5pm, closed Mondays and holidays.
Museu Alberto Sampaio. Open 10am–12.30pm and 2–5.30pm, closed Mondays and holidays
Paço dos Duques de Bragança. Open 9am–5.25pm.

Tourist Offices

Barcelos: Largo da Porto Nova (tel. 053 811 882).
Braga: Av. da Liberdade, 1 (tel. 053 22 550).
Esposende: Rua 1 de Dezembro (tel. 053 961 354).
Guimarães: Alameda de S. Dâmaso (tel. 053 412 450).
Vila do Conde: Cento de Artesanato, Rua 5 de Outubru (tel. 052 642 700).

10. COIMBRA

Lying on the banks of the Mondego river, Coimbra is crowned by the university buildings perched atop Alcácova hill. The city's foundations go back into misty prehistory but it became Roman Aeminium before taking the name Coimbra from the Roman settlement of Conimbriga close by. During more than 300 years of Moorish rule, it became an important centre of Mozarabic culture before succumbing to the Christians in 1064. Dom Afonso Henriques moved the capital of the emerging Portugal from Guimarães to Coimbra. Its spell as capital was relatively short lived, that honour being transferred to Lisbon about 1250.

After reconquest by the Christians, Coimbra became an important river port but there were problems with flood water and silt along the south bank of the river. Financed by the church as a means to produce more priests, the first university in Portugal was established in Lisbon (1290) by Dom Dinis I. Transferred to Coimbra in 1308, students were tutored by the monks of Santa Cruz Monastery but political wrangling, between the monarchy and church, caused the seat of the university to be moved back and forth between the two cities a number of times. The university was finally settled in Coimbra in 1537 and remained the only university in the country for nearly 400 years. Despite efforts by a succession of Portugal's kings to raise standards and put the University firmly on the map, the Church's stranglehold stifled development and caused serious students to pursue academic success outside Portugal. The country had to wait for the Marquês de Pombal finally to prise away the stagnant grip of the Church, in the 18th century, and lay the foundation for the University's reputation as a recognised seat of learning. Coimbra has developed and grown around its university which is the heartbeat of the city. Its reputation as a major learning centre remains intact, even though the more recently founded university in Lisbon now exceeds Coimbra in student numbers. The buzz of city life is highly charged whilst the students are in residence, with something going on somewhere almost all the time. Outside term time a much quieter ambience prevails.

Medieval traditions are an integral part of the fabric of everyday student life, which in themselves inject additional colour and interest. The usual form of lodging, which has survived down the centuries, is in *repúblicas* (republics) where a group of students share furnished accommodation. Many students now opt to wear casual dress but the sense of being transported to another time accompanies those who wear the traditional long, black capes. Faculty

Coimbra: view over the old town towards the cathedral

ribbons (*fitas*), pinned to the capes, denote the wearer's area of study with blue for arts, red for law and yellow for medicine. Perhaps more intriguing is to check a students' tally of amorous conquests by counting the number of tears around the bottom of his cloak. A carnival atmosphere accompanies the end of final exams in May, the highlight of which is a ceremony called *Queima das Fitas* (Burning the Ribbons) when faculty ribbons are ritually burnt.

Coimbra's greatest contribution to traditional folk music is the soulful and expressive musical art form, **fado**. This style of singing is an instinctive expression, which springs from the soul in the form of a lament about love, longing, life etc.,and a lone voice can often be heard winging through the night. These mournful sounds make sense if, as one story goes, *fado* in Coimbra developed around homesick students of yore; but its origins are thought to stem from the plaintive songs of African slaves, a lament which found an echo in the hearts of homesick Portuguese sailors on voyages of discovery. It is not really given to organised public performance, which probably accounts for the tradition of not applauding a rendition, although some restaurants employ a *fado* singer at weekends. Unlike the *fado* in Lisbon, which is more commercial and sung by men and women, Coimbra *fado* is performed only by men and has a more serious and intellectual content. Singers are accompanied by a twelve-string guitar although spontaneous snatches of a few bars of unaccompanied *fado* are not uncommon.

The Town

Approaching Coimbra from the Santa Clara side of the Mondego river, across the bridge of the same name, affords the best overall view of the old city. This south facing elevation, encompassing the main area of interest, is dominated by the hilltop university. What remains of the city's medieval past clings tenaciously to the steep gradients below. Fortunately, much of Salazar's more recent characterless, angular faculty blocks are somewhat masked from this angle. Even the Mondego river is a celebrity for, unlike the Douro and Tagus rivers, it springs from and flows its entire length through Portuguese soil. As such, it has fired the passions of writers and musicians over the centuries to the extent of becoming known as O Rio dos Poetas (The River of Poets). The spread of the city degenerates into a jumble of old and new, the new not always in harmony with its heritage, but this soon ceases to intrude.

Walking is the only way to absorb the sights and sounds of this fascinating city. Evening, especially, can be very atmospheric and a different experience again from a daytime jaunt over the same ground. Distance is not a problem, as the centre is fairly compact, but the steep inclines may be a deterrent to some. Pedestrianised shopping streets in the Baixa (lower town), which although outside the old city is almost as old, keep heavy traffic at bay. This effectively creates an island within which the original city streets are concentrated, although cars wend tortuously through some of the streets around the university. Cars are not really an option here as parking is limited. It is best to park along Avenida Emidio Navarro to the right on crossing the Ponte de Santa Clara or in the metered car park to the left. If these options fail, there is parking on the Santa Clara side before crossing the bridge.

The **Largo da Portagem**, immediately opposite on crossing Ponte de Santa Clara, is a good place to start a tour. Those who stay at *Hotel Astoria*, to the left of Largo da Portagem, are well placed for touring on foot. This friendly and recently refurbished hotel retains much of its 1920s ambience with modern day comforts. The restaurant is one of the best in town and the wine list includes the excellent but elusive Buçaco wines, only available in this hotel chain. To the right of Largo da Portagem is the helpful Turismo, which supplies a good map and can advise on other hotels and *residencials* close by.

Starting out along pedestrianised **Ferreira Borges** causes problems from the start. Cafés displaying trays of the delicious local speciality *arrufadas* — a cake wrapped in layers of filo-type pastry — act like a magnet. The cakes are not actually baked on the premises but transported daily by the trayful from the small village of Tentugal, near Figueira da Foz. The *Café Briosa* does particularly brisk business and offers other mouth-watering specialities such as *queijades* (cheese cakes), *manjares brancos* (coconut tart) and *pasteis de nata* (custard tarts). Temptation does not stop there, for Coimbra's large student population ensures a generous sprinkling of inviting cafés in this area. Rua Ferreira Borges becomes Rua Visconde da Luz, leading to Praça 8 de Maio, and is lined with fashionable shops. For now, head only as far as the **Arco de Almedina** (Almedina Gate), a few hundred metres along Rua Ferreira Borges on the right. Its name suggests a Moorish connection as 'medina' is the Arabic word for city. Once a gate in the medieval city walls, it leads into Rua do Quebra Costas (Street of the Broken Backs) which was then, as now, the main pedestrian route between the Sé Velha (old cathedral) and the Baixa. The tower above was the town hall until 1878 and is where the Sino de Correr (Warning Bell) is still housed along with the city's archives.

Artesanato (craft) shops lining the way, provide plenty of excuse for stops on the upward haul. Divert left into Rua Sobre Ripas to the **Casa de Sobre Ripas** on the left, just before the archway. A Manueline doorway and windows (attributed to João de Ruão) grace the external walls of this 16th century mansion but a glimpse of the plain interior suggests an earlier foundation. It is believed to be the site of the murder of Maria Teles, who had secretly married João, the eldest son of Inês de Castro, a tale of jealousy and intrigue which revolved around Maria's own sister, Queen Leonor of Portugal. With the promise of her own daughter in marriage, Leonor successfully persuaded João that Maria was being unfaithful. He dutifully disposed of his wife, only to find Leonor renege on her promise and have him banished from the country. The mansion is now the Archaeological Faculty of the University. Continue beneath the archway, whose façade is studded with sculpted cameos by João de Ruão, a prolific sculptor of the 16th century, to the Torre do Anto. The 12th century tower was once part of the city walls but now serves as the **Casa de Artesanato da Região de Coimbra** (Regional Craft Centre). It was the home of the 19th century poet António Nobre for a short

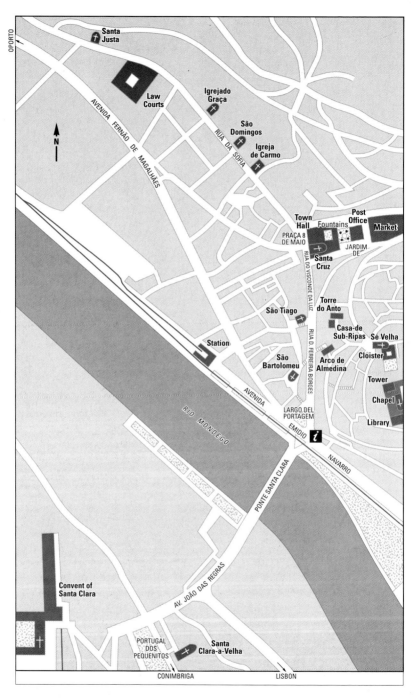

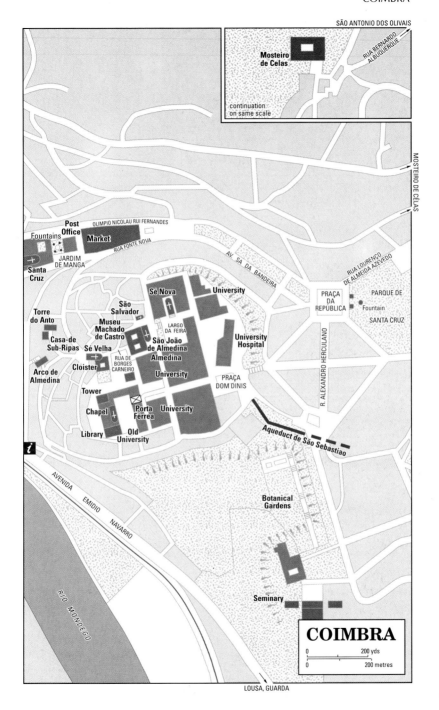

SÃO ANTONIO DOS OLIVAIS

Mosteiro
de Celas

RUA BERNARDO ALBUQUERQUE

continuation
on same scale

MOSTEIRO DE CÉLAS

OLIMPIO NICOLAU RUI FERNANDES

Post
Office

Fountains

Market

RUA FONTE NOVA

JARDIM
DE MANGA

Santa
Cruz

AV. SA DA BANDEIRA

Sé Nova

University

RUA LOURENÇO DE ALMEIDA AZEVEDO

PRAÇA
DA
REPUBLICA

PARQUE DE

Fountain

SANTA CRUZ

Torre
do Anto

São
Salvador

Museu
Machado
de Castro

LARGO
DA FEIRA

University
Hospital

Casa-de
Sub-Ripas

Sé Velha

São João
de Almedina
Almedina

R. ALEXANDRO HERCULANO

RUA DE
BORGES
CARNEIRO

Arco de
Almedina

Cloister

University

PRAÇA
DOM DINIS

Tower

Chapel

Porta
Ferrea

University

Library

Old
University

Aqueduct de São Sebastiao

AVENIDA

EMIDIO

NAVARRO

Botanical
Gardens

RIO MONDEGO

Seminary

COIMBRA

0	200 yds
0	200 metres

LOUSA, GUARDA

while when he attended the university. The multi-lingual curator offers expert guidance around the four floors of the tower. Two floors are dedicated as permanent salesrooms for local handicrafts whilst the other two are used for rotating craft displays from different areas. This is an ideal place to purchase local souvenirs of pottery, delicately carved white poplar, weaving and lace from local villages — all of good quality and at a reasonable price. From here return to continue climbing the steps to Largo da Sé Velha.

Infante Dom Pedro and Inês de Castro

The epic love story of Pedro and Inês has become inextricably bound up in the folklore of Portugal. Ideal subject matter for minstrels and poets, it is a classic tale of uncontrollable passion, jealousy, intrigue and gory revenge. The die was cast as soon as Inês arrived from Spain to attend her cousin Constanza, with whom she had been brought up and who had married Pedro in 1340. As soon as Pedro laid eyes on Inês he fell madly in love, which precipitated her banishment from court. When Constanza died in 1345, Inês returned and went to live with Pedro as his mistress and bore him several children.

Inês de Castro's only crime appears to have been her Spanish connections, a Galician nobleman for a father and ambitious brothers. Jealousy and suspicion over Inês' foreign connections gained momentum. Pedro's father, Afonso IV, forbade their marriage on the grounds that she was a potential Spanish influence over the heir to the throne. Ignoring his father's wishes, Pedro whisked Inês off to Bragança where, it is claimed, they married secretly in 1354. Prime movers in the political intrigue at court were three nobles, Pedro Coelho, Diogo Pacheco and Alvaro Gonçalves who persuaded Afonso that Inês would have to be disposed of permanently. At first the king gave his agreement but, when it came to the crunch, backed down. Fired up with zeal for their mission, the three nobles took matters into their own hands and sought out Inês in the grounds of what is now the Quinta das Lágrimas where they murdered her in cold blood on 7 January 1355.

Pedro was inconsolable and threatened revolt. Intervention by the archbishop of Braga ostensibly cooled the situation and, outwardly at least, an uneasy truce between Pedro and his father was negotiated. Two years later, when Pedro succeeded to the throne, he gave full reign to his vengeance. With a lust for justice uppermost in his mind, Pedro relentlessly hunted down the perpetrators of the crime. Pacheco managed to elude capture but Coelho and Gonçalves were tracked down and brutally executed at Santarém. In the meantime, Pedro swore before the *Cortes* (national assembly) that he had indeed married Inês at Bragança. The depth of his love for Inês was such that he had her body removed from its tomb in the church of Santa Clara (now Santa Clara-a-Velha). Setting her corpse on a throne at his side he crowned her as his queen and forced his courtiers to kiss her decomposing hand.

The elaborately sculpted 14th century tombs of Pedro and Inês lie opposite each other in the transepts of the Mosteiro de Alcobaço. Each is inscribed with the motto '*Ati ao Fim do Mundo*' (Until the End of the World). Pedro expressly left instructions that their tombs be placed foot to foot, so that on Judgement Day the first thing they see will be each other. During the ten years of his reign, Pedro I diverted his all consuming passion into the administration of justice and became known as the *Justeiro* (Justicer).

The sloping square is dominated by the **Sé Velha** (Old Cathedral), one of the finest Romanesque cathedrals in Portugal. Built between 1162 and 1184, its fortress-like appearance is testament to the need for continuing protection from Moorish incursions into the area at the time. Within its walls, the unfurling of history has included the coronations of Sancho I and João I and also the ordination of the Lisbon-born Saint Anthony of Padua (1195–1231). The main entrance was the work of João de Ruão who had a workshop close to the Casa de Sobre Ripas. Later embellishments attempted to soften the austere lines of the exterior, especially the Renaissance Porta Especiosa (north portal), which is unfortunately crumbling, and the door of the north transept which was altered at the same time. The 1837 domed belfry is more out of character, as domes are not a feature in Portuguese architecture, but it is only really noticeable from above. A stark interior comes as no surprise; maybe the warmth in the colour of the stone compensates for a lack of elaborate decoration but this church seems more welcoming than most. All that is left of the *azulejos*, bought from the Seville workshop of Quijarro in 1508, are unobtrusive panels along the side walls. The rest of the tiles once decorated the pillars of the nave where it is difficult to imagine them having done much in the way of interior enhancement.

The intricate and delicately carved Gothic main altarpiece, executed by the Flemish masters Olivier of Ghent and Jean d'Ypres, is aesthetically pleasing and blends well with the simple style of its surroundings. It was presented by Bishop Jorge de Almeida (1483–1543) whose tomb lies in the **chapel of São Pedro** (1537), in the north transept. This chapel is considered to be one of the most elegant and harmonious examples of Renaissance architecture in Portugal. Amongst a collection of mainly bishops tombs, lies that of Dona Vetaça, who was governess to Queen Santa Isabel. Steps lead from the south aisle to the Gothic cloister which once housed the university press. Giant conch shells, used to hold holy water, are an unusual reminder of the 'Age of Discoveries' and Portugal's exotic colonies. In 1772, the Episcopal see was moved to the Sé Nova but the impression is that, at least today, the old cathedral acts more as a focal point of city life than its later replacement.

Sculpting and Sculptors

A different quality of limestone 'Pedra de Ançã', from the village of Ançã to the north-west of Coimbra, was responsible for the town's development as a centre for sculpture. Being softer than limestone from other areas, Ançã stone lent itself particularly well to the art of the carver. It was used in abundance for decorative embellishment during a 200 year period from the 1300s onwards, until its popularity declined in favour of wood carving.

An early exponent of the art of stone carving was Pêro, who is said to have introduced the Gothic style to Coimbra. Frenchmen particularly, attracted to Coimbra as much by the wealth being poured into new building as by the quality of the local stone, were prolific exponents of the art during the 16th century. Of these, Nicolau Chanterène (c 1540) produced some of the finest Renaissance work whilst the carving of João de Ruão (Jean de Rouen), although extensive, never achieved the same acclaim.

A kaleidoscope of life swirls round the **Largo da Sé Velha**, an ideal place for people watching from one of the surrounding cafés. Music students from the nearby faculty practice their scales or perform in the cathedral but for a Saturday night *fado* treat with good food, the *Trovador restaurant* is a good choice.

Move on and up behind the Sé Velha along Rua do Norte, passing the 16th century Casa dos Melos, now the Faculty of Pharmacy, to the **Velha Universidade** (Old University). Enter the courtyard, known as Patio do Paço das Escolas (Patio of the Schools), through the 17th century Porta Férrea (Iron Gate). Niches on the top hold statues of Dom Dinis and Dom João III. Purchase tickets for the Sal dos Capelos and Biblioteca from the far side of the double stairway. Buildings fill three sides of the courtyard and have evolved from the original royal palace, donated by Dom João III in 1573. They still form the nucleus of the university. The south side is open, with elevated views over the River Mondego across to the convent of Santa Clara, and a portly statue of Dom João III, reminiscent of Henry VIII of England, takes centre stage in the courtyard. The double stairway, to the right on entering, leads to the Via Latina (Latin Way) gallery where students process to their graduation. Pass through the door marked '*reitoria*' on to the balcony of the Sal dos Capelos (Ceremonial Hall), one time throne room but now the setting for degree ceremonies, where portraits of Portugal's kings hang beneath a 17th century painted wooden ceiling. In the corner of the courtyard stands the 18th century Baroque clock tower which has become a national symbol. Christened '*cabra*' (goat) by the students, it was once used to summon them to lectures as well as being used to signal a dawn-to-dusk curfew. Further

The Manueline doorway of Casa de Subra Ripas, Coimbra

round is the 16th century **Capela de São Miguel** (University Chapel) entered via a Manueline portal. The elaborate interior decoration is a mix of styles added over the next 200 years. 'Carpet' style *azulejos* are placed alongside the painted and gilded altarpiece, which is highly regarded as a fine example of the Mannerist style, but the pièce de résistance, not to everyone's taste, is a heavily gilded Baroque organ which is apparently as 'loud' as it looks. Finally, the 18th century Biblioteca Joanina (library) is regarded as one of the world's most magnificent Baroque libraries. Ring the bell at the side for admittance. Constructed by Dom João V, whose coat of arms hangs above the entrance, the interior consists of three connecting gilded and painted rooms lined with double storey shelves of rare books. The elaborately framed connecting doors create a telescopic effect through all three rooms to the large portrait of Dom João V framed on the far wall.

Move through Praça da Porta Férrea between the nondescript modern university faculties to **Praça de Dom Dinis**. A large statue of Dom Dinis dominates the large open square where Coimbra Castle stood until its demolition in 1772. There is a small Turismo office located here. Steps lead down then along Oliveira Matos to the **Praça da República**, its bars and cafés a popular haunt of students, and beyond to the Parque de Santa Cruz. To the right, the 16th century São Sebastião Aqueduto (Aqueduct), built on the site of an earlier aqueduct, stretches across the edge of the **Jardim Botânico** (Botanical Gardens). The gardens were laid out to a circular design, at the instigation of the Marquês de Pombal, and although started in 1774 took over a hundred years to complete. Possibly of more immediate interest is the huge building dominating the landscape at the end of the aqueduct. This 18th century building, with 19th century additions, was once a seminary and is noted for its octagonal domed church but now does service as the local *Penitenciária* (prison).

From Praça de Dom Dinis, the **Sé Nova** (New Cathedral) is only a short walk down Rua dos Estudos. Originally founded in 1598 by the Jesuits, and taken from them when they were suppressed in 1759, it took 100 years to build. The bleak expanse of the Largo da Sé Nova matches the equally lacklustre Renaissance frontage of the cathedral whose interior confirms the ominous portent of its exterior. Inside, an eerie bluish tinge strikes a chill through the lofty emptiness. Paintings of the Life of the Virgin, mostly Italian copies and framed by carvings, line the walls behind the 17th century redwood choir stalls which were originally in the Sé Velha along with the Manueline font. Even the Jerómino Luís' gilded main altarpiece, two ornate Baroque organs and an abundance of gilded vine leaves, cherubs and further paintwork fail to have much impact on the pervading gloom.

By contrast to the Sé Nova, a visit to the **Machado de Castro Museum** is like a breath of fresh air. Not too surprisingly as Coimbra developed as a centre for sculpting the museum, founded in 1912, was named after an 18th century Portuguese sculptor. Housed in what served as the old Episcopal Palace and church of São João de Almedina, whose foundation stems from the 12th century, it was built on the site of the Roman forum. A two storey Roman cryptoporticus (crypt), built onto the side of the hill to support and give height to the forum which once stood here, was left to do similar service for the later building. This provides one of the most fascinating aspects of a visit here as it is possible to explore the passages of the upper storey; the lower storey is closed to the public. A torch is useful as the low but atmospheric lighting makes close inspection of the stonework difficult.

The tower by the main entrance and the church, probably built on the site of a mosque, provide a Moorish connection, but much of the building seen today is the result of 16th century additions and rebuilding. Besides sculpture, which includes an appealing 14th century knight on horseback attributed to Pêro, the museum contains paintings from as early as the 14th century, furniture, ceramics and the bishop's coach. The same ticket covers access to the gold, silver and jewellery treasures, via a separate entrance at the foot of the steps from the Sé Nova. Along the edge of the pleasant quadrangle runs a loggia, providing an elevated view of the city and connecting the museum café with the entrance to the cryptoporticus in the other part of the museum. There is no concession to foreign visitors and information on exhibits is presented in the Portuguese language only, a problem all too frequently encountered.

Soak up the atmosphere on the way down to Praça 8 de Maio, by making for the 18th century **Igreja de São Salvador** (Saviour), with its earlier Romanesque doorway, and wandering in the area of Rua de São Salvador and Rua da Matematica where many of the student *repúblicas* are located.

Down in Praça 8 de Maio at the end of Rua Visconde da Luz lies the **Igreja de Santa Cruz**, once a monastery and one of Coimbra's most important churches. Dom Afonso Henriques is reputed to have sanctioned its foundation as a monastery for Augustine monks in 1131, his confessor, São Teotónio, being installed as its first prior. Dom Manuel started enlarging the monastery in 1502 and exempted the priors from the jurisdiction of the bishop. This eventually led to Dom João III giving the priors automatic succession to the chancellorship of the new university, when it was moved from Lisbon in 1539. A privilege which lasted until monasteries were disbanded in 1834. The Portal da Majestade (frontage) is somewhat over the top, with the original 16th century doorway masked by an early 19th century arch. Floor level is now below street level, so steps lead down into the church which is lined with 18th century *azulejos*. It is not the ornate altarpiece which excites attention but Nicolau Chanterène's intricately carved pulpit of 1522 and, in the chancel, the tombs of Portugal's first two kings, Dom Afonso Henriques and his son Dom Sancho I, disinterred and placed here after lying 400 years in nearby graves. A door from the sacristy, which contains furniture and notable paintings, opens into the lovely Manueline **Casa do Capitulo** (Silent Cloister).

A favourite of the Portuguese is the *Café Santa Cruz* next door. Formerly a chapel attached to the church, as the Manueline ceiling and stained glass windows testify, it has served as a café for nearly 70 years.

Behind the church is the curiously named **Jardim de Manga** (Garden of the Sleeve), so named because Dom João III is reputed to have drawn the design for this oddity on his sleeve although its design is also attributed to João de Ruão. Curiously modernistic, this unwieldy construction was completed in 1535 as a representation of the fountain of life, and was originally a cloister of the Santa Cruz monastery.

Rua da Sofia (Street of Wisdom), so called because it was once lined with theological colleges, could be of interest to church collectors. The churches of Carmo (1597), Graça (1555) and Santa Justa (1710) were connected with the colleges when the university of Coimbra was established and, in an effort to preserve the 16th century architecture, this street has been declared a national monument.

A plunge into the bustling rabbit warren of streets leading off Praça 8 de Maio is a wonderful diversion from monuments and a journey of discovery in itself. When refreshment calls, the outdoor cafés in the irregularly shaped **Praça do Comércio**, a circus during the Roman period but now lined with shops in 17th and 18th century houses, seem an attractive proposition. Two more churches can be found here, the 12th century Romanesque church of **São Tiago** (James) and the nearby **São Bartolomeu**, the latter rebuilt in Baroque style in the 18th century, masking its 10th century foundations. The wiggle of narrow streets encompassed within a triangle marked by the squares of Comércio, Meias and Portagem contain a concentration of good and very reasonably priced eating places which includes the very Portuguese *Zé Manuel*.

On a hill across the Mondego lies the brooding bulk of the 17th century Convento de Santa Clara-a-Nova (New Santa Clara Convent), a shorter walk than it might appear, especially as there are diversions along the way. Here lies the body of Rainha Santa Isabel (Queen Saint Isabel), wife of Dom Dinis, who freely spent her husband's money on helping the poor and needy. Her canonisation was the result of a life spent founding hospitals and orphanages and the Miracle of the Roses. The miracle story relates to when Dom Dinis, annoyed with the extent of his wife's largess at his expense, waylaid her on one of her mercy missions, only to discover the bread and gold she had been carrying had turned into roses.

After crossing the bridge over the Mondego, keep heading up past Avenida Inês de Castro but take the next narrow road left to come up behind the sunken Gothic **Convento de Santa Clara-a-Velha** (Old Santa Clara Convent). Dona Mór Dias founded the convent in 1286 and it was refounded in 1330 by Santa Isabel and is where she and the ill-fated Inês de Castro were originally interred. Annual flooding of the Mondego river and consequent silting caused the convent to be finally abandoned in 1677, the tomb of Santa Isabel being transferred up the hill to the new convent whilst that of Inês now rests alongside that of Pedro I at Alcobaça. The absurdity of a sinking church, with the tops of arched vaulting wallowing in green weed covered water, is compounded by a recently renovated roof and cleaned stonework. To view the convent and its rose window from the front, approach from off Rua António Augusto Gonçalves down the side of the Portugal dos Pequenitos park. Further along the same road on the right is the 19th century *Quinta das Lágrimas* (House of Tears), earmarked for hotel development, and traditional site of the home Inés de Castro shared with her lover Pedro. Legend states that the Fonte dos Amores (Fountain of the Lovers), in the grounds of the *quinta*, gushed from the spot where Inés was murdered, a tale compounded no doubt by the poetic license of Camões in *The Lusiads*.

Luís de Camões

Portugal's greatest epic poet started life in the bosom of an impoverished aristocratic family. The probabilities are that he was born in Lisbon in 1524, the year Vasco da Gama died, and studied at Coimbra University where he would have received a thorough grounding in the classics, but the early part of his life tends to be based more on supposition than fact. The passionate nature of Camões can be gleaned from biographical elements in his early writing, and his indiscreet amours eventually led to his being banished from the Portuguese court at Lisbon, where he had gone in 1544 to write poetry and plays.

An adventurous life now beckoned, and Camões went off to Ceuta in Morocco around 1547 where he lost his right eye. Five years later he was imprisoned for being involved in a street brawl in Lisbon and injuring a royal official. His life over the next 17 years appears to have been fraught with danger and deprivation. After gaining an early release from prison, by agreeing to serve in Goa for an obligatory three year stretch, a stroke of good fortune saw his safe arrival in India on the *São Bento*, the only ship of the fleet to survive the journey. From there, he travelled on to Macau in the Far East when, on the journey either to or from Macau, he was shipwrecked in the Mekong estuary and lost everything except the half-completed manuscript of his epic poem. Eventually returning to Goa, he was again thrown into prison for some unknown transgression. Intent on returning home to have his poem published, Camões reached Mozambique where he lived for two years from 1567. Penniless by now, sympathetic compatriots funded his journey back to Portugal in 1570.

Os Lusíades (*The Lusiads*) was finally published in 1572. Named for the sons of Lusus, the mythical founder of Portugal, *Os Lusíades* was inspired by Camões' hero Vasco da Gama, whom he used in a similar manner to Homer's hero in the *Odyssey*. Unlike the *Odyssey*, where fact becomes immersed in ancient folklore, Camões' genius lay in his ability to blend historical accuracy whilst introducing mythical elements of classical Graeco-Roman culture. The poem reflects the Portuguese spirit of the time, a time when it was growing rich and powerful from the Voyages of Discovery.

Camões received scant acclaim when the poem was published although he managed to win a small royal pension. Now one of Portugal's most famous sons, he died in poverty and with no heirs in 1579.

The **Portugal dos Pequenitos** is a fanciful Lilliputian-style outdoor museum for, as the name implies, children. Individual displays of indigenous artefacts from Portugal's former colonies and small-scale models of Portuguese buildings, in which children are free to clamber around, make a worthwhile side-trip for all ages.

Keep heading up Rossio Santa Clara towards the new convent, passing the dilapidated and forlorn façade of the former monastery of São Francisco (1602), a chimney denoting its demotion to a factory. Cobbled Calçada Santa Isabel, wends steeply to the gate of the convent. One of the best overall views of Coimbra is from the terrace in front of the church. Except for a small Military Museum, the main body of the convent is now a barracks and barred to the public. The **Convento de Santa Clara-a-Nova**, constructed between 1649 and 1677, has become a shrine to Santa Isabel (1271–1336) since the relocation of her remains in the chancel in 1696 from the waterlogged old convent below. These remains now lie in the chancel in a silver casket purchased with donations from the people of Coimbra, whilst her original stone tomb lies empty in the lower choir. Gilded carvings and paintings, especially six panels depicting the removal of Santa Isabel's body from the old convent, adorn the interior. Dom João V is reputed to have had a fascination for nuns and it was he who provided the convent with its large cloister.

Excursions from Coimbra

Coimbra makes a good base from which to explore the surrounding area and a visit to Conimbriga is a must.

A 20 minute drive, south along the IC2 then off left through Condeixa onto the IC3, is all it takes to reach Conimbriga, the largest and most important Roman archaeological site on the Iberian Peninsula. Its natural defences, with gorges on two sides, implies its use as a settlement even before the Celts arrived.

Conimbriga

When the Romans first came along at the end of the 2nd century BC, Conimbriga's strategic position on the road between Lisbon (Olisipo) and Braga (Bracara Augusta) made it an obvious target for expansion. Over the

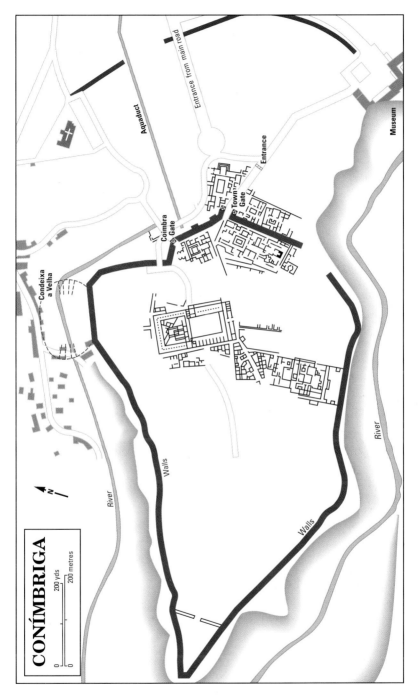

CONÍMBRIGA

0 — 200 yds
0 — 200 metres

N

Aqueduct

Entrance from main road

Entrance

Town Gate

Coimbra Gate

Condeixa a Velha

River

Walls

Walls

River

Museum

following centuries, the site grew to cover around 32 acres, much of which still lies waiting to be excavated. Conimbriga developed in importance to such an extent that Vespasian granted it municipium status around AD 70. Prosperity lasted until the Roman Empire began to crumble, towards the end of the 3rd century. Incursions by the Suevi (Swabians) increased in frequency and persistence and it became necessary to strengthen defences. The inhabited part of Conimbriga was drastically reduced and a large wall hurriedly constructed to protect a smaller area of the town. This wall, much of it still in evidence today, cut a swathe through existing housing. It is evident from the materials used to build the wall that it was constructed in haste, with rubble from destroyed buildings incorporated as building material. Heavier fortification failed to repel the Suevi who, after repeated attacks in the 5th century, eventually forced the inhabitants to succumb. Many of the townspeople were taken as slaves, including the wife and children of a nobleman who lived in Casa do Cantaber (House of Cantaber), the foundations of which now provide an insight into the lifestyle of the Roman nobility of the time.

After such a decimation of the population, many that were left removed to Aeminium (Coimbra) which was better defended, although a pocket of the inhabitants remained. It appears that the final abandonment of Conimbriga occurred around the time the Episcopal see was transferred to Aeminium, along with its name, some time during the 6th century. Those who did remain, formed a community on the site where the amphitheatre once stood, which eventually developed into modern-day Condeixa-a-Velha.

Pleasantly situated in countryside on the outskirts of Condeixa, Conimbriga is high on the list of places to visit. Most visitors are unaware on the approach to the car park that the accompanying wall to the right is actually a stretch of the original **Roman wall**. A modern building houses an imaginative **display of finds** in two parts. To one side, a series of windows open onto collections of artefacts depicting different aspects of Roman life; health and hygiene, personal adornment and military equipment to name but some. The other room contains mosaics, one of which is a picture of a minotaur's head in a maze, fragments of friezes, statuary and a scale model of the forum and temple. A good café/bar/restaurant is also part of the complex, where lunch is available; but those who prefer to eat alfresco will find a specially designated picnic area in the grounds.

The excellent plan of the site, on sale at the ticket office, is invaluable to have to hand. Access to the site is along the remains of the Lisbon to Braga Roman road, which passes through the previously mentioned heavy defensive wall at the main gate. On the right, just before reaching the wall, is the **Casa das Fontes** (House of Fountains). Excavations have revealed the function of the various rooms which surround the large ornamental pool and uncovered mosaics and wall paintings. A 50 *escudos* coin is all it takes to set the fountains playing again. Once through the gate, the largest and possibly the most luxurious villa on the site lies to the left, the **House of Cantaber**, with its own private baths. To the right is an aqueduct which ran underground from Alcabideque 3km (1¾ miles) away and was then raised on arches to cross the

The Roman site of Conimbriga

town to a distribution tower. At some time, possibly when Suevi attacks became more frequent, an underground cistern was brought into operation as insurance against deliberate sabotage of the aqueduct. Further along on the same side was the Roman Forum and other monumental buildings. It is quite easy to while away an hour or two enjoying this elevated country location.

Parque Nacional de Buçaco

A short trip north-east via Mealhada, famous for *leitão assado* (suckling pig), via the 234 to the spa town of Luso then south down the 235 leads to another countryside location, the Parque Nacional de Buçaco. This arboreal enclave was created by monks who had been on the site since the 6th century but were expelled when religious orders were suppressed in 1834. A map can be obtained from the hotel or tourist office in Coimbra which shows the layout of paths in the forest. The forest was first planted by the monks who built hermitages amongst the leafy fronds of the still flourishing collection of imported and native trees. The fanciful turreted confection, which is now the *Palace Hotel do Buçaco*, was built on the site of the former monastery as a summer palace for the royal family at the end of the 19th century. Now a five-star luxury hotel, it is rated as one of the finest in Europe with a service to match. A delectable menu is complemented by an impressive wine list, which includes the excellent quality Buçaco own label.

Enjoy the tang of the sea with trips north to **Aveiro**, off the IP1, for boat trips along the lagoon, where the beautiful *moliceiro* boats dredge for seaweed, or along the coast via the 111 to **Figueira da Foz**. For those intent on pursuing yet more monuments, the proximity of the IP1 makes trips south as far as Leira, Tomar, Batalha and Fatima viable propositions, these to be covered in the forthcoming regional guide to Lisbon and Central Portugal.

Practical Information

Hotels and Restaurants

COIMBRA

Hotel Tivoli, Rua João Machado (tel. 039 269 34). Four-star and fairly central, swimming pool, restaurant and disabled facilities.

Hotel Astoria, Avenida Emídio Navarro (tel. 039 220 55/6). Comfortable three-star hotel, very central with excellent restaurant.

Hotel Dom Luís, Quinta da Várzea, Santa Clara (tel. 039 813 196) Three-star, in country facing city across river, about 3km out. Restaurant.

Hotel Ibis, Avenida Emídio Navarro (tel. 039 491 559). Part of French chain, this two-star comfortable hotel is fairly central, restaurant.

Casa dos Quintais, Carvalhais de Cima, Assafarge (tel. 039 438 305). 6km outside Coimbra in quiet surroundings, part of the Turismo Rural scheme. Three rooms and swimming pool.

Trovador (tel. 039 254 75) next to Sé Velha. Atmospheric, good food and *fado*. Moderate.

Zé Manuel (tel. 039 237 90) behind Hotel Astoria in Beco do Forno, very Portuguese. Good and cheap.

Places of Interest

COIMBRA

Convento de Santa Clara-a-Nova: daily 9am–12.30pm & 2– 5.30pm

Moisteiro de Santa Cruz: daily 9am–12.30pm & 2–6pm.

Museu Machado de Castro: Tues–Sun 10am–1pm & 2.30–5pm, free Sunday morning. Closed Mondays.

Museu Militar (Military Museum next to Santa Clara-a-Nova) daily 10am–12 noon & 2–5pm.

Portugal dos Pequenitos: summer daily 9am–7pm & winter daily 9am–5.30 pm.

Sé Velha: daily 9.30am–12.30pm & 2–5.30pm.

Velha Universidade: daily 9.30am–12.30pm & 2–5pm.

Conimbriga: summer daily 10am–12.30pm & 2–6pm, closes one hour earlier in winter.

Tourist Offices

Região de Turismo do Centro, Largo da Portagem, 3000 Coimbra (tel. 039 330 19).
Tourism Posts
Coimbra: Largo Dom Dinis, (tel. 039 325 91).
Conimbriga: Condeixa-a-Nova, Câmera Municipal (tel. 039 941 114).

INDEX

Sandeman - Ruby Imperial
Tawny - Sociedade Agrícola
(wil) da Romaneira, S.A.
Rana - 1982 Aida + CA Maltos Filhos,
(L.B.V.) Lda